# RUSSIAN
## LANGUAGE AND PEOPLE

by Terry Culhane and Roy Bivon (University of Essex)

Based on the original series produced by Terry Doyle

Developed by BBC Language Unit

Project Manager: Phoenix Publishing Services

Designer: Giles Davies

Editorial Consultant: Sue Purcell

Producer of TV series *Russian Language and People*: Terry Doyle

Published by BBC Books
A division of BBC Worldwide Ltd
Woodlands, 80 Wood Lane, London W12 0TT

ISBN 0 563 40012 9

First edition published 1980

Revised edition © BBC Worldwide 1995

Reprinted 2001 (twice)

Printed and bound in Great Britain by
Martins the Printers Ltd, Berwick upon Tweed

# Contents

# Introduction

This is a revised edition of *Russian Language and People*, replacing the one first published by the BBC in 1980. It has been rewritten to take into account the changing face of Russia since the collapse of the Soviet Union.

The course is designed to provide a self-instructional introduction to the Russian language and Russian society. Based mainly on skills of *understanding* rather than *speaking,* it is also ideal for use in evening classes.

We have had three aims in mind in writing the course. Firstly, we hope to provide a stimulus for future study, by giving the student some insight into Russia and a painless and enjoyable introduction to the language. Secondly, we hope to provide something of immediate practical use to the person who wishes to visit Russia for business or pleasure, by using authentic materials in the course, and by using many language exercises based on the sort of situations that the visitor might find in a Russian environment. Timetables, newspapers, menus, signs, maps, have all been used to this end. Thirdly, we want the course to be accessible to the average person who does not have a particular 'gift for languages'. The course is largely based on skills of understanding, and many of the exercises, even in the later units of the course, are accessible to any student with a knowledge of the alphabet and a minimal amount of grammar.

The two cassettes, which have been re-edited and supplemented by additional recorded material, are an integral part of the course, and contain material for use in each lesson. Exercises recorded on the cassettes are marked 🔲.

The course has 20 units, each of which is divided into sections, as follows:

## ALPHABET (UNITS 1–5)

The alphabet is taught a few letters at a time, using simple words recorded on tape, many of which are similar to English words, and all of which are in current use in everyday Russian. Students are later taught the recognition of Russian script and Russian handwriting.

## LIFE IN RUSSIA

Each unit has a section devoted to some aspect of Russian life, and there are language exercises based on this, preparing the student for linguistic survival in these situations.

## LANGUAGE INFORMATION

Contains grammatical and other information about language, expressed in a concise way. Students who wish to study without the help of grammar are free to skip this section.

## LOOKING AT WORDS

Word-building is an important and fascinating aspect of the learning of Russian, and a great help in understanding Russian vocabulary. It is introduced gradually.

## A SITUATION TO REMEMBER

A 'situation setting' which acts as an aide-memoire for the student, this can be utilised for basic oral training, and for revision purposes. It contains some 'role-play' and other situations which might profitably also be used by a teacher in training speaking skills.

## WHAT YOU KNOW

A summary of the main points covered in the unit.

## KEY WORDS

Contains the most useful vocabulary in each unit. The words which occur here also appear in the vocabulary at the back of the book.

Units 5, 10, 15 and 20 are mainly concerned with the revision of the preceding four units, and contain exercises for revision purposes.

At the back of the book are the following reference sections:

- A transliteration and pronunciation guide
- A summary of the grammar contained in the course
- Tapescripts of all recorded material not printed in the units
- An answer key to the exercises
- A complete Russian-English vocabulary, containing all the words used in the course, together with the number of the unit in which they occur.

## ● TIPS FOR THE STUDENT

**1** Go at your own pace.

**2** Don't be afraid of stopping the cassette and going back over an exercise, or stopping in between items in an exercise if you need more time.

**3** Listen carefully to the recorded material and try and base your pronunciation on the sound, rather than what you think it should be from your reading of the words.

**4** Do not expect to understand every word or grammatical form that you meet. If, for example, you ask your way to somewhere, the reply you receive is likely to contain words and expressions that you do not understand in their entirety. This reply, however, will contain some key words and expressions, the understanding of which will enable you to get to your destination. It is the object of this course to teach you simple ways of expressing yourself in Russian, and provide you with enough understanding of language to decode more complex spoken and written Russian by selecting the essential, relevant items.

**5** Do not be put off if you do not understand a grammatical explanation. You may find that it falls into place later. In any case, you will find that you can do exercises later in the course without necessarily understanding absolutely everything that has gone before.

**6** In some of the early units examples of written Russian are given. Writing exercises are provided in Units 11–15 for those who wish to start writing Russian. If you do not, simply skip the exercises.

**7** When revising, think in terms of what to say or do in a given situation. Use the *Situation to remember* section to help you with your oral practice and do not be afraid of saying things out loud – in private, of course! Make use of the checklists in Units 5, 10, 15 and 20.

We sincerely hope that you will enjoy the experience of learning Russian with *Russian Language and People*.

# Getting started

NOMER ODIN

## ● The Russian alphabet

### Introduction

The Russian alphabet is called Cyrillic after the Greek missionary, St Cyril, who, along with his brother St Methodius, was said to have invented it in the late 9th century in order to write down the Gospels for the peoples around the area we now know as Moravia, in the Czech Republic.

Some letters are derived from Latin letters, others from Greek and some from Hebrew. Apart from Russian, versions of the Cyrillic alphabet are used for some other Slavonic languages, including Bulgarian, Serbian, and Ukrainian. Slavonic languages such as Polish and Czech use the Roman alphabet.

Once you have mastered the sound of a Russian letter, it usually stays the same, and in this respect Russian is much more 'logical' than English.

We shall introduce the letters a few at a time over the first five units. When there is a word which contains letters you have not met, we shall print it in small capitals. The stressed syllable will be indicated with an accent – SPASÍBO (meaning *thank you*). From Unit 5 onwards we shall write everything in Russian characters.

7

## Alphabet 1

There is a group of letters which look and sound very much like their English counterparts. Together they form a word – **KOMÉTA**, which means what you would expect it to. All the sounds of these letters are very close to English, but the **E** is pronounced 'ye' and the **T** is pronounced with the tongue touching the back of the teeth, with the teeth slightly apart.

**Here are some more Russian letters:**

# С П Р И Н В

The new letters have sounds very much like English sounds, but they look a little different.

**С** sounds like English 's'.

**П** sounds like English 'p'. This comes from the Greek letter 'pi', often used in mathematical formulae.

**Р** sounds like a Scottish 'r'. Please be careful: in English we often do not pronounce the letter 'r'; in Russian it is *always* pronounced.

**И** is pronounced 'ee'.

**Н** is like English 'n'.

**В** is like English 'v'.

All the letters explained in this unit are picked out in bold in the following list:

а **б в** г д **е** ё ж з **и** й к л м **н о п р с т** у ф х ц ч ш щ ъ ы ь э ю я

The words chosen below are the sort of words you might already know because of their similarity to English. All of them are common words in everyday use in Russia. They are recorded on your cassettes.

Notice that we have put stress marks (´) on the words. The part of the word under the stress is pronounced more strongly than the rest of the word, and Russian stress is heavier than English. It may also occur on a different part of the word than you might expect from the English, as in words 5, 7, 11, 12, 15, 16. Note this as you go along. Try to get the stress right from the very start.

| | | | | | |
|---|---|---|---|---|---|
| 1 | комéта ☐ | 8 | óпера ☐ | 15 | ресторáн ☐ |
| 2 | аппарáт ☐ | 9 | спорт ☐ | 16 | оркéстр ☐ |
| 3 | самовáр ☐ | 10 | парк ☐ | 17 | áвиа ☐ |
| 4 | кácса ☐ | 11 | таксú ☐ | 18 | мáрка ☐ |
| 5 | теáтр ☐ | 12 | пианúст ☐ | 19 | нет ☐ |
| 6 | áтом ☐ | 13 | винó ☐ | 20 | стоп ☐ |
| 7 | метрó ☐ | 14 | Москвá ☐ | 21 | пáспорт ☐ |

- **АППАРÁТ** is a camera. Many Japanese cameras are now available in Russia, and Russians, like many other people, are avid photographers.

- **САМОВÁР** is a device traditionally used by Russians for making tea. Don't forget to pronounce the 'r'. Russians usually drink tea from a **СТАКÁН** (*glass*).

- **КÁССА** is a cash desk or box-office. Most shops have them. It is also where you buy tickets for theatres, cinemas, museums, etc.
- **ТЕÁТР** is a theatre. Notice that the **Е** and **А** are pronounced separately, and the **Р** is rolled.
- **МОСКВÁ**, *Moscow*, will probably be the first word you see in big letters if you fly into Sheremetevo airport in Moscow. Note where the stress is, resulting in the **О** being pronounced almost as an 'a'.
- **ÓПЕРА**, **СПОРТ**, **ПАРК** are all good examples of rolled 'r' in Russian.

- **ÁВИА** means *airmail*. You will see it printed on envelopes.

- **МÁРКА** is a stamp. Russians love collecting them.
- **ПÁСПОРТ** can be a passport for travelling abroad, as well as a document that Russians carry at all times to prove who they are. Once again, don't forget to pronounce the 'r'.

You will probably have noticed that most Russian capital letters are very similar to the small letters: **Аа**, **Вв**, **Ее**, **Пп**.

· · · · · · · · · · · · · · · · · · · · · · · · ·

### 🔲 EXERCISE 1

Look at the list of words numbered 1–21 on the previous page.
First time round listen to the recording and repeat the word.
Second time round you say the word after you hear the number and check it with the tape. If you are satisfied with your attempt, put a tick in the box. If not, try again.

· · · · · · · · · · · · · · · · · · · · · · · · ·

## EXERCISE 2

**1** What would you do here?

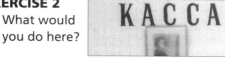

**2** What would you put in this?

**3** What happens here?

**4** When you follow this sign would you expect to go up or down?

**5** What would you wait for here?

**6** What would you make in this?

---

## ● Language information

### A, an, the

There is no word for *a* in Russian, and no word for *the*. This makes things simpler!

Éто **теáтр** means *This is **a** theatre* or *This is **the** theatre*.

Уа **пианúст** means *I am **a** pianist* or *I am **the** pianist*.

**Он таксúст** means *He is **a** taxi driver* or *He is **the** taxi driver*.

---

## Verb *to be*

You will also notice that you do not use the verb *to be* in the present tense. Even simpler! You are literally saying: *This theatre, I pianist, He taxi driver.*

## *What is, Who is*

Sнто éто? means *What is this?*
Кто éто? means *Who is this?* and *Who is it?*

---

### 🔊 EXERCISE 3

Listen to the tape and look at the pictures below.

You will be asked Sнто éто? *What is this?* or Кто éто? *Who is this?* You reply éто ...
The correct answer will then be given.
The pictures are numbered to help you.
Tick the box when you are satisfied with your answer.
If you are not sure what to do, play the tape through. For the first one you will hear **нómер** одín, *number one,* Sнто éто? You reply éto **таксú**, and you hear the correct answer éto **таксú**.

| | | | |
|---|---|---|---|
| 1 ☐ | 4 ☐ | 7 ☐ | 10 ☐ |
| 2 ☐ | 5 ☐ | 8 ☐ | |
| 3 ☐ | 6 ☐ | 9 ☐ | |

## Asking questions

You can change a statement into a question by making your voice go up on the word you are questioning. Compare a statement:

Э́то **ма́ма**.

with a question: Э́то **ма́ма**?

### 🔊 EXERCISE 4

Listen to the tape.
Now you should try to ask questions with Э́то and give replies.
Make sure that in the question your voice goes up on the word you are questioning.
Repeat the question and reply in the gaps provided.

## Saying *yes, no, not*

DA means *yes*, **нет** means *no*. The word **не** means *not*. Notice that Russian has the **т** on the Russian for *no*, and no **т** on the Russian for *not*. All you have to do is to add **не** to an ordinary sentence to make it negative:

Э́то **па́па**.   *This is dad.*
Э́то **не па́па**, э́то **ма́ма**.
*This is not dad, this is mum.*

### 🔊 EXERCISE 5

Look at the pictures in Exercise 3 and listen to the tape. This exercise requires negative answers.
You will be asked Э́то ...? (*Is this a ...?*)
You should answer **Нет**, э́то **не** ... (*No, it's not a ...*) Э́то ... (*It's a ...*)
You will then be given the correct answer.
Thus the first one would be as follows:
**но́мер** ODÍN, *number one*, э́то **па́па**?
You should reply **Нет**, э́то **не па́па**, э́то **такси́**.

### 🔊 EXERCISE 6

Replay Exercise 5.
In each example the wrong object or person is identified in the first part.
You should find the object or person identified and place the number in the box.
Thus in the first example you would hear **но́мер** ODÍN, *number one*, э́то **па́па**?
You find the picture of **па́па** and put the number in the box. This is done for you.
Notice that the examples are intentionally unrealistic!

| | | | | | | | |
|---|---|---|---|---|---|---|---|
| **1** | 7 | **4** | | **7** | | **10** | |
| **2** | | **5** | | **8** | | | |
| **3** | | **6** | | **9** | | | |

### EXERCISE 7

Here is a jumbled list of the words indicated by the pictures.
Place the number of the appropriate picture in the box at the side of each word. The first one is done for you.
We have left the stress marks off the words. See if you can put them in without looking at the original list.

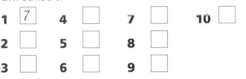

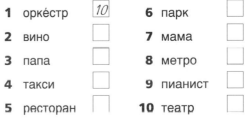

| | | | | | |
|---|---|---|---|---|---|
| **1** | оркестр | 10 | **6** | парк | |
| **2** | вино | | **7** | мама | |
| **3** | папа | | **8** | метро | |
| **4** | такси | | **9** | пианист | |
| **5** | ресторан | | **10** | театр | |

## Going by taxi

### EXERCISE 8

Here is a recording of a short conversation between a taxi driver and some people who have just called him to their flat. You will not understand all the conversation. Listen for the words for:

| | |
|---|---|
| *hello* | ZDRÁSTVUYTE |
| *please* | POZHÁLSTA |
| *thank you* | SPASÍBO |
| *good* | KHOROSHÓ |
| *goodbye* | DO SVIDÁNIYA |

Where are the people going to?

## ● Looking at words

Peter the Great founded St Petersburg in 1703 as 'a window on the West'. Since that time the Russian language has borrowed many words from Western European languages. This process was continued during the time of Catherine the Great (1729–1796), when it was considered sophisticated by Russian courtiers to speak French. Since the fall of communism more and more foreign words have come into the language, and many advertisements now even occur in English as well as Russian, as more trade takes place with the West.

### EXERCISE 9

Look at the following pictures.
Answer the question which follows each picture.
Don't expect to understand every word.

**1** What is the name of the shop?

**2** What is this cafe called?

**3** This is an advert for a bank. What is its name?

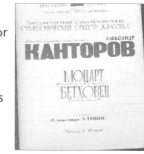

**4** This is a poster for a Mozart and Beethoven concert. What is the conductor's name?

**5** What would you find if you followed the arrow to the left?

## A situation to remember

### Identifying things

Here is a short conversation in which one person asks the other what an object is.

A: ZDRÁSTVUYTE!
B: ZDRÁSTVUYTE!
A: SHTO ÉTO?
B: ÉTO **винó**.
A: SPASÍBO. DO SVIDÁNIYA!
B: DO SVIDÁNIYA!

Now you ask your partner about:

**1** a restaurant
**2** a theatre
**3** Moscow
**4** the underground
**5** a stamp
Play both parts, if necessary

You can then vary the conversation by asking:

– ÉTO **винó**? and getting a reply:
– **Нет**, ÉTO **не винó**, ÉTO **пи́во** (beer).

## ● Playing with words

A number of the words you have met are concealed in the square below. See if you can find them and fill in the blanks on the right. You can move in any direction, sometimes changing direction in the middle of a word, and the last letter of a word starts the next word. You may use the same letter more than once. Start in the top left-hand corner.

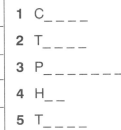

| С | И | Н | Е | Р |
|---|---|---|---|---|
| П | Н | Е | Т | Е |
| О | Т | А | С | И |
| Р | Е | К | Р | Т |
| Т | С | И | П | О |

**1** С_ _ _ _
**2** Т_ _ _ _
**3** Р_ _ _ _ _ _
**4** Н_ _
**5** Т_ _ _ _

## WHAT YOU KNOW

### Saying *hello, goodbye, please* and *thank you*

| | |
|---|---|
| *hello* | ZDRÁSTVUYTE |
| *please* | POZHÁLSTA |
| *thank you* | SPASÍBO |
| *goodbye* | DO SVIDÁNIYA |

### Identifying things and people

| | |
|---|---|
| *What is this (it)?* | SHTO ÉTO? |
| *Who is this (it)?* | **Кто** ÉTO? |
| *Is this (it) dad?* | ÉTO **пáпа**? |

### Understanding the replies

| | |
|---|---|
| *This (It) is dad.* | ÉTO **пáпа**. |

### Agreeing and disagreeing

| | |
|---|---|
| *yes* | DA |
| *no* | **нет** |
| *This (It) is dad.* | ÉTO **пáпа**. |
| *This (It) isn't dad.* | ÉTO **не пáпа**. |

## KEY VOCABULARY

| | |
|---|---|
| винó | wine |
| кто | who |
| мáма | mother, mum |
| Москвá | Moscow |
| нет | no |
| он | he |
| пáпа | father, dad |
| ресторáн | restaurant |
| теáтр | theatre |
| | |
| DA | yes |
| DO SVIDÁNIYA | goodbye |
| ÉTO | this, it |
| KHOROSHÓ | good |
| POZHÁLSTA | please |
| SHTO | what |
| SPASÍBO | thank you |
| YA | I |
| ZDRÁSTVUYTE | hello |

# 2

## номер два

---

**Asking where something is**

---

**Meeting somebody for the first time**

---

**Asking someone their name and how they are**

---

# Where is? How is?

NOMER DVA

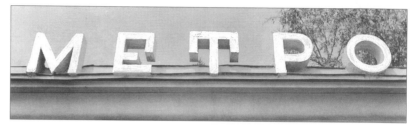

## ● Alphabet 2

**Here are the new letters for this unit:**

### З Д Л У Й

The letters you have met so far are picked out in the following list:

**а** б в **г** **д** **е** **ё** ж **з** и **й** **к** **л** **м** **н** **о** **п** **р** **с** **т** **у** ф
**х** ц ч ш щ ъ ы ь э ю я

So by the end of this unit you will already know half the letters!

**All of the letters have sounds similar to English sounds.**

**З** is similar to the English 'z'.
**Д** is similar to the English 'd'.
**Л** is the Russian version of the English 'l': listen carefully to the way it is pronounced in words 3–6 on the next page.
**У** is very like 'oo' in *mood*.
**Й** is like 'y' in *boy*.

Don't forget the stress! It is sometimes a good idea to exaggerate the stress when pronouncing Russian. It is stronger than in English and tends to affect the pronunciation of the unstressed vowels in a word. Thus the 'o' in the first syllable of **KOMÉTA**, the first word you learned in Unit 1, is pronounced almost like an 'a', whereas **METPÓ** sounds a bit like *mitro*.

Always try and get your pronunciation as close as possible to that on the tape, and make a habit of practising listening and repeating a little without the aid of the book to attune your ears to the stress patterns of Russian.

| | | | | | |
|---|---|---|---|---|---|
| 1 вода́ | ☐ | 9 пе́пси | ☐ | 17 апте́ка | ☐ |
| 2 во́дка | ☐ | 10 пра́вда | ☐ | 18 Марс | ☐ |
| 3 лимона́д | ☐ | 11 крокоди́л | ☐ | 19 кио́ск | ☐ |
| 4 литр | ☐ | 12 Кавка́з | ☐ | 20 Толсто́й | ☐ |
| 5 кило́ | ☐ | 13 зоопа́рк | ☐ | 21 Война́ и мир | ☐ |
| 6 киломе́тр | ☐ | 14 дом | ☐ | 22 росси́йский | ☐ |
| 7 университе́т | ☐ | 15 да́та | ☐ | 23 Украи́на | ☐ |
| 8 ко́ка ко́ла | ☐ | 16 квас | ☐ | 24 здра́вствуйте | ☐ |

- **ВОДА́** (*water*) and **ВО́ДКА** look very much alike, but do not mistake one for the other! The two words have the same root, **ВОД-**, and **-КА** here denotes something small that is endearing! It is important to work out what different parts of a word mean: you can often guess the meaning of a word you have never heard before.

- **КО́КА КО́ЛА** is a word that has come into common usage in recent years, as has its 'rival' **ПЕ́ПСИ**.

- **ПРА́ВДА** means *truth*. Before the fall of **КОММУНИ́ЗМ**, it was the name of the main daily newspaper, the circulation of which dropped considerably with the onset of **КАПИТАЛИ́ЗМ**. **Пра́вда?** is also used as a question meaning *Is that so?* or *Really?*

- **КРОКОДИ́Л**, besides meaning what you would expect it to mean, is the name of a satirical journal with political cartoons.

- **КАВКА́З**, the Caucasus, is the range of mountains to the south of Russia. Its highest point is Mount Elbrus, at 5633m. Probably the most spectacular in the range is Mount Kazbek.

- **ДОМ** literally means *house* or *home*, and in this sense **ДО́МА** can be used to mean *at home*. It is also used to refer to a large block or apartment building.

- **КВАС** is a traditional Russian drink made of fermented black bread. It is very slightly alcoholic.

- **АПТЕ́КА** is a chemist's. Compare the English *apothecary*.

- **МАРС**, besides the planet, has a new meaning, *Mars bar*.

- **ТОЛСТО́Й** is the famous Russian author of **ВОЙНА́ И МИР**, *War and Peace*.

- **РОССИ́ЙСКИЙ** has come to mean *belonging to the country of Russia*. The usual word for Russian is **ру́сский**, and *in Russian* is **по-ру́сски** – note the small letters. If you want to ask what a word is in Russian, you say: **Как по-ру́сски ...** (*What is the Russian for ...*).

- **УКРАИ́НА**, the Ukraine, one of Russia's largest neighbours.

- **ЗДРА́ВСТВУЙТЕ** is Russian for *hello*. If you have difficulty with the pronunciation, miss out both **в**'s and **у** and say ZDRÁSTYE.

## EXERCISE 1

Look at the list of words numbered 1–24 on the previous page.

First time round listen to the recording and repeat the word.

Second time round you say the word after you hear the number and check it with the tape. If you are satisfied with your attempt, put a tick in the box. If not, repeat your attempt.

## EXERCISE 2

Now we shall mix up the words.

Look at the list of words numbered 1–24 on the previous page.

Find the number of the word that has just been read.

Place it in the appropriate box below.

### Example

You hear **но́мер оди́н**, *number one*, **университе́т**, you find **университе́т** in the list and place 7 in the box next to number one.

| | | | |
|---|---|---|---|
| **1** | 7 | **6** | |
| **2** | | **7** | |
| **3** | | **8** | |
| **4** | | **9** | |
| **5** | | **10** | |

## EXERCISE 3

Here are some of the words written in the Roman alphabet. Identify them by their original numbers, using the boxes provided. The first one is done for you.

| | | | | | |
|---|---|---|---|---|---|
| **1** | LIMONÁD | *3* | **6** | KAVKÁZ | |
| **2** | KILÓ | | **7** | ZOOPÁRK | |
| **3** | PÉPSI | | **8** | VÓDKA | |
| **4** | PRÁVDA | | **9** | VODÁ | |
| **5** | KROKODÍL | | **10** | KILOMÉTR | |

## ● Language information

### ОН, ОНА, ОНО, ОНИ

You will have noticed that nouns have different endings. Nouns like **лимона́д**, **Кавка́з**, **крокоди́л** may be referred to by **ОН** (*he, it*). Those ending in **-А** (**пра́вда**, **во́дка**, **Москва́**) are usually referred to by **ОНА́** (*she, it*). **Па́па**, and other nouns referring to males, would be **ОН**. Nouns ending in **-О** or **-Е** (**вино́**, **кило́**) are referred to by **ОНО́** (*it*). Plural nouns are always referred to by **ОНИ́**.

## EXERCISE 4

Look at the picture below.

The question each time is *Where is ...?* (GDE ...?)

The answer is **Вот он**, **Вот она́** or **Вот оно́**. You choose which of these it is, underline it, then write the number on the correct object in the picture. The first one is done for you.

| | | | | |
|---|---|---|---|---|
| **1** | GDE оркéстр? | <u>Вот он.</u> | Вот онá. | Вот онó. |
| **2** | GDE пáпа? | Вот он. | Вот онá. | Вот онó. |
| **3** | GDE мáма? | Вот он. | Вот онá. | Вот онó. |
| **4** | GDE пианúст? | Вот он. | Вот онá. | Вот онó. |
| **5** | GDE стол? | Вот он. | Вот онá. | Вот онó. |
| **6** | GDE вóдка? | Вот он. | Вот онá. | Вот онó. |
| **7** | GDE водá? | Вот он. | Вот онá. | Вот онó. |
| **8** | GDE винó? | Вот он. | Вот онá. | Вот онó. |
| **9** | GDE пúво? | Вот он. | Вот онá. | Вот онó. |

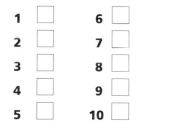 **EXERCISE 5**

On your recording is a series of questions asking you where objects are.
Supply the answers **Вот он, Вот онá** or **Вот онó**.

A space is provided on the recording for your answer and then the correct answer is given.
The boxes below are for you to tick your answers, if you are satisfied with your response. If not, try again.

| | | | |
|---|---|---|---|
| **1** | ☐ | **6** | ☐ |
| **2** | ☐ | **7** | ☐ |
| **3** | ☐ | **8** | ☐ |
| **4** | ☐ | **9** | ☐ |
| **5** | ☐ | **10** | ☐ |

## In, on, at

The nouns you have met up to now have been in the *nominative case*, which is the case you will find in a dictionary.

If you want to answer the question GDE STUDÉNT? with the response that he is in or at the university, **университéт**, you might reply **Он в университéте**.

Look at the picture in Exercise 4 above. You will see **Мáма и пáпа в ресторáне**. You will see **стол**, *a table*, and various things **на столé** (*on the table*). This is the *prepositional case*, sometimes called the *locative case* because it is used after **в** (*in*) and **на** (*on*) when we want to indicate where something is located.

The prepositional case normally ends in **-e**:

| | |
|---|---|
| ресторáн | в ресторáн**е** |
| аптéка | в аптéк**е** |

Some nouns, especially foreign ones, e.g. **таксú, кинó** (*cinema*), **метрó**, do not change at all.

| | |
|---|---|
| таксú | в таксú |
| кинó | в кинó |
| метрó | на метрó |

As you might expect, the prepositional is often used with places. Note that **на** occurs with some words where you might expect **в**. Sometimes you will see **и** as the ending of the prepositional case.

### EXERCISE 6

See if you can make out the following.

Торóнто в Канáде
Стадиóн «Динáмо» в Москвé
Ивáн в Лóндоне
Мадрúд в Испáнии
Нúна на Кавкáзе
Кúев на Украйне

# ● Looking at words

Russian will often change the ending to indicate that a person is female:

СТУДЕ́НТ    *a male student*
СТУДЕ́НТКА  *a female student*

Sometimes Russian will adopt a foreign word and then change it, as in the case of **СТУДЕ́НТ**. This sometimes leads to some strange words. **СПОРТСМЕ́Н** means a sportsman, in the sense of someone who participates in sport. The meaning of **СПОРТСМЕ́НКА** should be obvious. **РЕКОРДСМЕ́НКА** is a little less obvious: it means a female record holder.

---

### A situation to remember (1)

#### Introducing someone

You are introducing Victor to your parents.

| | |
|---|---|
| YOU: | **Ма́ма**, э́то **Ви́ктор**. |
| MAMA: | ZDRÁSTVUYTE, ÓCHEN' **ра́да**. |
| | *Hello, very pleased to meet you.* |
| VIKTOR: | ZDRÁSTVUYTE, ÓCHEN' **рад**. |
| YOU: | **Па́па**, э́то **Ви́ктор**. |
| PAPA: | ZDRÁSTVUYTE, ÓCHEN' **рад**. |
| VIKTOR: | ZDRÁSTVUYTE, ÓCHEN' **рад**. |

---

You might want to ask your friend (or someone else!) some questions. Here are some which involve the word **как** (*how*):

● **EXERCISE 7**

On your recording you will hear another 'meeting' dialogue. Listen carefully for the expressions in the table at the bottom of this page, and underline as many as you can in the table and in the dialogue in *A situation to remember*.

**EXERCISE 8**

Read through the following conversations and then make up some of your own.

| | |
|---|---|
| **Как вас зову́т?** | **Как дела́, Ни́на?** |
| MENYÁ зову́т | NICHEVÓ. |
| **Влади́мир**. | **А как до́ма?** |
| **А как вас зову́т?** | PLÓKHO. |
| **А́нна Петро́вна.** | |
| **Как дела́, Ви́ктор?** | **Как до́ма?** |
| SPASÍBO, KHOROSHÓ. | KHOROSHÓ. |
| **А как ма́ма?** | **А как Анто́н?** |
| NICHEVÓ. | NICHEVÓ, SPASÍBO. |

**Как** does not have to be part of a question. It may sometimes be used as part of an exclamation, as follows:

**Как** PRIYÁTNO ZDES'!  *How pleasant it is here!*
**Как** ZDES' KHOROSHÓ!  *How good it is here!*

| Question | | Answer | |
|---|---|---|---|
| Как вас зову́т? | *What is your name?* | Ви́ктор. | *Victor.* |
| | *(lit. how do they call you?)* | MENYÁ зову́т Ви́ктор. | *My name is Victor.* |
| Как дела́? | *How are things?* | SPASÍBO, KHOROSHÓ. | *Fine, thank you.* |
| Как до́ма? | *How are things at home?* | or NICHEVÓ. | *OK.* |
| Как ма́ма? | *How's your mum?* | | |
| И па́па? | *And your dad?* | or PLÓKHO. | *Terrible.* |

Notice how it can take many more words in English to express an idea!

## *A situation to remember (2)*

**Meeting your neighbour in the park**

If you have the chance to practise a conversation with someone, work as a pair. If you are on your own, remember the situation and the expressions you would use in it. There are some suggestions in the Key at the back of the book.

You meet your neighbour **Ива́н** in the park (**в па́рке**).
What do you say when you first meet?
He asks you how your mother (VÁSHA) is.
You thank him, say she is well and ask after **Ли́за**, his sister (**сестра́**).
You ask if she is at home, and he says no, she is in **Ки́ев**. She is a student at the university.
You say how nice it is in the park, and your friend agrees.

# ● **Playing with words**

## Word square 1

Here is another word square, slightly larger than the last one, and containing more words. The rules are the same as before. See how many words you can find, starting at the top left-hand corner. The last letter of a word starts the next one and letters may be used more than once. If you find you're at a 'dead-end', try a different route.

| К | Н | Е | Т | А | Р |
|---|---|---|---|---|---|
| А | Р | А | П | А | К |
| В | О | Т | П | М | И |
| К | Т | О | Р | А | Н |
| А | О | С | Е | П | О |
| З | О | Е | Р | Е | М |

## Word square 2

You may have noticed that there are a few words for drink in this lesson. Everyone knows the Russian word **ВО́ДКА**. The Russian for *beer* is **ПИ́ВО**. See how many more you can find hidden in the square below. This time all the words are in straight lines; they may be in any direction and may start anywhere. There are one or two you will have to guess, but they are very like English words, so it is not too difficult.

| К | А | К | А | О | П | Л |
|---|---|---|---|---|---|---|
| О | Л | В | О | Т | У | И |
| Р | И | А | Л | О | С | М |
| С | К | С | П | И | В | О |
| Е | С | В | И | Н | О | Н |
| В | И | Н | Т | О | Д | А |
| Л | В | О | Д | К | А | Д |

1  _ _ _ _ _ _
2  _ _ _ _ _ _
3  _ _ _ _
4  _ _ _ _
5  _ _ _ _ _ _
6  _ _ _ _ _
7  _ _ _ _ _ _ _
8  _ _ _ _ _

## WHAT YOU KNOW

**Asking where something is**

| GDE ...? | TEÁTP | OH |
|---|---|---|
|  | KÁCCA | OHÁ |
|  | METPÓ | OHÓ |

**Saying where something is**

| BOT | OH | HA CTOЛÉ |
|---|---|---|
|  | OHÁ | B ПÁPKE |
|  | OHÓ | B PECTOPÁHE |

**Asking after someone's health**

| KAK | ДЕЛÁ? |
|---|---|
|  | MÁMA? |

**Asking/Giving one's name**

| KAK | BAC ЗOBÝT? |
|---|---|

MENYÁ ЗOBÝT ...

**Saying how nice it is**

| KAK | PRIYÁTNO! |
|---|---|
|  | KHOROSHÓ! |

## KEY VOCABULARY

| аптéка | chemist |
|---|---|
| водá | water |
| вóдка | vodka |
| дáта | date |
| дом | house |
| дóма | at home |
| здрáвствуйте | hello |
| зоопáрк | zoo |
| килó | kilo |
| километр | kilometre |
| кинó | cinema |
| киóск | kiosk |
| литр | litre |
| метрó | metro |
| прáвда | truth, is it true? |
| рад | pleased |
| россíйский | Russian |
| стол | table |
| таксí | taxi |
| ÓCHEN' | very |
| NICHEVÓ | OK |
| PLÓKHO | terrible |

**НóМЕР ТРИ**

# Finding your way around

**Asking the way**

**Finding out when a place is open**

NÓMER TRI

## ● Alphabet 3

**There are five new letters in this unit:**

### Х Ю Б Ф Ь

The letters you have met so far are picked out in the
following list:

### а б **в** г **д** е ё ж з и **й** к л м н о п р с т у ф
### **х** ц ч ш щ ъ ы **ь** э **ю** я

**Х** is pronounced like 'ch' in Scottish *loch*. It is the first
letter in **хоккéй** (*ice-hockey*).

**Ю** is like 'yew'.

**Б** sounds like the English 'b'.

**Ф** sounds like the English 'f'.

**Ь** is called 'soft sign'. It does not have a sound of its own,
but 'softens' the sound before it. Listen carefully and see
if you can hear what happens when it occurs.

21

| | | | | | |
|---|---|---|---|---|---|
| 1 футбо́л | ☐ | 10 бюро́ | ☐ | 19 Дина́мо | ☐ |
| 2 клуб | ☐ | 11 фо́то | ☐ | 20 стадио́н | ☐ |
| 3 вход | ☐ | 12 Кремль | ☐ | 21 Спарта́к | ☐ |
| 4 костю́м | ☐ | 13 фильм | ☐ | 22 Торпе́до | ☐ |
| 5 меню́ | ☐ | 14 ю́мор | ☐ | 23 Локомоти́в | ☐ |
| 6 перехо́д | ☐ | 15 авто́бус | ☐ | 24 ремо́нт | ☐ |
| 7 телефо́н | ☐ | 16 буфе́т | ☐ | 25 администра́тор | ☐ |
| 8 бульо́н | ☐ | 17 узбе́к | ☐ | 26 хокке́й | ☐ |
| 9 кафе́ | ☐ | 18 кли́мат | ☐ | 27 кино́ | ☐ |

- Russians are very fond of **ФУТБО́Л**. There are several football grounds in Moscow, some of them shared by two or more teams. **Стадио́н «Дина́мо»** (*Dynamo Stadium*) is a sports complex, where, besides football, other sports are played under the auspices of the Dynamo club. Notice where the Russians put the stress on the words **СТАДИО́Н** and **ДИНА́МО**. Some teams are associated with trades or professions: for example, **ЛОКОМОТИ́В** is the team of the railway workers. Notice that all the words in this paragraph have the stress where you might least expect it.
- **КРЕМЛЬ**, the Kremlin. The word means *fortress* and there are lots of them in ancient Russian towns. The Moscow Kremlin is the seat of the Russian government, and is the site of some beautiful churches and cathedrals. Listen out for the soft **Л** at the end of the word.
- **УЗБЕ́К** is a native of **Узбекиста́н**. This was formerly one of the constituent republics of the Soviet Union and is now an independent country.
- **РЕМО́НТ** is a borrowed word from French and means *repair*. **На ремо́нте** outside a shop or public building means that it is closed for repairs.

- **АДМИНИСТРА́ТОР** is the manager of a hotel, restaurant or other large institution.
- **ХОККЕ́Й**, *ice-hockey*, is a popular sport in Russia, and **ДИНА́МО**, **СПАРТА́К** and **ТОРПЕ́ДО** all have teams in the national ice-hockey league. Other winter sports that are very popular are **ката́ние на конька́х**, *skating*, and **ката́ние на** LÝZHAKH, *skiing*. During winter months many Russians go cross-country skiing on the outskirts of Moscow and other cities.

● **КИНÓ**, *cinema*, is extremely popular in Russia. Most films shown these days are dubbed films from the West, which are also widely for sale on video. The Russian cinema industry now earns most of its money by providing facilities for Western film companies.

Most of the words listed above will easily be recognised by their similarity to English. **БЮРÓ** (*office*) and **БУЛЬÓН** (*clear soup*) are examples of words borrowed from French.

**EXERCISE 1**

Look at the list of words numbered 1–27 on the previous page.

## EXERCISE 1

Look at the list of words numbered 1–27 on the previous page.
First time round listen to the recording and repeat the word.
Second time round you say the word after you hear the number and check it with the tape. If you are satisfied with your attempt, put a tick in the box. If not, repeat your attempt.

## EXERCISE 2

Now we shall mix up the words.
Look at the list of words at the beginning of the unit.
Find the number of the word that has just been read.
Place it in the appropriate box below.
The first one is done for you.

### *Example*

You hear **нóмер одúн**, *number one*, **фóто**, you find **фóто** in the list and place 11 in the box next to number 1. The first one is done for you.

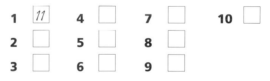

| | | | |
|---|---|---|---|
| **1** *11* | **4** ☐ | **7** ☐ | **10** ☐ |
| **2** ☐ | **5** ☐ | **8** ☐ | |
| **3** ☐ | **6** ☐ | **9** ☐ | |

## EXERCISE 3

Here are some of the words written in the Roman alphabet. Identify them by their original numbers, using the boxes provided. The first one is done for you.

| | | | | |
|---|---|---|---|---|
| **1** AVTOBUS | *15* | **6** KHOKKEY | ☐ |
| **2** PEREKHOD | ☐ | **7** UZBEK | ☐ |
| **3** STADION | ☐ | **8** BYURO | ☐ |
| **4** BULYON | ☐ | **9** YUMOR | ☐ |
| **5** TELEFON | ☐ | **10** TORPEDO | ☐ |

Try to mark the stress without referring to the list at the beginning of the unit. Then check your answers.

# ● Language information

## Directions

In the last unit the question GDE? was asked and you had to provide the answer **Вот он** or **Вот она́**, etc. You may also be given much more complicated replies. Knowing what to expect is important, and helps you to pick out the key bits of the answer. Words to watch out for are:

| | |
|---|---|
| нале́во | *on the left* |
| напра́во | *on the right* |
| PRYÁMO | *straight ahead* |
| далеко́ | *far* |
| недалеко́ | *near* |

........................................

### EXERCISE 4

Look at the sign showing where to find things in a park. Which are to the right and which to the left? Mark → for **напра́во** and ← for **нале́во**.

| | | | | |
|---|---|---|---|---|
| **1** | авто́бус | ☐ | **5** туале́т | ☐ |
| **2** | кино́ | ☐ | **6** кафе́ | ☐ |
| **3** | ка́сса | ☐ | **7** буфе́т | ☐ |
| **4** | телефо́н | ☐ | **8** рестора́н | ☐ |

Try inventing a few sentences of the type:
**авто́бус нале́во, телефо́н напра́во.**

........................................

### ▭ EXERCISE 5

Now listen to the recording. People are giving directions. Sometimes there is one direction indicated, sometimes two or more. If the first direction is to the right, put an arrow pointing to the right; if to the left, put an arrow pointing to the left. If the direction is straight on, put an arrow pointing straight upwards. If the place is a long way, put ✓ in the box under **далеко́?** Don't expect to understand every word, but pick out the key points. The first one is done for you.

**далеко́?**

| | | → | ← | ↑ | | |
|---|---|---|---|---|---|---|
| **1** | метро́ | | | | | |
| **2** | кино́ | | | | | |
| **3** | стадио́н | | | | | |
| **4** | рестора́н | | | | | |
| **5** | такси́ | | | | | |

........................................

### EXERCISE 6

At the top of the next page is a plan of a park. All the paths have been laid out in a squared pattern. We will give you directions using these squares, telling you which direction you have to follow. We will then ask you where you are, and you have to pick out the answer from the list on the left and put its number in the box provided. We have done the first one for you. Start at the same point (**ВХОД**) each time.

........................................

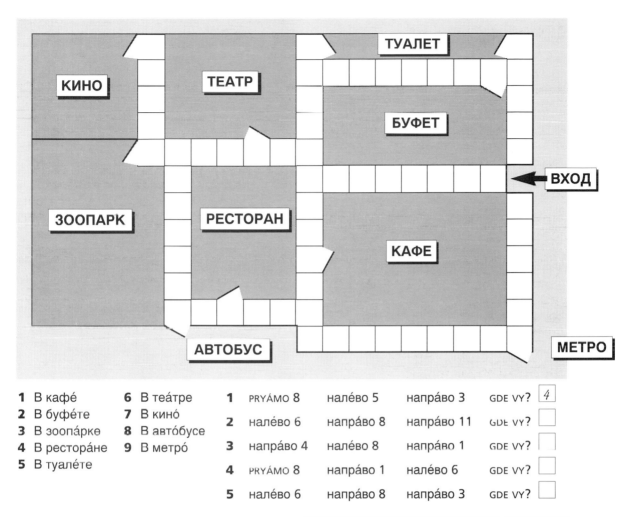

| | | | | | | | |
|---|---|---|---|---|---|---|---|
| **1** | В кафе́ | **6** | В теа́тре | | | | |
| **2** | В буфе́те | **7** | В кино́ | | | | |
| **3** | В зоопа́рке | **8** | В авто́бусе | | | | |
| **4** | В рестора́не | **9** | В метро́ | | | | |
| **5** | В туале́те | | | | | | |

| | | | | |
|---|---|---|---|---|
| **1** | PRYÁMO 8 | нале́во 5 | напра́во 3 | GDE VY? 4 |
| **2** | нале́во 6 | напра́во 8 | напра́во 11 | GDE VY? |
| **3** | напра́во 4 | нале́во 8 | напра́во 1 | GDE VY? |
| **4** | PRYÁMO 8 | напра́во 1 | нале́во 6 | GDE VY? |
| **5** | нале́во 6 | напра́во 8 | напра́во 3 | GDE VY? |

## When

The Russian for *when* is KOGDÁ. The reply may contain one of the following words:

| | |
|---|---|
| SEVÓDNYA | *today* |
| за́втра | *tomorrow* |
| SEYCHÁS | *now* |
| VSEGDÁ | *always* |

## Open, closed

When you want to say the restaurant is open, you say **рестора́н** OTKRÝT. To say it is closed, say **рестора́н** ZAKRÝT. If you want to say the same thing about **кафе́** you would need to add **-о**, or with **апте́ка** you would need to add **-а**. Watch out for this as you proceed in the course.

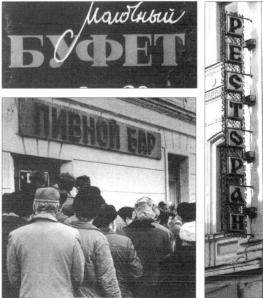

25

## EXERCISE 7

Answer the following questions, explaining when various places are open.
Underline the correct time word.
The first one is done for you.

**1** KOGDÁ **ГУМ** OTKRÝT? (*always*)
**Гум** _____ OTKRÝT
**всегда́**/за́втра/сего́дня/сейча́с.

**2** KOGDÁ **стадио́н** OTKRÝT? (*tomorrow*)
**Стадио́н** _____ OTKRÝT
всегда́/за́втра/сего́дня/сейча́с.

**3** KOGDÁ **кино́** OTKRÝTO? (*today*)
**Кино́** _____ OTKRÝTO
всегда́/за́втра/сего́дня/сейча́с.

**4** KOGDÁ **ка́сса** OTKRÝTA? (*now*)
**Ка́сса** _____ OTKRÝTA
всегда́/за́втра/сего́дня/сейча́с.

**5** KOGDÁ **клуб** OTKRÝT? (*always*)
**Клуб** _____ OTKRÝT
всегда́/за́втра/сего́дня/сейча́с.

## Being polite

Notice that when people want to be polite to one another they will say **извини́те** or **прости́те** (*excuse me*) and usually add POZHÁLSTA (*please*).

## ● Looking at words

### напра́во, нале́во

Notice that NALÉVO and NAPRÁVO have **на-** (*towards*) in common.

### -ход

There are lots of words ending in **-ход**. They are all connected with moving around on foot. **Вход** is an entrance (literally *going in*). The sign **ВХОД В МЕТРО́** tells you where to go into the underground.
**Перехо́д** is a crossing; **пере-** at the beginning of a word means *across*. You see the sign on the street to tell you where you can cross the road. In the centre of big cities in Russia you should only cross where you see this sign. You will also see it in the underground: follow this sign if you want to change lines.

## ● Listening

▭ **EXERCISE 8**

Listen to the recording. This time we are trying to find out whether or not a place is open, and if not when it will be. Answer the questions in English.

1 Is the restaurant open?
2 When is the cinema open?
3 When is the cafe open?
4 Why is the buffet closed?
5 What do they have in the cafe?

---

### A situation to remember (1)

**Finding your way in Russia**

If you have a partner, devise a conversation with him/her. If you are on your own, you will have to play both roles.
You have stopped a passer-by in the street.
Ask the way to GUM, politely, of course.
The directions are left, right and right again.
Ask if it is open.
Ask if it's far. (It isn't.)
End the conversation politely.

You can now devise some more conversations asking your way – in Moscow to BOLSHÓI TEÁTR or in St Petersburg to the Hermitage museum (ERMITÁZH) or to the main street of the city (NÉVSKY PROSPÉKT).

---

## A situation to remember (2)

### Directing a Russian in Britain

Use what you have learnt so far to work out directions in your own environment. Imagine, for example, a Russian friend is visiting you in Britain. She is going to your local town centre for the first time by herself. She asks you the way to the cinema, the chemist's, the park, the university. Give her as detailed directions as possible and don't forget to tell her if it is a long way.

## ● Playing with words

### Alphabet game

Here is another alphabet game. Fill in the blanks below to make up words, using each letter once only. Initial letters are given in bold.

к е а ю р д о о о о о о б **б в л ф ф** ф у х т т

1 **Ф** _ _ _ _ _

2 **К** _ _ _

3 **Ф** _ _ _

4 **Б** _ _ _

5 **В** _ _ _

### Jumbled words

Here are some jumbled words. See if you can decipher them. Use the boxes provided for your answers.

1 ЮМFН

2 НМДИОА

3 ЕХДПРОЕ

4 НФОТЛЕЕ

5 ИРЕЕНИУСВТТ

# 4

## Finding out whether or not something is allowed

## How to make a few words go a long way

## Asking for someone on the telephone

# Asking permission

NOMER CHETYRE

## ● Alphabet 4

### Here are the new letters for this unit:

## Э Г Я Ы Ё

The letters you have met so far are picked out in the following list:

## а б в г д е ё ж з и й к л м н о п р с т у
## ф х ц ч ш щ ъ ы ь э ю я

Most of the new letters are quite unlike any English letters.

**Э** is like the English 'e' in *extra*. Russian uses this letter rarely and usually only in foreign words. Don't confuse it with 'e', which is pronounced *ye*.

**Г** is like English 'g' in *god*.

**Я** is 'ya' as in *kayak*.

**Ы** is a bit like the 'i' sound in *fixture*, but made further back in the throat.

**Ё** is like the 'yo' sound in *yacht*. It is always stressed. The two dots are usually missed out in normal Russian print.

You have now seen all the Russian vowels. Russian has twice as many as English, many of them starting with a 'y' sound:

| English | a | e | i | o | u |
|---------|---|---|---|---|---|
| | | | | | |
| Russian | а | э | ы | о | у |
| | я | е | и | ё | ю |

| | | | | | |
|---|---|---|---|---|---|
| 1 го́род ☐ | 9 газе́та ☐ | 17 грибы́ ☐ |
| 2 телегра́мма ☐ | 10 Росси́я ☐ | 18 О́льга ☐ |
| 3 год ☐ | 11 ГУМ ☐ | 19 май ☐ |
| 4 тури́сты ☐ | 12 экспре́сс ☐ | 20 неде́ля ☐ |
| 5 Аэрофло́т ☐ | 13 эне́ргия ☐ | 21 ряд ☐ |
| 6 самолёт ☐ | 14 програ́мма ☐ | 22 бланк ☐ |
| 7 экску́рсия ☐ | 15 вы́ход ☐ | 23 МГУ ☐ |
| 8 изве́стия ☐ | 16 выходи́ть ☐ | 24 ме́сто ☐ |

- **АЭРОФЛО́Т** is the Russian airline. It used to have the monopoly on all flights in Russia. Internal flights are now operated by a large number of small private companies. The name is still used for international flights. It is a two-part word: **флот** is the Russian word for *fleet*. Notice that the **А** and **Э** in Aeroflot are pronounced separately.

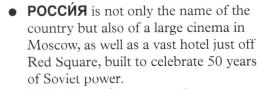

- **ИЗВЕ́СТИЯ** is the word for *news*. It is also the name of a Russian newspaper.

- **ГАЗЕ́ТА**, *a newspaper,* can easily be recognised from the English *gazette*. **Литерату́рная газе́та** is the main literary newspaper, which contains articles on sociological problems, theatre, cinema, television and foreign affairs, as well as on literature.

- **РОССИ́Я** is not only the name of the country but also of a large cinema in Moscow, as well as a vast hotel just off Red Square, built to celebrate 50 years of Soviet power.

- **ГУМ (Госуда́рственный Универса́льный Магази́н)** – *The State Universal Store.* This is perhaps the most famous Russian shop, situated on one side of Red Square. It was built at the end of the last century as a vast shopping arcade. It is now a private company and many famous Western shops have rented space in GUM.

- **МГУ** If you mix the letters of **ГУМ** you have **МГУ**, *Moscow State University,* pronounced **эм-гэ-у́** (EM-GE-Ú). It is situated on the highest point in Moscow and the view from there is a must for most tourists. It is the most prestigious Russian university and there is great competition to get a place to study there. You may need a pass (**про́пуск**) to enter the buildings.

- **ПРОГРА́ММА** is a theatre or football programme, and it is also used to indicate a TV or radio channel.

- **ГРИБЫ́**, *mushrooms*, are one of the Russians' favourite foods. There is a huge variety in the woods and forests, and regular expeditions are organised to collect them. The mushrooms are salted, dried, bottled, boiled, fried or stewed. Perhaps the best place to enjoy them is in a Russian home.
- **НЕДЕ́ЛЯ**, *a week*, is also the weekly supplement of **Изве́стия**.
- **РЯД** is a row. You will see it on a theatre ticket (**билет**). Apart from the date and time of the performance you also need to know if you are in the stalls (**партер**) or the balcony (**балкон**). You may be lucky and be in a box (LÓZHA) or out of luck and be in the Gods (**я́рус**). Watch out for **МЕ́СТО**: on a theatre ticket it gives you your seat number and is found next to your **ряд**. Otherwise **ме́сто** simply means *a place*.

Most of the words here are like English, and you should recognise them. Be careful, though: **бланк** means *a form*, blank until you fill it in! Ones you will not be able to guess are **го́род** (*town, city*), **самолёт** (*plane*) and **год** (*year*). **го́род** and a related form are seen as the second part of the names of a number of Russian towns and cities: **Но́вгород** and **Ленингра́д**, the previous name for **Санкт-Петербу́рг**. **Год** is often shortened to **г.**, and you will see 1996 **г.** or **в ма́е** 1996 **г.** (*in May, 1996*).

···················································

###  EXERCISE 1

Look at the list of words numbered 1–24 on the previous page.
First time round listen to the recording and repeat the word.
Second time round you say the word after you hear the number and check it with the tape. If you are satisfied with your attempt, put a tick in the box. If not, repeat your attempt.

···················································

### EXERCISE 2

Now we shall mix up the words.
Look at the list of words numbered 1–24 on the previous page.
Find the number of the word that has just been read.
Place it in the appropriate box below.

#### *Example*

You hear **но́мер оди́н**, *number one*, **вы́ход**, you find **вы́ход** in the list and place 15 in the box next to number 1. The first one is done for you.

| 1 | 15 | 4 | | 7 | | 10 | |
|---|----|---|---|---|---|----|---|
| 2 | | 5 | | 8 | | | |
| 3 | | 6 | | 9 | | | |

···················································

## EXERCISE 3

Here are some of the words written in the Roman alphabet. Identify them by their original numbers, using the boxes provided. The first one is done for you. Put in the stress marks and check your answers from the original list.

| | | | | | |
|---|---|---|---|---|---|
| **1** | GRIBY | 17 | **6** | ROSSIYA | |
| **2** | IZVESTIYA | | **7** | TELEGRAMMA | |
| **3** | VYKHOD | | **8** | SAMOLYOT | |
| **4** | RYAD | | **9** | ENERGIYA | |
| **5** | VYKHODIT' | | **10** | AEROFLOT | |

# ● Life in Russia

It is important to know what you can and cannot do in Russia, a country very different from our own. Smoking, for example, is forbidden in all public buildings and on public transport. The word *to smoke* is **кури́ть**: the most common notice is: **НЕ КУРИ́ТЬ!**

If you need to smoke, you will usually find a smoking room: look for the sign **кури́тельная ко́мната** (*smoking room*). It is usually by the toilets. On a train, you can smoke at the open section where two carriages join.

If you are unsure about whether something is permitted, you should use the word MÓZHNO. Make your voice go up when you ask:

MÓZHNO **кури́ть**? *Can I smoke?*
MÓZHNO **фотографи́ровать**? *Can I take photographs?*

or just simply say MÓZHNO?
Listen for the answer.
MÓZHNO or MÓZHNO, POZHÁLSTA means that it is allowed; **нельзя́**, or **нет, нельзя́** means that it is not, that it is forbidden.

## EXERCISE 4

The man in the drawing is arranging some notices forbidding things. See if you can guess what they mean. The first one is done for you.

**1** по газо́нам не ходи́ть!
   *Don't walk on the grass!*

**2** вхо́да нет! _____

**3** не фотографи́ровать! _____

   _____

**4** нет вы́хода! _____

**5** здесь не ку́рят! _____

**6** перехо́да нет! _____

**7** не кури́ть! _____

# ● Language information

## MÓZHNO

As we have pointed out earlier, some Russian words are especially useful in expressing a lot of information. One of these words is MÓZHNO. You may use it as a way of asking permission, or asking for the loan of something, as in the examples below.

| | |
|---|---|
| **Бланк** MÓZHNO? | *May I have a form?* |
| **Газéту** MÓZHNO? | *May I read your newspaper?* |
| **Телефóн** MÓZHNO? | *May I use your telephone?* |
| **Нúну** MÓZHNO? | *May I speak to Nina?* |
| **Винó** MÓZHNO? | *May I have some wine?* |

Russian simply misses out the verbs (*have, read, use, speak*), as it is obvious from the context.

Notice that **газéта**, *newspaper*, changes to **газéту**. **Бланк**, **телефóн** and **винó** do not change. You are using the *accusative case*.

Granting permission often includes the word POZHÁLSTA (*please*), which is used in many more situations than its English counterpart (see Unit 6).

## EXERCISE 5

Here is a sample conversation:

A: **Газéту** MÓZHNO?
B: POZHÁLSTA. **Вот онá**.
A: **Спасúбо**.

Here are some pictures of some objects. Using the conversation as a model, ask if you can have it, then reconstruct the rest of the conversation for yourself. Look back at the *Language information* in Unit 2 to make sure you know when to use **Вот он, онá, онó** or **онú**.

**1** билéт

**2** вóдка

**3** грибы́

**5** стакáн

**4** мáрка

**6** телефóн

## Plural

You may have noticed that some of the words in this unit end in **-ы** (**грибы́**, **тури́сты**). You add **ы** for the plural just like you add *s* in English to make a word plural. **Грибы́**, for example, means *mushrooms* and **тури́сты** means *tourists*. You can casily work out when you see **тури́ст** that it means one tourist, and that **гриб** means one mushroom.

Words ending in **-а** also have **-ы** in the plural, e.g. **газе́та – газе́ты** (*newspapers*). **И** is used instead of **ы** after **к** and a few other letters: **студе́нтка – студе́нтки** (*female students*). The ending **и** is also found in **они́** (see Unit 2). Sometimes, with 'borrowed' or 'imported' words, the result looks strange. **Бу́тсы**, taken from the English, means *football boots*. The singular is hardly ever used.

## ● Looking at words

In Unit 3 you met the words **вход** (*entrance*) and **перехо́д** (*crossing*). There is another similar word in this unit: **вы́ход** (*exit*). Be careful with this one, as it means exactly the opposite of **вход**, and you don't want to confuse one with the other! You may also have noticed **выходи́ть** (*to exit*). This gives you a three-part word: **вы-** (*out*), **ход** (*go*) and **-ить**, which tells you that it is a verb, that an action is involved. Most words ending in **-ать** or **-ить** are verbs, meaning *to do* something: e.g. **фотографи́ровать** (*to photograph*).

## ● Listening

### On the telephone

### ▭ EXERCISE 6

On your recording is a telephone conversation. A man is trying to make a date with a woman (Olga). Listen to the conversation and see if you can answer the questions in English or Russian.

1   Who does the man speak to first?
2   Does she know him?
3   What is the man's name?
4   What does he want Olga to do?
5   What is her reply?
6   When do they intend to go to the theatre?

### *A situation to remember*

You ring someone up on the phone and arrange to go to the theatre. Devise a conversation with a partner. Here are some prompts:

**Person 1**

- Say hello and give your name.
- Suggest that you go to the cinema (**Пойдём в кино́**).
- Say today.
- Say that's fine, we'll go tomorrow.

**Person 2**

- Say hello and ask how your friend is.
- Ask when.
- Say you can't go today, suggest tomorrow.

Next time round, suggest that you go to the theatre, to GUM, to a cafe or to a restaurant.

## ● Playing with words

### Jumbled words 1

Here, in jumbled form, are some of the words introduced in this lesson. Work out what they are, using the boxes provided. There is a hidden word in one of the vertical columns. What is it?

1  ырбиг
2  гмраомарп
3  нгяэире
4  торфоалэ
5  хывдо

Hidden word:

### Jumbled words 2

Here is another game like the last one.

1  азгтае
2  усотвба
3  сскэрепс
4  исрясо
5  кярскиэус
6  ятвзисие

Hidden word:

### Matching symbols

Pick out the matching symbols and form words with the letters inside them. You are given the first letter in each word.

1  С _ _ _ _ _ _
2  Б _ _ _ _
3  Р _ _ _ _
4  В _ _ _ _
5  Н _ _ _ _ _

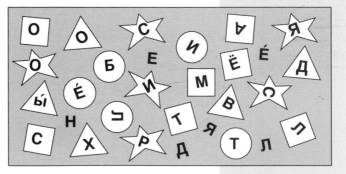

# Revision

**NOMER PYAT**

## ● Alphabet 5

**There are six new letters in this unit, and they are all quite unlike any English letters:**

**Ж Ч Ш Щ Ц Ъ**

Now you have seen the whole alphabet:

**а б в г д е ё ж з и й к л м н о п р с т у ф
х ц ч ш щ ъ ы ь э ю я**

Notice the order of the alphabet. The order from **и** (i) to **у** (u) is very similar to the order of the Roman alphabet, and most of the 'exotic' letters occur towards the end.

**Ж** is pronounced much like the 's' in *measure*.
**Ч** is similar to 'ch' in *Charles*.
**Ш** resembles 'sh' in *shush*.
**Щ** is like the 'shch' in *fresh cheese*.
**Ц** is pronounced like the last two letters in *cats*.
**Ъ** the hard sign, the rarest letter in the Russian alphabet, only occurs in the middle of words and does not have a sound of its own.

35

| | | | | | |
|---|---|---|---|---|---|
| 1 Чéхов | ☐ | 11 москви́ч | ☐ | 20 щи | ☐ |
| 2 чáйка | ☐ | 12 этáж | ☐ | 21 шáпка | ☐ |
| 3 маши́на | ☐ | 13 мóжно | ☐ | 22 жéнщина | ☐ |
| 4 электри́чество | ☐ | 14 хорошó | ☐ | 23 цирк | ☐ |
| 5 информáция | ☐ | 15 шоссé | ☐ | 24 пóчта | ☐ |
| 6 бифштéкс | ☐ | 16 цветы́ | ☐ | 25 центр | ☐ |
| 7 шашлы́к | ☐ | 17 вéчер | ☐ | 26 концéрт | ☐ |
| 8 демонстрáция | ☐ | 18 ночь | ☐ | 27 подъéзд | ☐ |
| 9 матч | ☐ | 19 Крáсная | | | |
| 10 Большóй теáтр | ☐ | плóщадь | ☐ | | |

- **ЧÉХОВ.** Антóн Пáвлович Чéхов (Chekhov) wrote a large number of mainly humorous short stories and a few famous plays, revealing the changes in society at the end of 19th-century Russia. He died in 1904, aged 44.
- **ЧÁЙКА** is a seagull and the name of a play by Chekhov. It also used to be a very grand Russian car (**маши́на**), used by communist party members under the old regime. Other Russian makes of car are **Москви́ч** (*Muscovite*), **Вóлга** and **Жигули́**. The **Жигули́** is made in a factory built by Fiat. We know the export version in this country as **Лáда**. You will also see many imported cars in Russia nowadays.
- **БИФШТÉКС** is usually used to describe a hamburger or rissole of some sort. **ЩИ** is the traditional Russian *cabbage soup*. There is more information about food in Unit 9.
- **ШАШЛЫ́К**, or more often referred to in the plural **шашлыки́** (notice the shift in stress) are barbecued pieces of meat on a spit, larger than kebabs, which are often served with spring onions. They may be obtained at a **шашлы́чная**, a specialist restaurant, and you will see them on most restaurant menus.

Bolshoi Theatre

- **БОЛЬШÓЙ ТЕÁТР** is the most famous theatre in Russia, with its own ballet and opera companies. **Большóй** means *big*. Of course, nowadays there are bigger theatres, but none with the same atmosphere as the Bolshoi. The theatre also has a huge stage, big enough even to accommodate people on horseback.
- **ЭТÁЖ** has been borrowed from French and means a *floor* or *storey* in a building. Most Russians live in flats and you will need to know which **этáж** they live on to find their flat.
- **ШОССÉ** is another French borrowing: it is a *highway*, leading out of one town towards another. Russians pronounce the 'e', as if it was spelt with **э**. This makes it sound foreign to a Russian. Listen out for it on the tape.

ЦИРК | представления для детей

- **ВЕ́ЧЕР** means *evening* and **НОЧЬ** means *night*. You wish someone **до́брый ве́чер** (*good evening*) when you go to see them in the evening and **споко́йной но́чи** (*good night*) when they are going to bed.

- **КРА́СНАЯ ПЛО́ЩАДЬ** was called Red Square long before the advent of communism. **Кра́сный** used to have the meaning *beautiful*. Today **краси́вый** is the usual word for *beautiful*.

- **ША́ПКА** is a traditional Russian cap or hat made out of fur, with or without ear-flaps to keep out the cold.

- **ЖЕ́НЩИНА**, *woman*. The sign you see on ladies' toilets is **Ж**, occasionally **Д** (the word **да́ма** means *lady*). Men's toilets are marked **М** (the word **мужчи́на** means *man*).

- **ЦИРК**: Russians love the circus. The Moscow State Circus is the most famous in the world. It has two permanent buildings: **Ста́рый цирк**, the old building on the inner ring road, and the new building, **Но́вый цирк**, near **МГУ**.

- **ПО́ЧТА**, a *post office*, is where you buy **ма́рки** (*stamps*) and **откры́тки** (*postcards*). Notice the similarity between **откры́тки** and **откры́т** (*open*). **ПО́ЧТА** is also written on letterboxes, as in the example in the photograph.

- **КОНЦЕ́РТ**, besides *concert*, means *concerto*.

- **ПОДЪЕ́ЗД** is the entrance to a block of flats. You will find that the entrance that you require is not from the street, but from a **двор** (*courtyard*). If you are lost, ask one of the old women (**ба́бушки**) who are usually to be found sitting on the benches. You may see a few old men, but women of this age tend to outnumber men, many of whom died during the second world war.

Look at the list of words numbered 1–27 on page 36.

First time round listen and repeat.

Second time round you say the word after you hear the number and check it with the tape.

If you are satisfied with your attempt, put a tick in the box. If not, repeat your attempt.

⌨ **EXERCISE 2**

Now we shall mix up the words. Look at the list of words, find the number of the word that has just been read in the list on page 36 and place the number in the box below.

### Example

You hear **но́мер оди́н**, *number one,* **электри́чество**. You find **электри́чество** in the list and place 4 in the box next to number 1. The first one is done for you.

| | | | | | | | |
|---|---|---|---|---|---|---|---|
| **1** | *4* | **4** | ☐ | **7** | ☐ | **10** | ☐ |
| **2** | ☐ | **5** | ☐ | **8** | ☐ | | |
| **3** | ☐ | **6** | ☐ | **9** | ☐ | | |

**EXERCISE 3**

Here are some of the words written in the Roman alphabet. Identify them by their original numbers, using the boxes provided. The first one is done for you.

| | | | | | |
|---|---|---|---|---|---|
| **1** | TSVETÝ | *16* | **6** | SHCHI | ☐ |
| **2** | BIFSHTEKS | ☐ | **7** | ZHENSHCHINA | ☐ |
| **3** | SHOSSE | ☐ | **8** | VECHER | ☐ |
| **4** | SHAPKA | ☐ | **9** | TSENTR | ☐ |
| **5** | ETAZH | ☐ | **10** | SHASHLYK | ☐ |

When you have put in all your numbers see if you can mark all the stresses in the correct position from memory. Check your answers from the list.

⌨ **EXERCISE 4**

On your cassette is a conversation about what is going on in various places in Moscow. Each time one person asks the question **Что идёт в …?** The other person looks in the newspaper and provides the answer. You have to make sentences by joining up the words below.

| | | |
|---|---|---|
| В па́рке | идёт | о́пера |
| В кино́ | идёт | концёрт |
| В Большо́м теа́тре | идёт | ле́кция |
| В университе́те | идёт | фильм |

## ● Language information

### Alphabet

You have now met the whole of the Russian alphabet, so we shall not use any more transcriptions. You may have noticed that very often one letter in Russian can take several letters in English.

Some names for well-known Russians now have a standard spelling in English. **Чайко́вский** is spelt Tchaikovsky (and not Chaykovsky, which is a more accurate transliteration).

The Cyrillic alphabet has definite advantages when it comes to the representation of Slavonic sounds. The Polish language does not use it, and it has sz for **ш**, cz for **ч**, and szcz for **щ**! The Russian word **щипцы́** (*tongs, forceps*) in Polish is *szczypce* (eight letters).

## ● Looking at words

### -ЦИЯ

The meaning of **информа́ция** should be obvious. The ending **-ция** on this word as well as on the end of the words **демонстра́ция** and **конститу́ция** corresponds to the English *-tion*. The ending **-ство** in **электри́чество** (*electricity*) corresponds to the English *-ity*. **-ство** can have a variety of translations in English: *-ity*, *-cy* or *-ism*.

### EXERCISE 5

Here are some examples of words ending in **-ство** or **-ция**, where foreign words are 'Russified'. See if you can guess what they mean.

1 аге́нтство _____

2 пира́тство _____

3 хулига́нство _____

4 администра́ция _____

5 мобилиза́ция _____

6 концентра́ция _____

7 конфедера́ция _____

8 револю́ция _____

## Prefixes

The most frequent initial letter in Russian is **п**. This is because most prefixes begin with this letter. See the Grammar section for further information.

| | | |
|---|---|---|
| пере- | перехо́д | *crossing* |
| про- | про́пуск | *pass* |
| по- | пойдём | *let's go* |
| под- | подъе́зд | *entrance* |
| при- | приходи́ть | *to arrive* |

## ● Revision

### EXERCISE 6
Listen to the tape.
You will hear **Э́то рестора́н** (*This is a restaurant*) and then **Вот Ви́ктор** (*Here is Viktor*). You have to say that *He is in the restaurant* – **Он в рестора́не**. You will be given the correct answer on the tape.

### EXERCISE 7
Underline the correct alternative. The first one is done for you.

1 Москва́
   в Росси́и
   в А́нглии
   в Аме́рике

2 Кра́сная пло́щадь
   в Ло́ндоне
   на стадио́не
   в це́нтре Москвы́

3 Э́то вы́ход. Здесь нельзя́
   переходи́ть
   выходи́ть
   входи́ть

4 Э́то вход. Здесь мо́жно
   входи́ть
   выходи́ть
   кури́ть

5 Э́то вы́ход. Здесь нет
   перехо́да
   вы́хода
   вхо́да

6 На стадио́не сейча́с идёт
   матч
   конце́рт
   крокоди́л

## EXERCISE 8

Here is a drawing with some signs on it.
Match the Russian words to the drawing by
placing the appropriate number in the box.

автобусы   `4`    не курить   ☐

туалет(м)   ☐    такси   ☐

касса   ☐    Нина   ☐

выход   ☐    туалет(ж)   ☐

метро   ☐    телефон-автомат   ☐

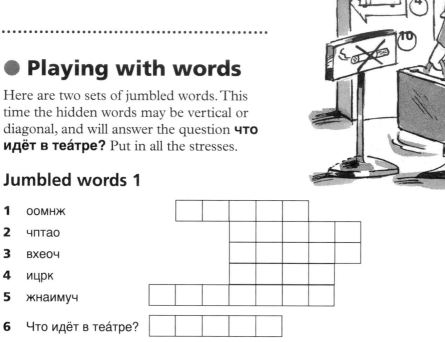

## ● Playing with words

Here are two sets of jumbled words. This
time the hidden words may be vertical or
diagonal, and will answer the question **что
идёт в театре?** Put in all the stresses.

### Jumbled words 1

**1** оомнж

**2** чптао

**3** вхеоч

**4** ицрк

**5** жнаимуч

**6** Что идёт в театре?

### Jumbled words 2

**1** кйача

**2** сеошс

**3** фцмярииноа

**4** ртнце

**5** щанижен

**6** ршхооо

**7** чтма

**8** Что идёт в театре?

## LANGUAGE REVIEW

You now know all the alphabet. Here are some important words and phrases that we have transliterated until now. The unit where they first occurred is given in brackets. Write in the English translation.

До свида́ния! (1) _____

закры́т (3) _____

Здра́вствуйте! (1) _____

Когда́ (3) _____

Кто э́то? (1) _____

мо́жно (4) _____

ничего́ (2) _____

откры́т (3) _____

пожа́луйста (1) _____

пря́мо (3) _____

сего́дня (3) _____

сейча́с (3) _____

спаси́бо (1) _____

Что э́то? (1) _____

Note that **ничего́** and **сего́дня** are spelt with a **г** but pronounced with a 'v': NICHE<u>VÓ</u>, SE<u>VÓ</u>DNYA.

## Questions and answers

You should know how to ask the following questions and understand the answers. If you need to remind yourself of how to say any of these things, the unit where we first practised the phrases is given on the right.

## KEY VOCABULARY

| | |
|---|---|
| Большо́й теа́тр | Bolshoi Theatre |
| же́нщина | woman |
| конце́рт | concert |
| Кра́сная пло́щадь | Red Square |
| маши́на | car |
| москви́ч | Muscovite |
| по́чта | post office |
| туале́т | toilet |
| хорошо́ | good |
| цветы́ | flowers |
| центр | centre |
| цирк | circus |
| ча́йка | seagull |
| Че́хов | Chekhov |
| ша́пка | hat |
| шашлы́к | kebab |
| шоссе́ | highway |
| щи | cabbage soup |
| электри́чество | electricity |
| эта́ж | floor, storey |

| Question | Answer | Unit |
|---|---|---|
| What is this?/Who is this? | This is ... | 1 |
| Where is it? | Here it is. | 2 |
| | It is in the restaurant/on the table. | 2 |
| | It is straight ahead/on the left/ on the right. | 3 |
| | It is a long way away/nearby. | 3 |
| When is it open/closed? | today/tomorrow/now | 3 |
| Can I smoke? Can I have the paper? | You can/can't ... | 4 |

# Travelling around town

## ● Life in Russia

### Travelling around a town

There are three types of public transport in most large Russian towns:

| | |
|---|---|
| *bus* | авто́бус |
| *trolleybus* | тролле́йбус |
| *tram* | трамва́й |

Moscow, St Petersburg and a few other large cities in Russia also have an underground (**метро́**).

It doesn't matter how far you want to go, there is a standard fare covering any distance in a town. If you go by metro, you can change lines (**де́лать переса́дку**) as often as you want, you still pay the standard fare.

If you are being given directions, listen out for the phrases:

| | |
|---|---|
| *by bus* | на автóбусе |
| *by trolleybus* | на троллéйбусе |
| *by tram* | на трамвáе |
| *by underground* | на метрó |

You will need to know where the nearest stop (**останóвка**) is, or how to find the underground station (**стáнция метрó**).

If you want to find your way to Red Square, ask:

Как мне пройти́ на Крáсную плóщадь?
*How can I get to Red Square?*

A typical answer might be:

Иди́те *(go)* пря́мо и потóм *(then)* налéво.

You should recognise the direction words from Unit 3.

Another direction word you might hear is **напрóтив** *(opposite)*.

If you are a long way from Red Square, ask instead:

Как мне проéхать на Крáсную плóщадь?

This is the answer that you night hear:

Лу́чше *(it is better)* на автóбусе. Там напрóтив останóвка.

.......................................................

## EXERCISE 1

Using the sample questions and answers given above, work with a partner and ask your way to the following places:

### в Москвé
1 в Большóй теáтр
2 в Третьякóвскую галерéю (the Tretyakov Gallery, the biggest collection of Russian art in Moscow)
3 на Арбáт (one of the main streets in Moscow)

### в Санкт-Петербу́рге
4 в Мари́инский теáтр (this is the theatre in St Petersburg that used to be known as the Kirov)
5 на Нéвский проспéкт (one of the main streets in St Petersburg)
6 в Эрмитáж (the Hermitage museum: the finest collection of Western art in Russia)

.......................................................

To travel by bus, trolleybus or tram you need to buy some tickets (**талóны**). They are usually sold in strips of ten and you can get them from the driver (**води́тель**) or from a kiosk (**киóск**) or cash desk (**кáсса**) in big shops. When you get on, you need to punch your ticket at one of the machines (**компóстер**), one for each journey. If you don't do this, you may get fined by an inspector (**контролёр**). You will only find conductors on country buses.

Public transport tends to be very crowded: you will be amazed at how many people can get into a Russian bus! You may need to be forceful in elbowing your way on and off. As you are getting near your stop, position yourself near the exit. If the person in front doesn't appear to be getting off, ask him or her: **Вы сейча́с выхо́дите?** Listen out for the answer **Да, выхожу́**: this means they are getting off. Alternatively they will try to move aside to let you past. It may be a very tight squeeze. If *you* get asked the question, don't forget to move out of the way if you are not getting off, or you may find yourself getting off, even if you don't want to!

The first Russian underground was started in Moscow in 1935 and the early stations are very grand affairs with lots of marble, mosaics, statues, etc. The stations on the circle line in Moscow (**кольцева́я ли́ния**) are fine examples of this style. The first underground line in St Petersburg was opened in 1955 and is much simpler. Many central stations have doors in the wall that open when the train arrives. It is very deep and you can't usually see the top of the escalator (**эскала́тор**) from the bottom.

The underground is the fastest and most efficient way of travelling round a big Russian city. Trains are very frequent, every two minutes or even less in the rush hour. You will usually find buses, trolleybuses or trams at the underground stations to take you on further. The underground closes between 12.30 and 1.00 a.m.

To use the underground, you have to buy a token (**жето́н**) from the **ка́сса** at the station. You can save time and buy more than one. You then put the **жето́н** into a machine and you go through the barrier when you see the green light or the word **ИДИ́ТЕ**. If you go through when it says **СТО́ЙТЕ**, or when the red light is on, you will be grabbed by a set of mechanical arms!

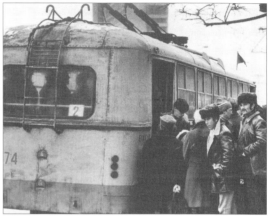

**Петербургский Метрополитен. Схема линий**

ПРОСПЕКТ ПРОСВЕЩЕНИЯ
ОЗЕРКИ
УДЕЛЬНАЯ
ПИОНЕРСКАЯ
ЧЕРНАЯ РЕЧКА
ПЕТРОГРАДСКАЯ
ГОРЬКОВСКАЯ

ДЕВЯТКИНО
ГРАЖДАНСКИЙ ПРОСПЕКТ
АКАДЕМИЧЕСКАЯ
ПОЛИТЕХНИЧЕСКАЯ
ПЛ. МУЖЕСТВА
ЛЕСНАЯ
ВЫБОРГСКАЯ
ПЛ. ЛЕНИНА

ПРИМОРСКАЯ
ВАСИЛЕОСТРОВСКАЯ
ГОСТИНЫЙ ДВОР
НЕВСКИЙ ПРОСПЕКТ
МАЯКОВСКАЯ
ЧЕРНЫШЕВСКАЯ
ПЛ. ВОССТАНИЯ
ДОСТОЕВСКАЯ
ЛИГОВСКИЙ ПР.
СЕННАЯ ПЛ.
САДОВАЯ
ПЛ. АЛЕКСАНДРА НЕВСКОГО
ВЛАДИМИРСКАЯ
НОВОЧЕРКАССКАЯ
ПУШКИНСКАЯ
ТЕХНОЛОГИЧЕСКИЙ ИНСТИТУТ
ЕЛИЗАРОВСКАЯ
ЛАДОЖСКАЯ

БАЛТИЙСКАЯ
ФРУНЗЕНСКАЯ
ЛОМОНОСОВСКАЯ
НАРВСКАЯ
МОСКОВСКИЕ ВОРОТА
ПРОСПЕКТ БОЛЬШЕВИКОВ
КИРОВСКИЙ ЗАВОД
ЭЛЕКТРОСИЛА
ПРОЛЕТАРСКАЯ
АВТОВО
ПАРК ПОБЕДЫ
УЛ. ДЫБЕНКО
ЛЕНИНСКИЙ ПРОСПЕКТ
МОСКОВСКАЯ
ОБУХОВО
**4-я линия**
ПРОСПЕКТ ВЕТЕРАНОВ
ЗВЕЗДНАЯ
КУПЧИНО
РЫБАЦКОЕ

**1-я линия**      **2-я линия**      **3-я линия**

There are maps of the underground network in each station and on each platform you will see a list of stations for the current line, with interchanges indicated. The station names on the platform are not as clear as in London; you will have to listen out for the recorded announcements given at each station. The phrase **сле́дующая ста́нция** means *the next station is*. The other message you will hear at every station is **Осторо́жно, две́ри закрыва́ются!** (*Careful, the doors are closing.*)

Metro token

If you are in Russia for a long time, it is worth buying a season tickct (**проездно́й биле́т**). They are sold towards the end of every month and are valid for one month from the 1st of the following month. You can also buy **еди́ный биле́т**, which covers you for a month for all forms of transport.

## Shopping

If you go into one of the old-style shops, you will find that standards of service have not improved with the collapse of communism. To attract a woman shop assistant's attention, say: **Дéвушка!** You would also use it to a waitress in a restaurant. Don't confuse it with the word **дéвочка**, who is a girl far too young to be working in a shop! A **дéвушка** may be insulted if you call her a **дéвочка**!

Here are the sort of expressions you might need in a shop.

If you were trying to buy a metro map (**план метрó**), you might have the following conversation:

– Дéвушка, у вас есть (*do you have*) план метрó?
– Есть.

If you can see the metro map, but want to look at it before you buy, the conversation might start as follows:

– Дéвушка, покажи́те план метрó!
– Вот он, пожáлуйста.

The assistant will usually tell you how much it costs (**скóлько стóит**). Don't worry at this stage if you can't understand the answer, just ask her to write it down for you:

– Напиши́те, пожáлуйста.

Having decided what you want, the assistant will usually ask you to pay at the cash-desk, as assistants in old-style shops rarely take the money.

– Плати́те, пожáлуйста, в кáссу!

At the **кáсса** you will be given a receipt (**чек**), which you take back to the assistant to claim your goods.

Of course, most transactions will not be as complicated as this. Here is someone buying something in a cafe (**кафé**) or snack bar (**буфéт**):

A: Дéвушка, у вас есть винó?
B: Нет.
A: А что у вас есть?
B: У нас коньяќ, пи́во, шампáнское, чай и кóфе.
A: Дáйте (*Give*), пожáлуйста, чай и пи́во.
B: Вот, пожáлуйста, чай и пи́во.

You will notice that the prices of many goods (particularly expensive imported goods) are quoted in US dollars because of the instability of the rouble. You will, however, be expected to pay in roubles at the current exchange rate. Please note that the present volatile nature of the Russian economy makes any statement about exchange rates or trading practices subject to change with very little notice.

## ● Language information

### Numbers 1–10

| The Russian numbers from 1–10 are: | | | |
|---|---|---|---|
| оди́н | 1 | шесть | 6 |
| два | 2 | семь | 7 |
| три | 3 | во́семь | 8 |
| четы́ре | 4 | де́вять | 9 |
| пять | 5 | де́сять | 10 |

When Russians count they start **раз**, **два**, **три** instead of using **оди́н**, **два**, **три**. **Раз** literally means *once*, **два ра́за** *twice*, etc.

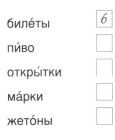

**раз**          **два**

**три**          **четы́ре**

Notice that **два** starts with the same letter as *duet*, *double* and *duo*, and **три** is like English.

Make sure that you distinguish the number 9 (**де́вять**) from 10 (**де́сять**). **Де́сять** is related to the English *decimal*.

Five short conversations are recorded on your cassette. Each one involves a young woman (**де́вушка**) at a kiosk and a customer. He asks for an item and she asks him how many (**ско́лько**) he wants. You have to put the quantity he asks for in the box. The first one is done for you.

биле́ты    | *6* |

пи́во    | |

откры́тки    | |

ма́рки    | |

жето́ны    | |

Russian numerals might at first sight appear daunting, but they are not as difficult as they might first appear. If you know the numbers up to nine, with a little bit of help you can work out numbers all the way up to 1000.

## Numbers 11–19

### EXERCISE 3

Look at the following list of numbers and see if you can identify them. They are the numbers from 11–19, but not in order. Fill in the blanks.

восемна́дцать        1__
двена́дцать          1__
девятна́дцать        1__
оди́ннадцать         1__
пятна́дцать          1__
семна́дцать          1__
трина́дцать          1__
четы́рнадцать        1__
шестна́дцать         1__

## Numbers 20–90

### EXERCISE 4

Now try to work out the numbers from 20–90. You should be able to recognise the numbers **два** through to **де́вять** in the first part of all but the last number. The numbers are not in order.

во́семьдесят         __0
два́дцать            __0
девяно́сто           __0
пятьдеся́т           __0
се́мьдесят           __0
три́дцать            __0
шестьдеся́т          __0
со́рок               __0

## Numbers 100–900

### EXERCISE 5

Finally, try the numbers from 100–900. As usual they are all jumbled up. The one that you may not guess is left until the end. What does it mean?

две́сти              __00
пятьсо́т             __00
семьсо́т             __00
три́ста              __00
восемьсо́т           __00
четы́реста           __00
девятьсо́т           __00
шестьсо́т            __00
сто                 __00

## Going to a place

Russian uses the same words for *to* (**в**, **на**) as it does for *in, on, at*. The only difference is the ending on the noun. If the noun ends in **-e** or **-и** (prepositional case), the meaning will be *in, on, at*. We have looked at this construction in Unit 2. If the noun does not change, or ends in **-у** instead of **-а**, the meaning is *to*. This is another use of the accusative case, which we first met in Unit 4.

### EXERCISE 6

Look at the phrases with **в** or **на**, then check the ending of the following word. Write down *in, on, at, to* in the box to indicate the meaning of **в** or **на**. The first one is done for you.

1 в Москве́    *in*      6 в кварти́ру    ☐
2 в Эрмита́же  ☐         7 на конце́рте   ☐
3 в ГУМ       ☐         8 в Ло́ндон      ☐
4 на Арба́т    ☐         9 на пло́щадь    ☐
5 во дворе́    ☐         10 в Росси́и     ☐

## Asking for things

If you want to look at an article in a shop, you use the phrase:

Покажи́те, пожа́луйста (*Show me, please*)
or
Да́йте, пожа́луйста (*Give me, please*).

This is followed by the accusative case (the object of the verb):

– Покажи́те, пожа́луйста, журна́л и кни́гу.
– Вот, пожа́луйста, журна́л и вот кни́га.

If you are certain that you want to buy them, say simply:

– Да́йте, пожа́луйста, журна́л и кни́гу.

### EXERCISE 7

Now you make up some conversations asking for the following articles. Use either **Покажи́те, пожа́луйста** or **Да́йте, пожа́луйста**.

1 во́дка и вино́
2 ма́рка и откры́тка
3 кни́га и газе́та
4 стака́н и ча́шка (*cup*)
5 самова́р и чай

## Пожа́луйста

**Пожа́луйста** has got a variety of meanings. It can mean *please*:

Покажи́те, пожа́луйста  *Show me, please*
Извини́те, пожа́луйста  *Excuse me, please*

Besides meaning *please*, **пожа́луйста** means *don't mention it* when used in response to **спаси́бо**.

It is also used as a polite word when handing things over, as in the phrase **вот пожа́луйста**. You have already seen it in the responses by the shop assistant and the waitress when handing over the metro map and the drinks. When not on its own, **пожа́луйста** usually occurs as the second item in a sentence.

## У меня́, у тебя́, у вас, у нас

**У меня́, у тебя́, у вас, у нас** can mean: *I have, you have* (informal), *you have* (formal or plural), *we have*. In this meaning they are often followed by **есть**.

У меня́ есть кварти́ра в Москве́.
*I've got a flat in Moscow.*
У тебя́ (вас) есть кварти́ра в Санкт-Петербу́рге.
*You've got a flat in St Petersburg.*
У нас всё есть!  *We've got everything!*

They are also used in the sense of *in our place, in our country*, etc.

у нас до́ма       *in our house*
у нас в А́нглии    *with us in England*
у нас в Москве́    *with us in Moscow*
This is very similar to the French '*chez*'.

**У вас есть ...?** (*Have you got ...?/Do you have ...?*) is the usual way of asking for something in a shop.

# ● Looking at words

## Russian numbers

If you have done Exercises 3, 4 and 5, you will realise that you can easily recognise Russian numbers after ten.

The numbers from eleven to twenty all end in **-надцать**. This is a distorted form of **на де́сять** (*on ten*) and is the equivalent of the English *-teen*.

Most of the numbers from twenty to ninety end in **-де́сят** or an abbreviated form, **-дцать**. The only exceptions are **девяно́сто** (*ninety*), which starts with a shortened form of **де́вять**, and **со́рок** (*forty*). This is an oddity and we are told that it comes from Russians' love of hunting and that it originally meant a bundle of forty sable furs.

The hundreds all end in a form of the word for a hundred (**сто**). The word for a thousand is **ты́сяча** – this has become a popular word in the current inflationary times!

# ● Listening

Hotels have a service desk (**Бюро́ обслу́живания**) where the staff will provide advice and information on booking cars, restaurants, theatre tickets and flights, as well as arranging tourist excursions. The guides often speak English well but will, no doubt, be pleased if you can speak to them in Russian.

## ▱ EXERCISE 8

This is a conversation between a woman in a **бюро́ обслу́живания** and a tourist. Answer the following questions in English or Russian.

1 What does the guest want?
2 Why can't he get it?
3 What does he suggest as an alternative?
4 What is the reply?
5 How many tickets does he finally order?

## *A situation to remember*

### Shopping in Russia

Here is a typical situation in a Russian shop. Devise a conversation with a partner.

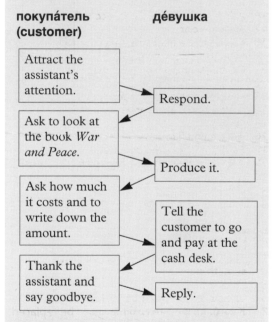

**покупа́тель (customer)**     **де́вушка**

Attract the assistant's attention. → Respond.

Ask to look at the book *War and Peace*. → Produce it.

Ask how much it costs and to write down the amount. → Tell the customer to go and pay at the cash desk.

Thank the assistant and say goodbye. → Reply.

Now try to buy a samovar, vodka and some flowers.

### Doing your sums

Practise counting from 1–10 in Russian.

Ask a friend the answer to some simple sums in Russian:

два плюс два, пять ми́нус три, три плюс семь, де́вять ми́нус во́семь, четы́ре плюс два

# ● Playing with words

## Кроссво́рд

Here is a Russian crossword. You have met almost all the words. The clues for the ones you have not met are marked with *. You should be able to guess them fairly easily, by solving adjacent clues.

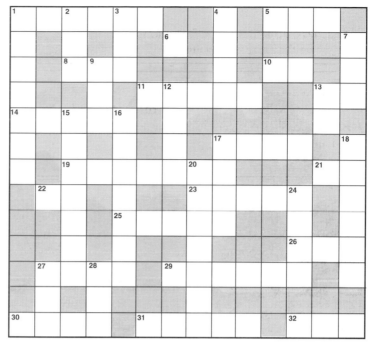

### Across
**1** семь, во́семь _____
**5** No
**6** I
**8** раз, два, _____ , четы́ре
**10** Opposite of **нет**
**11** *Swan Lake*, for instance
**13** In, into in some places
**14** A fur one to keep out the cold
**17** Storey, floor
**19** A telephone might be this, though not automatically
**21** Cabbage soup
**22** He, it
**23** A telephone has one, and so does a room in a hotel
**25** Eating place
**26** Where you live
**27** Former Soviet press agency*
**29** Port on the Black Sea, famous for its steps*
**30** Halt!
**31** Every footballer has them
**32** She

### Down
**1** Young lady
**2** The thing to say when you point at something
**3** Three
**4** Where to go for a meal or just a drink
**7** Кино́, кафе́, метро́ may each be replaced by this but not by 32 across
**9** A kind of pop music*
**12** This for peace in a power station
**13** You
**15** Марс, Юпи́тер, for example*
**16** You catch this when you cannot afford a такси́
**17** This
**18** Moscow football club
**20** Joke or anecdote*
**24** When a woman is pleased
**27** That, not quite э́тот
**28** * щи and бульо́н are examples of a Russian one

## Put things in their place

Complete the following, using the crossword as a reference. Look up the word on the left and put it *in* or *on* the word on the right. Don't forget to change the ending of the word on the right to make it into the prepositional case. The first one is done for you.

1 down **Де́вушка** в 29 across **Оде́ссе**

14 across _____ на 1 down _____

31 across _____ в 16 down _____

32 across _____ в 23 across _____

# Find the clue

Look at the clues below, find their numbers in the list of clues in the crossword and print the number of the clue in Russian. The first one is done for you.

| | |
|---|---|
| I | номер шесть |
| Young lady | номер _____ |
| раз, два, _____, четы́ре | номер _____ |
| The thing to say when you point at something | номер _____ |
| A kind of pop music | номер _____ |
| No! | номер _____ |
| Three | номер _____ |
| Opposite of **нет** | номер _____ |

Which numbers between 1 and 10 are missing?

но́мер _____        но́мер _____

---

## WHAT YOU KNOW

### How to get to places
Как мне пройти́/прое́хать на Кра́сную пло́щадь?
Иди́те напра́во, нале́во, пря́мо.

Лу́чше на авто́бусе/на троллейбусе/на трамва́е/на метро́.
Там напро́тив остано́вка.

### Asking for things in shops
У вас есть план метро́?
Есть.

Покажи́те (Да́йте), пожа́луйста, план метро́.
Вот он.

### Having things
У меня́ есть план метро́.
У тебя́ есть проездно́й биле́т.
У нас есть тало́ны.
У вас есть жето́ны.

### Numbers
оди́н, два, три, четы́ре, пять, шесть, семь, во́семь, де́вять, де́сять, сто, ты́сяча

## KEY VOCABULARY

| | |
|---|---|
| авто́бус | bus |
| Да́йте пожа́луйста ...? | Give (me), please |
| де́вушка | girl (form of address in shop) |
| жето́н | token (on underground) |
| Как мне прое́хать ... | How do I get to (by vehicle) |
| Как мне пройти́ ... | How do I get to (on foot) |
| конья́к | brandy |
| лу́чше | (it is better) |
| метро́ | metro, underground |
| напро́тив | opposite |
| остано́вка | stop |
| план | map |
| Покажи́те, пожа́луйста ... | Show me, please |
| ста́нция | station |
| тало́н | ticket (on bus) |
| трамва́й | tram |
| троллейбус | trolley bus |
| У вас есть ...? | Have you got ...? |
| чай | tea |
| четы́ре | four |
| шампа́нское | champagne |

# Being introduced to people

**Russian names**

**How to address close friends and children**

**Different nationalities**

## ● Life in Russia

### Russian names

If you have read a Russian novel in translation, you will probably at some stage have been confused, because the same person can have a bewildering variety of names. All Russians have three names. A man might be called **Ива́н Петро́вич Па́влов**, his sister **Ната́лья Петро́вна Па́влова**.

**Russian surnames typically end in:**

**-ов** for a man, **-ова** for a woman (see the above example)
**-ин** for a man, **-ина** for a woman (e.g. **Воро́нин**, man, **Воро́нина**, woman)
**-ский** for a man, **-ская** for a woman (e.g. **Ма́йский**, man, **Ма́йская**, woman)

In addition to a surname (**фами́лия**) and first name (**и́мя**), each Russian has a *patronymic* (**о́тчество**) derived, as its name implies, from the name of one's father (**оте́ц**) by adding **-ович** or **-евич** for a man and **-овна** or **-евна** for a woman.

| Father | Son | Daughter |
|---|---|---|
| Ива́н | Ива́нович | Ива́новна |
| Серге́й | Серге́евич | Серге́евна |
| Алекса́ндр | Алекса́ндрович | Алекса́ндровна |
| Алексе́й | Алексе́евич | Алексе́евна |
| Пётр | Петро́вич | Петро́вна |

In the spoken language the male versions of these patronymics are often shortened by missing out the **-ов** or **-ев**.

Russian does not have any equivalent of Mr, Mrs, Miss, Ms. The combination of the first name and patronymic (**и́мя-о́тчество**) is used instead. Schoolchildren address their teachers by their **и́мя-о́тчество**. Politicians are also often referred to by their **и́мя-о́тчество**. Their surnames are often omitted.

## EXERCISE 1

The following are the **и́мя-о́тчество** of some of the leaders of the Soviet Union or Russia. Can you supply their surnames? The first one is done for you.

| | | |
|---|---|---|
| 1 | Влади́мир Ильи́ч | <u>Ле́нин</u> |
| 2 | Ио́сиф Виссарио́нович | _____ |
| 3 | Ники́та Серге́евич | _____ |
| 4 | Михаи́л Серге́евич | _____ |
| 5 | Бори́с Никола́евич | _____ |

## EXERCISE 2

Here is a family tree for the Ivanov family.

Complete the Ivanov family tree.
Look for the name of the father and match it with the patronymic below. Put the number in the right box.
The first one is done for you.

| | |
|---|---|
| Алексе́й Бори́сович | 1 |
| Ива́н Никола́евич | ☐ |
| Ни́на Алексе́евна | ☐ |
| А́нна Ива́новна | ☐ |
| Серге́й Па́влович | ☐ |

Russian first names usually have two different forms, the standard one used together with the **о́тчество** and a so-called *diminutive* one. This is used immediately you are on informal terms with someone. When talking to foreigners, Russians often just refer to themselves by the diminutive form of their first name. You are then spared the problem of remembering their **и́мя-о́тчество**.

### Examples of diminutive forms are:

| Male | Diminutive |
|---|---|
| Алексе́й | Алёша |
| Бори́с | Бо́ря |
| Ви́ктор | Ви́тя |
| Влади́мир | Воло́дя |
| Ива́н | Ва́ня |
| Михаи́л | Ми́ша |
| Пётр | Пе́тя |
| Серге́й | Серёжа |
| Ю́рий | Ю́ра |
| Алекса́ндр | Са́ша |
| Евге́ний | Же́ня |

| Female | Diminutive |
|---|---|
| О́льга | О́ля |
| А́нна | А́ня |
| Гали́на | Га́ля |
| Ири́на | И́ра |
| Ната́лья | Ната́ша |
| Еле́на | Ле́на |
| Алекса́ндра | Са́ша |
| Евге́ния | Же́ня |

Note that Са́ша and Же́ня can be either a man or a woman.

English also has shortened forms of first names (James = Jim, Jimmy, etc.). In English the use of a shortened form depends on the individual. In Russian it is normal to use the diminutive form, once you have decided you are on informal terms with someone.

If you were introduced to **Ива́н Петро́вич Ле́вин**, your new teacher, you would call him **Ива́н Петро́вич**. On the other hand if he turned out to be a fellow student and not your teacher, you would call him **Ва́ня**. Nowadays, young people usually use the diminutive form straight away when meeting people of the same age and status. You always use diminutive forms when talking to children.

Russian first names can have a whole range of forms indicating endearment, affection, and occasionally, contempt. The endearment forms often end in **-ечка**, **-очка**, **-енька**, **-ушка** or **-юшка**. Many names have more than one form. **Ива́н,** for example, has at least five 'endearment' forms (**Ваню́ша**, **Ва́нечка**, **Ваню́шечка**, **Ваню́шка** and **Ива́нушка**) but only one 'contempt' form (**Ва́нька**). It is advisable to stick to the basic diminutive form, or you might end up suggesting a close relationship that you do not intend!

### ты or вы

Russian has two words meaning *you*: **ты** and **вы**. This has a parallel with many other European languages (compare French *tu/vous*, German *du/Sie*).

You always use **вы** if you are talking to a group of people. Talking to one person, a Russian would use **ты**, if using the diminutive form of the first name. If a Russian uses **и́мя-о́тчество** when talking to a person, he or she would normally use the **вы** form. **Вы** is always used to people of an older generation or to superiors at work, **ты** is used to friends and is always

used to children. Alternatively you can ask **Мо́жно на ты?** *Can I use* **ты?** A Russian may suggest **Дава́йте на ты!** (*Let's use* **ты** *to one another.*)

You should listen to how a Russian addresses you and reply with the same word **ты** or **вы** as the Russian used to you. If in doubt, use **вы**.

## ● Language information

### Forms with ты and вы

A number of words have got different forms, depending on whether you are using **ты** or **вы**:

| ты form | вы form | |
|---|---|---|
| здра́вствуй[1] | здра́вствуйте | *hello* |
| извини́ | извини́те | *excuse me* |
| скажи́ | скажи́те | *tell me* |
| Как ты пожива́ешь? | Как вы пожива́ете? | *How are you?* |
| Как тебя́ зову́т? | Как вас зову́т?[2] | *What's your name?* |
| Ско́лько тебе́ лет? | Ско́лько вам лет?[3] | *How old are you?* |

1  As an alternative to **здра́вствуй** in informal language, you can say **Приве́т!**
2  **Как тебя́ зову́т?** means literally *How do they call you?* Your reply should start off with the phrase **Меня́ зову́т ...** (*They call me ...*)
3  The answer is **Мне ... лет.** (*I am ... years old.*)

A useful word when getting to know people is **Познако́мьтесь!** It is said by someone when introducing two strangers. It means literally *Get acquainted.* It has only one (**вы**) form, as two people are being addressed.

Look at the following telephone conversations. The first one is formal, the second one informal. The versions are not meant as exact translations, but as an indication of what is likely in formal and informal situations.

## Formal

– Здра́вствуйте, Ви́ктор Ива́нович!
– Говори́т Ивано́в. Как вы пожива́ете?
– Бори́с Миха́йлович, как дела́ у вас в Санкт-Петербу́рге?

## Informal

– Здра́вствуй, Ви́тя! Как пожива́ешь? Э́то Бо́ря.
– Бо́ря, приве́т! Как там у тебя́ в Санкт-Петербу́рге?

### EXERCISE 3

You are staying with a Russian family. They decide to have a party.
The following people come in through the door. Greet each of them by underlining either **здра́вствуй** or **здра́вствуйте**.

1 Меня́ зову́т Ми́ша.
Здра́вствуй! Здра́вствуйте!

2 Здра́вствуй! Здра́вствуйте!
Меня́ зову́т Влади́мир Ива́нович.

3 Меня́ зову́т Ната́лья Миха́йловна.
Здра́вствуй! Здра́вствуйте!

4 Меня́ зову́т Ле́на.
Здра́вствуй! Здра́вствуйте!

5 Меня́ зову́т Ири́на Влади́мировна.
Здра́вствуй! Здра́вствуйте!

### EXERCISE 4

On your recording an older person is talking to a small child.
Listen to the conversation. Then answer the questions.

1 What is the child's name?
2 How old is she?
3 What is she playing with?
4 How many has she got?
5 What does her father do?
6 What does her mother do?

Are they on **ты** or **вы** terms?

## Adjectives

Adjective endings change depending on the noun which follows.

'**Он**' nouns (masculine) have adjectives ending in:
**-ый**: вку́сн**ый** чай (*tasty tea*)
**-ий** after **к** or **ш**: Не́вск**ий** проспе́кт; хоро́ш**ий** студе́нт
**-о́й** if the ending is stressed: Больш**о́й** теа́тр

'**Она́**' nouns (feminine) have adjectives ending in **-ая**: Кра́сн**ая** пло́щадь

'**Оно́**' nouns (neuter) have endings in **-ое**: кра́сн**ое** вино́

If the noun is plural, the ending is: **-ые**: краси́в**ые** же́нщины (*beautiful women*)
**-ие** after **к** and **ш**: русск**ие** же́нщины (*Russian women*); хоро́ш**ие** студе́нты (*good students*)

6 Меня́ зову́т А́ня.
Здра́вствуй! Здра́вствуйте!

7 Меня́ зову́т Алекса́ндр Серге́евич.
Здра́вствуй! Здра́вствуйте!

**EXERCISE 5**
Look at the following and join them up to make sentences. The first one is done for you.
**Страна́** means *country*, **столи́ца** means *capital city*.

| | | | |
|---|---|---|---|
| 1 | Росси́я | ру́сский | футболи́сты |
| 2 | Оли́мпус | англи́йский | порт |
| 3 | Де́вушка, у вас есть | америка́нская | шампа́нское |
| 4 | Москва́ | япо́нский | столи́ца |
| 5 | На столе́ | росси́йская | газе́та |
| 6 | Дина́мовцы | кра́сное | царь |
| 7 | Нью-Йорк Таймс | украи́нский | вино́ |
| 8 | Бори́с Годуно́в | францу́зское | фотоаппара́т |
| 9 | Оде́сса | больша́я | го́род |
| 10 | Ма́нчестер | хоро́шие | страна́ |

# ● Looking at words

Many of the adjectives in this unit are to do with nationalities – **ру́сский**, **брита́нский**, **америка́нский**, etc. Notice that nationality words start with a small letter. Only names of countries start with a capital, e.g. **Аме́рика**. Look at these examples:

| Country | Adjective | Male | Female |
|---|---|---|---|
| А́нглия *England* | англи́йский | англича́нин | англича́нка |
| Аме́рика *America* | америка́нский | америка́нец | америка́нка |
| Герма́ния *Germany* | неме́цкий | не́мец | не́мка |
| Ирла́ндия *Ireland* | ирла́ндский | ирла́ндец | ирла́ндка |
| Кана́да *Canada* | кана́дский | кана́дец | кана́дка |
| По́льша *Poland* | по́льский | поля́к | по́лька |
| Росси́я *Russia* | ру́сский | ру́сский | ру́сская |
| Уэльс *Wales* | валли́йский | валли́ец | валли́йка |
| Украи́на *Ukraine* | украи́нский | украи́нец | украи́нка |
| Фра́нция *France* | францу́зский | францу́з | францу́женка |
| Шотла́ндия *Scotland* | шотла́ндский | шотла́ндец | шотла́ндка |

Only **Герма́ния**, *Germany*, has a nationality word (**не́мец**, *a German*) from a different source. This comes from the word **немо́й**, *dumb*, and was originally applied to all foreigners who could not speak Russian. **Аме́рика** refers to the whole continent. The USA is **США** in Russian, short for **Соединённые Шта́ты Аме́рики**.

Alongside **ру́сский** there is a second adjective, **росси́йский**, mentioned in Unit 2. Since the collapse of the Soviet Union this word has become very popular. The country's full title is **Росси́йская федера́ция**. However, note that **ру́сский** and **ру́сская** are always used for citizens of the country: this is the only nationality to use an adjective for the citizen of a country.

## EXERCISE 6

Look at the map and insert the number of the country in the correct place on the map. The first one is done for you.

| | |
|---|---|
| 1 Россия | 5 Украина |
| 2 Áнглия | 6 Польша |
| 3 США | 7 Кана́да |
| 4 Герма́ния | 8 Фра́нция |

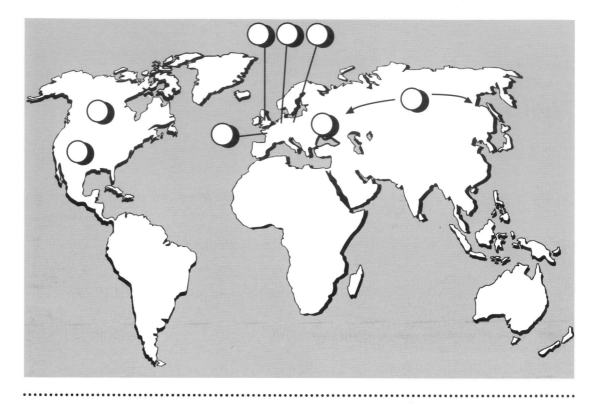

## A situation to remember

### Getting to know each other

You are staying at a Russian's flat. Your host decides to have a party.

Each of the characters from Exercise 3 comes through the door. They say 'hello' and give their name.

You give yours, say that you are pleased to meet them (**Óчень прия́тно!**). Ask them how they are.

Use **ты** or **вы**, taking your cue from the Russian.

### Talking on the telephone

Useful key phrases when talking on the phone are:

Алло́ *or* Слу́шаю вас  *hello*
Вы не туда́ попа́ли *or* Не тот но́мер
*wrong number*
Перезвони́те  *try again*

📼 Now turn once more to your recording. A man is trying to make a call from a phone box (**телефо́н-автома́т**).
He gets the wrong number at the first attempt.
Listen out for the key phrases given above. Re-enact the conversation, if possible, with the help of a friend.

## Reading handwriting

Decipher the illustrated written forms and print them underneath the photographs.

_____

_____

**Russian weather**

**Time zones**

**What's on television**

**Likes and dislikes**

# Russian weather and Russian television

## ● Life in Russia

### The Russian climate

Russia is the biggest country in the world, stretching almost half way round it.

There are eleven time zones from one side to the other. Moscow is roughly on the same latitude as Edinburgh, and St Petersburg is on the same latitude as the Shetland Islands, the southern tip of Greenland and the most northerly point of Newfoundland. Moscow is usually thought of as being very cold. In fact it has a continental climate, cold in winter and hot in summer.

As you travel eastward on any latitude the average temperature goes down, and the coldest area is around **Верхоя́нск**, where the average winter temperature is below minus 50 degrees Celsius in January. The subsoil remains frozen all the year round in over 45 per cent of Russia, making difficult the exploitation of the vast mineral resources. The fact that the major rivers in Siberian Russia flow from south to north creates difficult conditions in spring and makes it impossible fully to exploit the rivers as sources of hydro-electricity.

Russians like talking about the weather (**пого́да**): they complain as much as the British do! If you want to say you are hot or cold, use the following phrases:

Мне хо́лодно *I'm cold.*   Мне тепло́ *I'm warm.*
Мне жа́рко *I'm hot.*   Мне о́чень хо́лодно means *I am very cold.*

Literally these phrases mean *it is cold/warm/hot to me*. If you simply want to state that the weather is cold, warm or hot, use the same words without **мне**.

You have met most Russian numbers in Unit 6. If you need the intervening ones, simply combine the numbers **один** to **девять** with **двадцать**, **тридцать**, etc. as you would in English:

двадцать один *21*    тридцать два *32*    сорок три *43*    пятьдесят четыре *54*

## EXERCISE 1

Here are some temperatures from a weather forecast for October.
Read the temperatures and write them in (**градус** means *degree*).
State if you feel hot, warm or cold. The first one is done for you.

**1** В Москве плюс один градус.                Мне холодно. _____  +1 ___

**2** В Мурманске минус два градуса.            _____  ___

**3** В Волгограде плюс семь градусов.          _____  ___

**4** Во Владивостоке плюс шестнадцать градусов. _____  ___

**5** В Верхоянске минус двадцать два градуса.  _____  ___

**6** В Краснодаре плюс двадцать три градуса.   _____  ___

# Telling the time

The 24-hour clock is widely used for official purposes: e.g. in railway and air timetables and for television and radio programmes.

## EXERCISE 2

Here are some times written out in full. Write them in numbers.
The first one is done for you.
**Сколько сейчас времени**? *What time is it?*

**1** Восемнадцать часов двадцать минут      *18.20*

**2** Двадцать один час пять минут           _____

**3** Двадцать два часа десять минут         _____

**4** Девятнадцать часов пятнадцать минут    _____

**5** Двенадцать часов двадцать две минуты   _____

**6** Пятнадцать часов двадцать пять минут   _____

**7** Семнадцать часов три минуты            _____

**8** Тринадцать часов тридцать пять минут   _____

**9** Два часа сорок девять минут            _____

**10** Десять часов пятьдесят пять минут     _____

Note that after numbers 2–4 and 22–24 **часа** is used. After **один** the form **час** is used. In every other case the form is **часов**.

Look at the time zone map below. The time in west European Russia is called Moscow time (**моско́вское вре́мя**), even if you are in St Petersburg!

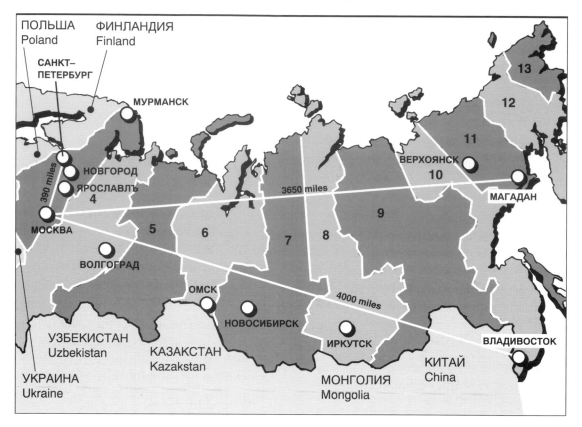

..........................................................................................

## EXERCISE 3

You are given **моско́вское вре́мя**, *Moscow time*. You are then asked what time it is in another town.
Write down the correct time.
The first one is done for you.

**1** Моско́вское вре́мя 12 часо́в.
А в Ло́ндоне ско́лько сейча́с вре́мени?
<u>9</u> час<u>о́в</u>

**2** Моско́вское вре́мя 11 часо́в.
А в Новосиби́рске ско́лько сейча́с вре́мени?     __ час__

**3** Моско́вское вре́мя 4 часа́.
А в Пари́же ско́лько сейча́с вре́мени?     __ час__

**4** Моско́вское вре́мя 17 часо́в.
А в Ирку́тске ско́лько сейча́с вре́мени?     __ час__

**5** Моско́вское вре́мя 15 часо́в.
А в Му́рманске ско́лько сейча́с вре́мени?     __ час__

**6** Моско́вское вре́мя 7 часо́в.
А в Волгогра́де ско́лько сейча́с вре́мени?     __ час__

**7** Моско́вское вре́мя 3 часа́.
А в О́мске ско́лько сейча́с вре́мени?     __ час__

**8** Моско́вское вре́мя 12 часо́в.
А в Магада́не ско́лько сейча́с вре́мени?     __ час__

**9** Моско́вское вре́мя 21 час.
А во Владивосто́ке ско́лько сейча́с вре́мени?     __ час__

# Russian television

Russian television has changed radically since the fall of communism. **Пе́рвый кана́л** (*first channel*) is often referred to as **Оста́нкино** after the area of Moscow where the channel has its headquarters and its television tower with revolving restaurant.

In Moscow you can also watch **Кана́л «Росси́я»**, **Моско́вская програ́мма** and **ТВ «Петербу́рг»**. There is also a daytime educational channel **«Росси́йские университе́ты»**, which gives way after 6 p.m. to the newest channel **НТВ**, short for **Незави́симое телеви́дение** (*independent television*). All channels are financed by advertising (**рекла́ма**) and many programmes have sponsors. Now look at the list of TV programmes on the right, adapted from a recent TV schedule for the Ostankino channel for 19th September. Russian has a variety of words for *news*. On the above schedule the word is **но́вости**, derived from the word **но́вый**, *new* (compare the English *novel*). You will also hear **изве́стия**. If you are watching **Кана́л «Росси́я»**, they call their programme **Ве́сти**.

A feature of Ostankino's schedules that has not changed for many years is the evening children's programme **«Споко́йной ночи, малыши́!»** (*Good night, children*). Another item that appears in most programme schedules is **мультфи́льмы** (*cartoons*). Russians are now very interested in the world of business and most schedules include a programme about the business world. Can you spot one in the programmes for 19th September?

---

**Программа телепередач**
**1 КАНАЛ ОСТАНКИНО**
------------------------------------
**понедельник, 19-ое сентября**

| | |
|---|---|
| **18.00** | **Новости** |
| **18.25** | **Бизнес-класс** |
| **18.40** | **Америка с М. Таратутой** |
| **19.00** | **Час пик** |
| **19.55** | **Говорит А. И. Солженицын.** |
| **20.40** | **«Спокойной ночи, малыши!»** |
| **21.00** | **Новости** |
| **21.35** | **Прогноз погоды** |
| **21.40** | **Концерт музыки Чайковского. Играет Владимир Ашкенази.** |
| **23.00** | **«Баллада о солдате» художественный фильм** |
| **12.30** | **Мультфильмы** |
| **1.00** | **Пресс-экспресс** |

...........................................

## EXERCISE 4

Look at the TV programmes for Ostankino for Monday 19th September. Answer the questions which follow in English.
**Что идёт в** means *What is on at ...?*
Place the time in the left-hand box and the programme title in the right-hand one.

**1** Что идёт в восемна́дцать часо́в?

**2** Что идёт в два́дцать оди́н час?

**3** Что идёт в восемна́дцать часо́в два́дцать пять мину́т?

**4** Что идёт в два́дцать три часа́?

**5** Что идёт в два́дцать оди́н час три́дцать пять мину́т?

**6** Что идёт в девятна́дцать часо́в пятьдеся́т пять мину́т?

**7** Что идёт в два́дцать оди́н час со́рок мину́т?

Now listen to your recording.
A television announcer is giving the programmes for the evening.
The announcement finishes with
«Передаём после́дние изве́стия» – *Here is the latest news.*
Answer the following questions:

1  When can you enjoy music by Tchaikovsky?
2  When should football fans tune in?
3  When should all children watch television?
4  What programme is on at 9.00?
5  After which programme do you get the weather forecast?
6  Which film are they showing tonight?

Ostankino TV tower, Moscow

## ● Language information

### Present tense of verbs

Just like French, German, Spanish or Italian, Russian verbs change their forms, depending on who is performing the action.

| игра́ть *to play* | | | |
|---|---|---|---|
| я (I) | игра́ю | мы (we) | игра́ем |
| ты (you) | игра́ешь | вы (you) | игра́ете |
| он (he) | игра́ет | они́ (they) | игра́ют |
| она́ (she) | | | |

| говори́ть *to say* | | | |
|---|---|---|---|
| я (I) | говорю́ | мы (we) | говори́м |
| ты (you) | говори́шь | вы (you) | говори́те |
| он (he) | говори́т | они́ (they) | говоря́т |
| она́ (she) | | | |

The dictionary form of verbs usually ends in **-ть**: this is the equivalent of the 'to' form in English. From now on this is the form we will use in the vocabulary lists in this book. Verbs ending in **-ать** or **-ять** have forms like **игра́ть**, those ending in **-ить** like **говори́ть**. Common verbs ending in **-еть** also usually have endings like **говори́ть**.

Я игра́ю в футбо́л, а Ми́ша игра́ет в хокке́й.
*I play football and Misha plays ice-hockey.*

**Ты говори́шь по-ру́сски?**
*Do you speak Russian?*

**Она́ чита́ет рома́н «Война́ и мир».**
*She is reading the novel 'War and Peace'.*

**Мы не ку́рим.**
*We don't smoke.*

**Вы лю́бите смотре́ть телеви́зор?**
*Do you like watching television?*

**Они́ гуля́ют в па́рке.**
*They are walking in the park.*

As you can see from the above translations, English has more than one present tense. Russian is much simpler: there is only one! You can deny things very easily in Russian: just add **не** to the verb. The best answer to a question, if you are not sure of something, is **Не зна́ю** (*I don't know*).

## EXERCISE 6

Here is a matching exercise. Join the words together to make complete sentences. The first one is done for you.

| 1 | Я | говоря́т по-ру́сски |
|---|---|---|
| 2 | Она́ | игра́ю в футбо́л |
| 3 | Вы | лю́бит игра́ть на гита́ре |
| 4 | Они́ | гуля́ете в па́рке |
| 5 | Он | смо́тришь телеви́зор |
| 6 | Ты | не зна́ем |
| 7 | Мы | говори́т по-англи́йски |

## По

A very common word in Russian is **по**. It can mean *along*: **по коридо́ру** (*along the corridor*); **по у́лице** (*along the street*). You will also see it with a number of communication words: **по телеви́зору** (*on television*); **по ра́дио** (*on the radio*), **по телефо́ну** (*on the telephone*). Note the endings:

add **у** to 'он' (masculine) nouns
change **а** to **е** on 'она́' (feminine) nouns.

This is the *dative case*.

**По** is also used to make new words, often hyphenated. *You speak Russian* is **Вы говори́те по-ру́сски**. *In English* is **по-англи́йски**. Look at the table in Unit 7 and work out how to say *in French*, *in German* or even *in Ukrainian*!
If you have an opinion you will need to know **по-мо́ему** (*in my opinion*), **по-тво́ему** or **по-ва́шему** (*in your opinion*).

Sometimes it becomes part of a new word: **почему́?** (*why?*) to which the answer is **потому́ что** (*because*).

## EXERCISE 7

Here are a number of questions asking 'why' and a number of answers beginning with the word 'because'. Match up question and answer. The first one is done for you.

| **Question** | **Answer** |
|---|---|
| 1 Почему́ рестора́н закры́т? | Потому́ что хорошо́ игра́ю. |
| 2 Почему́ вы гуля́ете в па́рке? | Потому́ что она́ краси́вая. |
| 3 Почему́ вы лю́бите те́ннис? | Потому́ что он о́чень краси́вый го́род. |
| 4 Почему́ вы лю́бите Ни́ну? | Потому́ что там хорошо́. |
| 5 Почему́ вам хо́лодно? | Потому́ что идёт ремо́нт. |
| 6 Почему́ вы лю́бите Санкт-Петербу́рг? | Потому́ что сего́дня ми́нус два́дцать гра́дусов. |

## ● Talking about words

Я тебя
люблю

### Liking/loving

There are two ways of saying *I like* or *I love* in Russian: **я люблю́** or **мне нра́вится**. **Мне нра́вится** means that I like something specific and is never as passionate as *I love*. *You like* is **Вам (Тебе́) нра́вится**. **Люблю́** is more general and can mean *I like* or *I love*, depending on the passion in your voice. You should be careful about how you say **Люблю́ тебя́** to a Russian! **Люблю́** comes from **люби́ть** and has forms like **говори́ть**. Note the extra **л** in the 'I' form only.

Look at the following examples:

| | |
|---|---|
| Я люблю́ му́зыку | Вам нра́вится конце́рт? |
| Я люблю́ теа́тр | Вам нра́вится пье́са? *(play)* |
| Он лю́бит спорт | Мне нра́вится матч |
| Вы лю́бите те́ннис? | Вам нра́вится переда́ча? |
| Вы лю́бите кино́? | Мне нра́вится э́тот фильм. |

Notice that if you want to say 'very much' you simply add the word **о́чень** (*very*), e.g. **Я о́чень люблю́ теа́тр** (*I like the theatre very much*).

Вам нра́вится Москва́? Да, о́чень.
Я о́чень люблю́ Ло́ндон.
Вам нра́вится э́та де́вушка? Не о́чень.

You can also use both forms to say that you like *doing* something, in which case the pattern looks like this:

Я люблю́ чита́ть.
Мне нра́вится смотре́ть телеви́зор.

If you want to say that you don't like doing something, simply add **не**: **я не люблю́** or **мне не нра́вится**.

### игра́ть *to play*

If you play a game in Russian, add the word **в**:

Он игра́ет в футбо́л.
Мы игра́ем в те́ннис.

If you play a musical instrument, use **на** and the **е** form of the noun (prepositional case):

Ми́ша игра́ет на гита́ре, а Са́ша игра́ет на балала́йке.

## ● Looking at words

### New words

Russian has been changing rapidly since the collapse of the old Soviet Union. New borrowings from English and other Western European languages are flooding into the language.

## EXERCISE 8

Every week Russians receive free newspapers, either delivered to their home or handed out in the street or at metro stations. Here are some words taken from adverts in a newspaper which describes itself as **Газе́та росси́йского бизнесме́на**. See if you can work out what they mean.

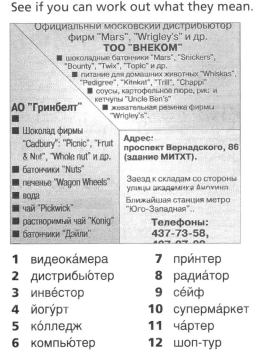

| | |
|---|---|
| 1 видеока́мера | 7 при́нтер |
| 2 дистрибью́тер | 8 радиа́тор |
| 3 инве́стор | 9 сейф |
| 4 йогу́рт | 10 суперма́ркет |
| 5 ко́лледж | 11 ча́ртер |
| 6 компью́тер | 12 шоп-тур |

## ● Listening

## What you do in your spare time

### ▭ EXERCISE 9

Listen to the recording. Four people are talking about leisure and work. Their names are **Са́ша**, **Ви́ктор**, **А́нна** and **Ни́на**. Listen particularly for the information asked for in the questions below, and answer the questions.

1 What is Nina's occupation?
2 What does Anna like doing?
3 What does Sasha do in his spare time?
4 Which TV programmes do they all like?
5 Which does Victor like very much?

---

## ● Playing with words

### Reading handwriting

Russians sometimes use handwriting-style typefaces in advertisements. Here are a few from a free newspaper.

Try to work out what the adverts mean. Have a go at writing out the slogans, copying the Russian handwriting.

Decipher the illustrated written forms, and print the words beneath the photographs.

# Word square

Here is a word square with ten Russian words, borrowed from English. There are ten in all for you to find.

| | | | | | |
|---|---|---|---|---|---|
| ф | д | о | к | м | к |
| а | и | д | с | а | о |
| к | л | и | е | н | т |
| с | е | с | р | г | т |
| т | р | к | о | о | е |
| р | п | н | к | о | д |
| о | ф | и | с | ш | ж |

## WHAT YOU KNOW

### Temperature
Мне хо́лодно/тепло́/жа́рко.

### Present tense of verbs

| игра́ть *to play* | |
|---|---|
| игра́ю | игра́ем |
| игра́ешь | игра́ете |
| игра́ет | игра́ют |

| говори́ть *to say* | |
|---|---|
| говорю́ | говори́м |
| говори́шь | говори́те |
| говори́т | говоря́т |

### По
по у́лице, по коридо́ру
по телеви́зору, по ра́дио, по телефо́ну

Я говорю́ по-ру́сски/по-англи́йски.

по-мо́ему/по-тво́ему/по-ва́шему
Почему́ рестора́н закры́т?
Потому́ что идёт ремо́нт.

### Like/love
Я (о́чень) люблю́ спорт.
Мне (о́чень) нра́вится футбо́л.

### Play
Я игра́ю в футбо́л.
Я игра́ю на балала́йке.

## KEY VOCABULARY

| | |
|---|---|
| вре́мя | time |
| говори́ть | to say |
| гуля́ть | to walk |
| жа́рко | hot |
| знать | to know |
| игра́ть (в футбо́л) | to play (football) |
| (на балала́йке) | (the balalaika) |
| идёт | is on |
| изве́стия | news |
| люби́ть | to like, to love |
| но́вости | news |
| мне нра́вится | (I) like |
| переда́ча | broadcast |
| по | along, on (TV, radio ...) |
| по-англи́йски | in English |
| по-ва́шему | in your opinion |
| по-мо́ему | in my opinion |
| по-ру́сски | in Russian |
| по-тво́ему | in your opinion |
| потому́ что | because |
| почему́ | why |
| Ско́лько сейча́с вре́мени? | What's the time? |
| смотре́ть (телеви́зор) | to watch (television) |
| телеви́зор | television |
| тепло́ | warm |
| хо́лодно | cold |
| час | hour, o'clock |
| чита́ть | to read |

# Russian cooking

## ● Life in Russia

### Eating out

Eating out in Russia can be an interesting experience. You may want to try one of the old-established restaurants such as **Славя́нский база́р**, or go to one of the many private restaurants which have opened since the fall of communism. Beware of high prices in some of them. There are also many fast food outlets such as McDonald's and Pizza Hut which appeared in the final years of communism. These are very popular.

If the restaurant you choose is a popular one, it might be as well to book a table (**заказа́ть стол**). Reasons why you might not be able to get into a restaurant may be as follows:

Рестора́н закры́т   (e.g. на ремо́нт – *for repair*)
Сва́дьба   *wedding*
Сего́дня приём   *reception*
Рестора́н откры́т то́лько с 4 до 10 часо́в   *from 4 until 10*
Все места́ за́няты.   *All the seats are taken.*
or simply
Мест нет!

**69**

Assuming that you have found your way into a restaurant these are the exchanges that might take place. Notice that there may be a variety of ways your question could be answered.

| Question | Answer |
|---|---|
| Здесь свобо́дно? | Свобо́дно. (*free*) |
| | Нет, за́нято. (*occupied*) |
| Мо́жно? | Мо́жно. |
| | Сади́тесь, пожа́луйста. |
| | *Please take a seat.* |

You might just hear **пожа́луйста** to show it is all right to sit down.

Don't forget, **Мо́жно?** is a very useful way of asking if you can do something (see Unit 4).

The waitress asks you what you want. You give the first part of your order – caviar and champagne.

She assumes that you want something to follow. You ask for beetroot soup and zander, after checking they are on the menu.

She brings you the first part of your meal and wishes you 'bon appetit'.

Yuu enter the restaurant and look for a free table

You call over the waitress

You ask for the menu, which the waitress produces

You ask for the bill.

Useful words and phrases in a restaurant are:

| | |
|---|---|
| свобо́дно | *free* |
| де́вушка | (used to address a waitress) |
| Слу́шаю вас. | (said by waiter/ waitress when ready to take your order) |
| пото́м | *next* |
| Да́йте, пожа́луйста... | *Can I please have ...* |
| *or* Мне, пожа́луйста... | |
| Сади́тесь, пожа́луйста. | *Please sit down.* |
| Да́йте, пожа́луйста, счёт. | *Can I have the bill, please?* |
| Прия́тного аппети́та! | *Enjoy your meal / 'Bon appetit'.* |

# МЕНЮ

## закуски

1. салат из помидоров
2. салат мясной
3. осетрина
4. сардины в масле
5. огурцы со сметаной
6. грибы
7. икра красная

## первые блюда

8. щи
9. борщ украинский
10. бульон
11. суп грибной

## вторые блюда

12. судак жареный
13. бефстроганов
14. филе «Космос»
15. шашлык
16. бифштекс натуральный
17. котлеты с рисом
18. свинина
19. курица с картошкой

## сладкое

20. фрукты
21. мороженое
22. торт
23. компот

## напитки

24. водка «Столичная»
25. коньяк
26. шампанское
27. вино грузинское, красное
28. вино французское, белое
29. портвейн
30. виски

31. чай с лимоном
32. кофе
33. сок
34. лимонад
35. минеральная вода

---

A **меню́** in a Russian restaurant is divided into:

| | |
|---|---|
| заку́ски | *hors d'oeuvre* |
| пе́рвые блю́да | *soups* (literally *first dishes*) |
| вторы́е блю́да | *main course* (literally *second dishes*) |
| сла́дкое | *dessert* |
| напи́тки | *drinks* |

You will notice from the menu above that many items of food have names that are recognisable from their (mainly) French equivalents. **Борщ** and **щи** are two types of soup and **грибы́** are mushrooms. **Суда́к**, zander, is a popular freshwater fish related to the perch. **Котле́та** can be a cutlet or chop, but is more often a rissole made of meat with a variety of additives. **Бифште́кс** can be superior **котле́ты**. If you see **котле́ты натура́льные** on the menu, you can expect steak. **Ма́сло** can mean either *oil* or *butter*. **Портве́йн** is a sweet fortified wine related to our port. Other menu items are:

| | |
|---|---|
| помидо́ры | *tomatoes* |
| огурцы́ | *cucumbers* |
| мя́со/мясно́й | *meat* |
| осетри́на | *sturgeon* |
| икра́ | *caviar* |
| филе́ | *fillet steak* |
| шашлы́к | *kebab* |
| свини́на | *pork* |
| ку́рица | *chicken* |
| карто́шка | *potatoes* |
| плов | *rice based stew (pilaf)* |
| моро́женое | *ice-cream* |
| компо́т | *stewed fruit* |
| грузи́нское вино́ | *Georgian wine* |
| сок | *juice* |
| торт | *gateau* |

## EXERCISE 1

You are a waiter in a Moscow hotel, and a group of four business people (**бизнесмéны**) arrive from Britain. You are taking their order.

Here is a list of what they choose. From the menu on page 71 put the number of each item in the box next to their choice.

**Miss Benson**

lemonade ☐

sardines ☐

beetroot soup ☐

steak ☐

stewed fruit ☐

French wine ☐

**Mr Brown**

vodka ☐

caviar ☐

cabbage soup ☐

fillet steak ☐

gateau ☐

brandy ☐

**Mr Smith**

mineral water ☐

mushroom soup ☐

kebabs ☐

fruit ☐

coffee ☐

Georgian wine ☐

**Mr Hart**

juice ☐

cucumbers in
sour cream ☐

fried zander ☐

ice-cream ☐

lemon tea ☐

champagne ☐

## 🔊 EXERCISE 2

Listen to your tape. It contains the dialogue from page 70, but each time something else is added.

Listen carefully and see if you can understand what is being said. The questions will help you understand the recording.

1 Does the man like the restaurant?
2 What time do they serve dinner?
3 What type of food does he look for on the menu?
4 What is missing from the menu?
5 What does he order to finish off with?
6 What does he think of Russian champagne?
7 What does he think of the bill?

## EXERCISE 3

Look at the picture below and match the food to the words below by putting the correct numbers in the boxes.

чёрная икрá ☐

шампáнское ☐

кýрица ☐

фрýкты ☐

ры́ба ☐

водá ☐

салáт ☐

шашлы́к ☐

кóфе ☐

морóженое ☐

грибы́ ☐

вóдка ☐

# Eating in

Of course, you will want to try genuine Russian cooking, and the best place to do this is in a Russian home. If you are lucky enough to be invited for a meal or to be staying in a Russian home, you will experience the generous hospitality for which Russians are famous.

Russian meals are as follows:

**За́втрак**. This is the equivalent of breakfast but is far more substantial than in Britain. Here are some dishes you might be given for breakfast:

| | |
|---|---|
| кефи́р | *a kind of yoghurt* |
| сыр | *cheese* |
| тво́рог | *curd cheese* |
| блины́ со смета́ной | *pancakes with sour cream* |
| яйцо́ | *egg* |
| яи́чница | *a fried egg dish, often with ham* (**ветчина́**) |
| сок | |
| чай, ко́фе | |

**Обе́д** is a large meal served in the middle of the day; **у́жин** is served in the evening. **Обе́д** or **у́жин** will usually start with **заку́ски** (*snacks* or *hors-d'oeuvre*) often washed down with glasses of vodka, brandy or juice. There is often a large variety of these **заку́ски**.

## Заку́ски

**Ры́ба** (*fish*)
**Шпро́ты** (*sprats*), **сельдь** (*salted herring*), **креве́тки** (*prawns*)
**Икра́** (*caviar*), **кра́сная** (red) from Pacific salmon, or **чёрная** (black) from sturgeon if your hosts can afford it.

**Мя́со** (*meat*)
**Колбаса́** (*continental sausage*), or **ветчина́**

**Сала́т** (*salad*)
**Помидо́ры**, **огурцы́** often in dill or salted (**солёные**).

Both are often accompanied by **смета́на** (*sour cream*), a bowl of which usually remains on the table for use with the soup course.

## Супы́ (*soup*)

Russians love to eat hearty soups full of vegetables. Perhaps the most famous are **щи** (*cabbage soup*) and **борщ** (*beetroot soup*). **Суп-лапша́** (*noodle soup*) and **бульо́н** (*clear soup*) are also popular. Soup is usually served during **обе́д** rather than **у́жин**.

**Вторы́е блю́да** will contain meat or fish dishes and may be followed by **сла́дкие**, often a very sweet gateau (**торт**) or ice-cream (**моро́женое**).

**Обе́д** or **у́жин** in a Russian household will often take much longer to consume than a similar event in most other countries, as Russians love conversation. So if you are invited out for a meal by Russian friends, make sure you do not have any appointments afterwards!

Some Russians will eat large quantities on certain special occasions, e.g. when they are entertaining foreigners! They will sometimes also drink a fair amount, and accompany each drink with a **тост**. A general toast would be **За ва́ше здоро́вье!** *Your health!* Besides **во́дка**, **пи́во** and **вино́**, they will often drink **шампа́нское**. **Сухо́е** is *dry*, **полусухо́е** *medium-dry* and **сла́дкое** *sweet*.

The word for *ready* is **гото́в**; thus you might hear **У́жин/обе́д гото́в**. In a domestic situation you might hear the expression **Ку́шайте** or **Ку́шайте на здоро́вье!** (literally *eat for the good of your health*). **Ку́шать** is an old word for *eat*, and is an expression that you will certainly hear but should not try and use, as it is limited in its use. **Ку́шайте!** is an encouragement to eat, almost like the English *Tuck in!*

Russians tend to eat more freshwater species of fish than we do. **Щу́ка** (*pike*), **суда́к** and **карп** are all popular dishes, and sturgeon (**осетри́на**) is a great delicacy. Carp and catfish (**сом**) are sometimes sold live in the markets and some Russian recipes will give special instructions on how the fish should be treated before it is killed, to give it the best taste.

If you have enjoyed your meal, besides saying **Большо́е спаси́бо** you might tell your host how tasty the meal was – **О́чень вку́сно!**

Whether in a restaurant or in a Russian home you will always find **хлеб** (*bread*) on the table. Bread and salt (**соль**) are a traditional symbol of hospitality. There is a wide variety of bread, but the ones that appear most frequently are **бе́лый хлеб** and **чёрный хлеб**.

**Чёрный хлеб** is usually prepared with rye flour, wheat germ and molasses and traditionally made by the sourdough method. It is much heavier than white bread, though much tastier and, of course, more typically Russian. Some Russians will

not serve black bread to non-Russians, as many foreigners do not like it, and city-dwellers often consider it to be a 'peasant' food. If you want butter with your bread (it is normally served without), you simply ask for **хлеб с ма́слом**.

Russian and foreign **моро́женое** (ice-cream) is sold all the year round on the streets. Russian ice-cream may be very good, but not always!

## EXERCISE 4

Listen to the tape. You are in a Russian home and your Russian host is asking you to take your place at the table.
See how many of the **заку́ски** you can recognise. What is the main course?

## ● Language information

### *Want*

| я | хочу́ | мы | хоти́м |
|---|---|---|---|
| ты | хо́чешь | вы | хоти́те |
| он, она́ | хо́чет | они́ | хотя́т |

You can ask people if they want something with the word **Хоти́те?** Reply with **(не) хочу́**. Try to make your voice go up on the **и** of **хоти́те**.

Хоти́те вино́? *Do you want some wine?*
Хоти́те осетри́ну? *Do you want some sturgeon?*
Хочу́ *or* Не хочу́. *I do or I don't.*

To ask if you are hungry or thirsty you say:
Хоти́те есть? *Are you hungry?*
Хоти́те пить? *Are you thirsty?*

You reply simply:
Хочу́ *Yes, I am.*
or
Не хочу́ *No, I'm not.*

The sentences mean literally *Do you want to eat? Do you want to drink?*

You will often hear Russians changing the word order to give the sentence a bit more emphasis: **Есть хоти́те?** They also frequently miss out the words **я**, **вы**, etc.

## Requests

If you want to be more direct, you can request someone to give you something. It may be food or drink or any object:

Да́йте мне, пожа́луйста, смета́ну.
*Give me the sour cream, please.*
Мне, пожа́луйста, ку́рицу.
*I would like the chicken, please.*

Russians often say **пожа́луйста** when they hand the object over.

### EXERCISE 5

Below is a list of things that you would like. Identify the object by placing the number of the Russian word in the circles in the picture.

Дайте, пожалуйста,

| | | | |
|---|---|---|---|
| **1** | грибы́ | **6** | ку́рицу |
| **2** | счёт | **7** | хлеб |
| **3** | газе́ту | **8** | самова́р |
| **4** | биле́т | **9** | пи́во |
| **5** | цветы́ | **10** | жето́н |

Да́йте, пожа́луйста.

Пожа́луйста.

## With

**С лимо́ном, со смета́ной, с гриба́ми** are all examples of **с** meaning *with*. **с** is followed by the *instrumental case*. This ends in:

| masculine and neuter | -ОМ | чай с лимо́н**ом** *tea with lemon* |
|---|---|---|
| feminine | -ОЙ | огурцы́ со смета́н**ой** *cucumbers with sour cream* |
| plural | -АМИ | свини́на с гриб**а́ми** *pork with mushrooms* |

## ● Looking at words

### Having breakfast, dinner, supper

**За́втрак**, **обе́д** and **у́жин** can all be turned into verbs by simply adding **-ать**.

за́втракать    *to have breakfast*
обе́дать    *to have dinner*
у́жинать    *to have supper*

They also sometimes appear with **по-** at the beginning of the verbal form. **Хоти́те поза́втракать?** means *Would you like a little breakfast?* Again notice the economy of Russian.

## A situation to remember

### Ordering food

Look again at Exercise 1 in this unit.
You are the only Russian speaker out of a group of British people.
You have found out what they want.
Explain to the waiter what each of them wants to eat for each course:

Ми́стер Джо́унс хо́чет сарди́ны ...
Мисс Бе́нсон хо́чет ... (etc.)

Then you tell the waiter what you want:

Да́йте мне, пожа́луйста, ...

The drinks have already been ordered.

### Are you hungry? Are you thirsty?

Ask a friend if he/she is hungry or thirsty.
Ask if he/she wants specific items of food or drink, choosing items from the menu in this unit.

## ● Playing with words

### Word square

See how many items of food and drink you can find in the square.

| А | С | К | А | Р | П | И | М |
|---|---|---|---|---|---|---|---|
| З | А | К | У | С | К | И | Ю |
| П | Л | О | В | И | П | К | С |
| Ж | А | Т | Л | И | У | Р | У |
| О | Т | Л | И | Р | Н | А | М |
| Ц | Ж | Е | М | Я | С | О | К |
| Й | Н | Т | О | С | С | У | П |
| Я | И | Ч | Н | И | Ц | А | К |

## Missing letters

Now here are some more items of food and drink. This time you have to insert the missing letters and then match the words on the left with the words or phrases on the right. The first one is done for you.

1 Шам*па́н*ское    из помидо́ров
2 С_рд_ны    (кра́сная)
3 С_ла_    минера́льная
4 С_к    ру́сское (полусухо́е)
5 Би_шт_кс    с ма́слом
6 И_ра́    в ма́сле
7 Вод_    тома́тный
8 _ай    с лимо́ном
9 _ле_    н_т_ра́льный

## Reading handwriting

Decipher the illustrated written forms and print the words beneath the photograph.

## WHAT YOU KNOW

### Saying what you want and what you want to do

| | |
|---|---|
| Я хочу́ | чай. |
| Хоти́те | сала́т? |
| | пиво? |
| Я хочу́ | есть |
| Хоти́те | пить? |

### Asking for things

| | |
|---|---|
| Да́йте (мне), пожа́луйста, | сок. |
| Мне, пожа́луйста, | ку́рицу. |
| | счёт. |

### What do you like with things?

| | | |
|---|---|---|
| Чай | с | лимо́ном |
| Суп | с | гриба́ми |
| Блины́ | со | смета́ной |

### KEY VOCABULARY

| | |
|---|---|
| вку́сно | tasty |
| вторы́е блю́да | main courses |
| есть | to eat |
| за́втрак | breakfast |
| заку́ски | hors d'oeuvre |
| за́нято | occupied |
| ко́фе | coffee |
| ма́сло | butter, oil |
| мя́со | meat |
| напи́тки | drinks |
| обе́д | dinner |
| пе́рвые блю́да | soup courses |
| пить | to drink |
| ры́ба | fish |
| Сади́тесь! | Sit down! |
| свобо́дно | free |
| сла́дкие | dessert |
| счёт | bill |
| у́жин | supper |
| чёрный хлеб | black bread |
| бе́лый хлеб | white bread |

Going to church

Visiting art galleries
and museums

Talking about
things

# Revision

## ● Life in Russia

### Russian churches

After the 1917 revolution the majority of the churches in Moscow and St Petersburg were used for a variety of non-religious purposes. Some were turned into museums, some used as warehouses, some were allowed to decay, some were demolished. After the fall of communism many churches have been returned to the church authorities and they are gradually being reinstated as working churches.

A visit to a church during a service can be a very moving experience. The Orthodox church (**Правосла́вие**) has very different rituals from a Catholic or Protestant Christian service. The congregation is separated from the priest by a door and screen or iconostasis (**иконоста́с**) and there are no statues or three-dimensional images in the church. Instead the walls are covered with icons (**ико́ны**) which are revered by the members of the congregation. The nave of the church is usually open, and the rich decorations add to the atmosphere.

The most famous of icon painters was **Андре́й Рублёв**, who lived and worked around the beginning of the 15th century. His work is to be found on many church interiors in and around Moscow, and his masterpiece is the icon of the Trinity (**Тро́ица**). There were earlier icon painters, notably Theophanes the Greek (**Феофа́н Грек**), who arrived in Novgorod from Constantinople in the 1370s. Many icons are of unknown origin and have miraculous powers ascribed to them.

Don't expect to understand the words of the prayers. The language used is called *Church Slavonic*: it is related to Russian and the most you can expect to do is to pick out a few words. Listen out for **Бог** or **Бо́же** (*God*) and the verb **моли́ться** (*to pray*). Be careful, Russian church services can go on for a very long time and there are no seats in an Orthodox church.

If you are looking at religious buildings, you will need to know the following words:

| | |
|---|---|
| собо́р | *cathedral* |
| це́рковь | *church* |
| храм | *church, cathedral* |
| монасты́рь | *monastery, convent* |
| ла́вра | *(large) monastery* |

You will find many **собо́ры** in the Kremlin in Moscow. The oldest and most famous is Assumption Cathedral (**Успе́нский собо́р**). Outside the walls of the Kremlin on Red Square, you will find St Basil's Cathedral (**Храм Васи́лия Блаже́нного**).
Besides the cathedrals and churches there are many **монастыри́** in and around

Moscow. One of the most important of these, **Новоде́вичий монасты́рь**, is situated close to the centre of Moscow. This is in fact a convent, as the Russian word, though related to the English *monastery*, can refer to a religious community either for men or for women. Many famous Russians are buried in the adjoining cemetery, including **Го́голь**, **Че́хов**, **Станисла́вский** and others. The tradition was continued in the communist period: there is a secular part of the cemetery where leading politicians such as **Хрущёв** and **Мо́лотов** were buried.

If you are interested in church architecture, you should visit one of the towns in the **Золото́е кольцо́** (*Golden Ring*). If, for example, you travel north-east of Moscow, you will find the towns of **Влади́мир** and **Су́здаль**, which have a collection of churches and monasteries, some of them older than any Moscow church. Possibly the most famous of all the monasteries near Moscow is Trinity-St Sergius Monastery (**Тро́ице-Се́ргиева Ла́вра**) in the town of **Се́ргиев Поса́д**, formerly **Заго́рск**. This monastery had the unique distinction that for many years in the communist period it housed the only seminary for training Orthodox priests.

## Museums and art galleries

The best place to see icons is in the Tretyakov Gallery (**Третьяко́вская галере́я**) in Moscow. You can you see the Virgin of Vladimir (**Влади́мирская богома́терь**) painted in the early 12th century and many of the works of Rublyov, Feofan Grek and others. There are also many paintings by Russian artists in the Tretyakov.

The Pushkin Museum (**Музе́й и́мени Пу́шкина**) in Moscow contains a large collection of world art, including Dutch paintings and French impressionists as well as Matisse and Picasso. Moscow's 'crown jewels' are on view in the Armoury Palace (**Оруже́йная пала́та**) in the Kremlin, along with many other precious artefacts from tsarist times.

The largest collection of art in Russia is in St Petersburg at the Hermitage (**Эрмита́ж**), which is housed in the Winter Palace. The collection of Dutch paintings is the largest in existence and these and other works are exhibited in 1000 rooms, so allow plenty of time!

## ● Language information

### o *about*

The word **o** means *about* and is followed by the prepositional case ('**e**' form). It has an alternative form **об** used before most vowels.

Са́ша говори́т **o** Москве́.
*Sasha is talking about Moscow.*
Ната́ша говори́т **об** Эрмита́же.
*Natasha is talking about the Hermitage.*
Ни́на зна́ет **o** футбо́ле.
*Nina knows about football.*
Ми́ша зна́ет **об** А́нглии.
*Misha knows about England.*

The word **в** sometimes has an alternative form **во**, e.g. **во** Владивосто́ке.

### писа́ть *to write*

In Unit 8 you discovered the present tense forms of verbs. Inevitably some verbs have irregular forms. One such verb is:

| писа́ть *to write* | | | |
|---|---|---|---|
| я | пишу́ | мы | пи́шем |
| ты | пи́шешь | вы | пи́шете |
| он, она́ | пи́шет | они́ | пи́шут |

### ну́жно, на́до *must*

Мне на́до бежа́ть. *I have to run.*
Вам (Тебе́) ну́жно прийти́ за́втра?
*Do you have to come tomorrow?*

The words mean literally *it is necessary*. Russians are saying: *It is necessary for me to run, Is it necessary for you to come tomorrow?*

They can also be used as the equivalent of the English *need*:

Э́то не то, что мне ну́жно (на́до).
*It is not what I need. (Literally It is not what is necessary for me.)*

You have already seen the forms **мне**, **тебе** and **вам** in Unit 8. They are the dative case of the words **я**, **ты** and **вы**, and mean *to* or *for me/you*.

# ● Revision exercises

## EXERCISE 1

Read the following letter. It is written by a young visitor to Moscow to a girl who is in his class at school in Vladimir. Answer the questions by ticking the correct box. The first one is done for you.

> Дорогая Óля!
> Вот я и в Москве! У меня очень хорошая комната в гостинице «Россия» недалеко от Красной площади. У меня в комнате есть телевизор, радио и телефон. Всё, что нужно. Сейчас по телевизору идёт американский фильм. Очень хороший фильм. Главную роль играет очень красивая актриса, англичанка. Как дела у тебя дома? Как папа и мама? Моя мама сейчас в Санкт-Петербурге, а папа работает в Иркутске. Он очень любит спорт и пишет, что играет в теннис. Пиши! Мой адрес Москва 107642, гостиница «Россия», комната 524 Телефон 298-65 24.
>
> С приветом,
> Саша

## New vocabulary

| | |
|---|---|
| дорогой | *dear* |
| комната | *room* |
| гостиница | *hotel* |
| недалеко от | *not far from* |
| главный | *main* |
| роль | *part* |
| с приветом | *best wishes* |

**1**   Где Саша?

A   В Кремле ☐
Б   В гостинице «Москва» ☐
В   В гостинице «Россия» ✓
Г   В театре ☐

**2**   Где гостиница?

A   В Санкт-Петербурге ☐
Б   Во Владимире ☐
В   В Америке ☐
Г   Недалеко от Красной площади ☐

**3**   Что Саша сейчас делает?

A   Гуляет по Москве ☐
Б   Смотрит фильм по телевизору ☐
В   Читает американскую газету ☐
Г   Обедает в хорошем ресторане ☐

**4**   Что идёт по телевизору?

A   Американский фильм ☐
Б   Английский фильм ☐
В   Играет красивая англичанка ☐
Г   Он не говорит по-английски ☐

**5**   Почему папа в Иркутске?

A   Он смотрит телевизор ☐
Б   Он там работает ☐
В   Он играет в теннис ☐
Г   Он играет в футбол ☐

**6**   Почему Саше нравится гостиница?

A   Потому что он в Москве ☐
Б   Потому что в комнате всё, что нужно ☐
В   Потому что папа играет в теннис ☐
Г   Потому что Óля красивая англичанка ☐

## EXERCISE 2

Look at the picture above and complete the sentences by supplying the missing word from the box below. The first one is done for you.

1 На _столе́_ цветы́.
2 Оди́н мужчи́на _____ телеви́зор.
3 Оди́н мужчи́на _____ газе́ту.
4 По телеви́зору _____ футбо́льный матч.
5 Же́нщина говори́т _____ телефо́ну.

| идёт по смо́трит столе́ чита́ет |
| --- |

## EXERCISE 3

Here is a matching exercise, using some of the times you met in Unit 8, and the time zone chart in the same unit (page 62). For each item you are given the Moscow time and you have to say what time it is in another town by picking out the appropriate clock and putting its letter in the box. The first one is done for you.

1 Моско́вское вре́мя пятна́дцать часо́в.
  Ско́лько сейча́с вре́мени в Ирку́тске?

2 Моско́вское вре́мя двена́дцать часо́в.
  Ско́лько сейча́с вре́мени во Владивосто́ке?

3 Моско́вское вре́мя семна́дцать часо́в.
  Ско́лько сейча́с вре́мени в Волгогра́де?

4 Моско́вское вре́мя два́дцать оди́н час.
  Ско́лько сейча́с вре́мени в Санкт-Петербу́рге?

5 Моско́вское вре́мя семь часо́в.
  Ско́лько сейча́с вре́мени в О́мске?

6 Моско́вское вре́мя де́вять часо́в.
  Ско́лько сейча́с вре́мени в Новосиби́рске?

7 Моско́вское вре́мя шестна́дцать часо́в.
  Ско́лько сейча́с вре́мени в Магада́не?

## EXERCISE 4

Here is a dialogue, recorded on your cassette, that takes place in a photographic shop. It is between a shop assistant and a tourist who is looking for a camera.
The shop assistant asks the tourist what he wants (**что вам ну́жно?** literally, *what do you need?*)
Answer the questions which follow.

Тури́ст: Здра́вствуйте.
Де́вушка: Здра́вствуйте.
Тури́ст: У вас есть но́вые ма́рки фотоаппара́тов?
Де́вушка: Да, есть.
Тури́ст: Мо́жно посмотре́ть?
Де́вушка: Пожа́луйста. Вот хоро́ший аппара́т «Зени́т».
Тури́ст: Я зна́ю о «Зени́те», но э́то не то, что мне ну́жно! Мо́жно посмотре́ть япо́нские ма́рки?
Де́вушка: Япо́нских аппара́тов у нас нет.
Тури́ст: Покажи́те, пожа́луйста, вот э́тот.
Де́вушка: (*Пока́зывает*) Это но́вый неме́цкий аппара́т. Очень хоро́ший.
Тури́ст: Хм ... Пожа́луй, я его́ возьму́ ... То́лько ... мо́жно прийти́ за́втра? Сейча́с мне ну́жно бежа́ть. (*Смо́трит на часы́*)
Де́вушка: Мо́жно.
Тури́ст: Спаси́бо! До свида́ния!
Де́вушка: Пожа́луйста!

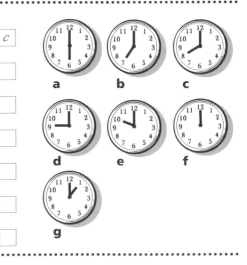

a     b     c

d     e     f

g

**New vocabulary**

| | |
|---|---|
| ма́рка | model |
| Зени́т | Zenith (make of Russian camera) |
| пока́зывать | to show |
| я его́ возьму́ | I'll take it |
| прийти́ | to come |
| смотре́ть на | to look at |
| посмотре́ть | to have a look |
| но | but |
| пожа́луй | perhaps, very likely |
| то́лько | only |
| бежа́ть | to run |
| часы́ | watch |

1  What does the man want?
2  What does the woman offer him?
3  What is his reply to this?
4  What does he finally decide on?
5  Why doesn't he take the camera immediately?

## EXERCISE 5

On your recording you will hear a number followed by a statement or question.
As soon as you hear the statement or question stop the recording and pick out the appropriate response below.
Put the number in the box.
The first one is done for you.
(It is a good idea to look first at the responses below and see if you can anticipate what sort of thing would fit before listening to each one.)

Хорошо́, а вы? ☐

Нет, сейча́с закры́т. ☐

Иди́те пря́мо, пото́м нале́во. [1]

Нет, то́лько лимона́д. ☐

Ничего́, а ты? ☐

Здра́вствуйте, о́чень рад. ☐

Нет, да́йте, пожа́луйста, ко́фе. ☐

Нет, не хочу́. Я сего́дня занята́. ☐

Нет, не моя́. ☐

Нет, да́йте, пожа́луйста, чай. ☐

О́ля, приве́т! Как дела́? ☐

## EXERCISE 6

Look back at the metro map of St Petersburg in Unit 6. Your hotel is situated near the station **Технологи́ческий институ́т**, which is on the first (**пе́рвая ли́ния**) and second (**втора́я ли́ния**) lines. If you need a station on the third (**тре́тья ли́ния**) or fourth (**четвёртая ли́ния**) lines, you will need to change (**де́лать переса́дку**). You have to plan the number of stops to get to each of the stations (**ста́нция**) below from your station, **Технологи́ческий институ́т**. Go the shortest way each time.
Write the number of stops in the first column. If you have to change tick the second column. The first one is done for you.

| | | | |
|---|---|---|---|
| 1 | Рыба́цкое | 9 | ✓ |
| 2 | Чёрная речка | | |
| 3 | Ла́дожская | | |
| 4 | Академи́ческая | | |
| 5 | пл. Алекса́ндра Не́вского | | |
| 6 | Моско́вская | | |
| 7 | Не́вский проспе́кт | | |
| 8 | На́рвская | | |
| 9 | Политехни́ческая | | |
| 10 | Примо́рская | | |
| 11 | Ломоно́совская | | |
| 12 | Достое́вская | | |

Why do most of the station names end in -ая?
Try to work out the meaning of the station names.

## A situation to remember

### Staying in Moscow

You are staying in a nice hotel in Moscow. You have a television in your room and some beautiful flowers on the table. Tell this to your friend over the telephone. Tell him/her about the museums and churches in Moscow, and the nice food you have in the hotel restaurant. Say how much you like Moscow.

## Playing with words

### Кроссворд

Note: This crossword consists mainly of words that you already know or can easily guess. New or difficult words are marked with an asterisk in the clues. If you have difficulty, solve them after you have solved the adjacent clues.

**Across**

1 Excuse me = **извините** or _____
7 And
10 _____ **о́чень нра́вится смотре́ть телеви́зор**
12 Aha! Russian style
14 **Ско́лько** _____ **э́та ша́пка**
16 Not the boxing kind of blow. More like a stunning drink.
17 **Вам нра́вится** _____ **фильм**
19 But
20 This is what happens before you get thrown into gaol*
22 Same as 19
23 Abbreviation for **Акаде́мия Нау́к** (Academy o Sciences)
24 In the Latvian capital = **в** _____
25 From*
27 – **Как вы пожива́ете?**
   – **Спаси́бо** _____ OK, Fine, Alright
29 So
33 **Ива́н гуля́ет** _____ **Москве́**
35 **Как вам** _____ **Москва́?**
37 Famous river in Rostov with Cossack connections
38 Not
39 Short for **О́льга**
41 State Universal Store
42 On, at or to
43 To go walking
45 **Они́** love **грибы́**
51 You can drink **пи́во** here*
52 Russian choir. Starts with **x**
53 I'm for it = **я** _____ (do this after 42 and 43 down)*
54 Volume or tome*
55 **Моско́вское вре́мя двена́дцать** _____

**Down**

1 _ _ _ **о** – it means *beer*
2 **В** _____ **о́чень хоро́шее меню́**
3 **гла́сн** _ _ _ **ь**
4 **Я** _____ **телеви́зор**
5 Genghis Khan was one – ends in **-ин**
6 Moscow University
7 And
8 Not
9 Ten
11 Russian girl
13 Same as 23 across
15 Metric ton (feminine)*
16 First syllable of the verbs *to arrive* and *to come*
18 _____ **говоря́т о футбо́ле**
21 _____ **буфе́т откры́т в три часа́** (not **за́втра**)
22 Musical note (feminine)*
26 Nine
28 One o'clock or hour
30 Not breast-stroke. Ends in a **-ь***
31 **Э́то вход. Мо́жно войти́?** _____ , **пожа́луйста.**
32 The coldest place in Russia: **Верх** _ _ _ **ск**
33 **Ива́н говори́т** _____ **-ру́сски**
34 **Ири́на студе́нтка.** _____ **в университе́те.**
36 Where samovars are made (near Tolstoy's home)
40 Musical note 'A'. (Do 39 and 43 across first)*
43 We get this from the North Sea – it's the first part of a newspaper
44 Russian *Hooray!* (guess!)
46 Short for **Ю́рий**
47 What the Russians (and the French) shout for *Encore!*
48 **Э́то не** _____ , **что ну́жно**
49 Short for **Ири́на**
50 **Сего́дня** _____ **телеви́зору о́чень интере́сная програ́мма**
51 _ _ **ази́лия**. Where the coffee comes from.

## WHAT YOU KNOW

**Talking about things**
Он говори́т о Москве́.

**Having to do things**
Мне ну́жно (на́до) смотре́ть телеви́зор.

## LANGUAGE REVIEW

Here are some words and phrases we have had in Units 6–10. Check that you understand what they mean. If you are not sure you know what they mean, look back to the unit where they first occurred: this is given on the right.

| | |
|---|---|
| Как пройти́ на Кра́сную пло́щадь? | |
| Иди́те напра́во/нале́во/пря́мо. | **6** |
| У вас есть план метро́? | |
| Есть. | **6** |
| Покажи́те, пожа́луйста ... Да́йте, пожа́луйста ... | **6** |
| оди́н, два, три, четы́ре, пять, шесть, семь, во́семь, де́вять, де́сять, сто, ты́сяча | **6** |
| Как тебя́/вас зову́т? | |
| Меня́ зову́т Ната́ша. | **7** |
| Как ты пожива́ешь? Как вы пожива́ете? | **7** |
| Здра́вствуй! Здра́вствуйте! | **7** |
| кра́сный авто́бус, кра́сная ма́рка, кра́сное вино́, кра́сные авто́бусы | **7** |
| Мне хо́лодно, тепло́, жа́рко. | **8** |
| игра́ю, игра́ешь, игра́ет, игра́ем, игра́ете, игра́ют | **8** |
| говорю́, говори́шь, говори́т, говори́м, говори́те, говоря́т | **8** |
| Я иду́ по у́лице. | **8** |
| по телеви́зору, по ра́дио, по телефо́ну | **8** |
| Я люблю́ спорт. Мне нра́вится футбо́л. | **8** |
| хочу́, хо́чешь, хо́чет, хоти́м, хоти́те, хотя́т | **9** |
| чай с лимо́ном, огурцы́ со смета́ной | **9** |
| Са́ша говори́т о Москве́. | **10** |
| Мне на́до бежа́ть. Мне ну́жно прийти́ за́втра. | **10** |

## KEY VOCABULARY

| | |
|---|---|
| гости́ница | hotel |
| дорого́й | dear |
| ко́мната | room |
| монасты́рь | monastery |
| но | but |
| ну́жно | must |
| о (об) | about |
| писа́ть | to write |
| собо́р | cathedral |
| то́лько | only |
| часы́ | watch |

# Times and seasons

## ● Life in Russia

### The Russian winter (Ру́сская зима́)

Russians celebrate winter, rather than just cope with it. The temperature in Moscow can get down as low as minus 30 degrees Celsius, although it is not usually this cold for very long. Russians have adapted to these low temperatures and wear warm clothing. A Russian fur hat with ear flaps (**уша́нка**) is not just a tourist souvenir, it is a practical necessity in such temperatures. You will also need a warm coat (**пальто́**).

Houses and all public buildings are, of course, double-glazed and very well centrally heated. The inside of Russian buildings often seems too hot for the non-Russian. Make sure that, like Russians, you remove all your warm clothes when you go inside.

Theatres, museums and most public buildings in Russia are equipped with a cloakroom (**гардеро́б**), and you are always expected to check in your overcoat before entering the building. When you enter someone's house you usually take off your coat, hat and your outdoor shoes, particularly if you are wearing galoshes or overshoes (**гало́ши**). Slippers (**та́почки**) will usually be provided for visitors in a normal Russian household. When you go round palaces and stately homes, you will be required to put on **та́почки** over your outdoor shoes to protect the floors and carpets.

The national sport in winter is ice hockey. Soccer is played in the summer, as grounds are not fit for play in the winter. The surface of rivers and lakes is frozen hard and skating is a popular pastime, as is skiing and tobogganing. Fishing is also a popular sport in winter. Anglers drill holes in the ice for their lines and may be seen sitting patiently waiting for a bite.

Useful words for winter activities:

| | |
|---|---|
| игра́ть в хокке́й | *to play ice-hockey* |
| ката́ться на лы́жах | *to ski* |
| ката́ться на конька́х | *to skate* |
| ката́ться на саня́х | *to toboggan* |
| лови́ть ры́бу | *to fish* |

## Ру́сское ле́то (Russian summer)

Russians who live in small flats in big cities like to get away as often as they can to the country. Moscow, for example, is surrounded by vast areas of woodland and it is here, in **Подмоско́вье**, that many Russians own or rent a dacha (**да́ча**). This can vary from a tiny single-storeyed wooden house with few facilities to a two-storeyed brick-built house with all the usual modern conveniences.

The dachas are usually situated in beautiful countryside and are surrounded by a plot of land (**уча́сток**), on which the owners will grow potatoes (**карто́шка**) and other vegetables, as well as fruit such as apples, raspberries and gooseberries. Russians will not waste fresh vegetables and fruit. They are expert at pickling and salting vegetables

and making **варе́нье**, a type of whole fruit jam. In difficult economic times, this is a useful supplement to the family's diet. Some of the food that we talked about in Unit 9 may have come from the family's **да́ча**.

When not cultivating their plot Russians will relax and maybe go for a swim (**купа́ться**) in the local river or lake. Alternatively they will simply sunbathe (**загора́ть**). Some very hardy Russians will swim out in the open air even in winter in sub-zero temperatures. These are known as **моржи́** (*walruses*). They have a theory that to swim in extreme conditions is good for the health. They also beat themselves with birch twigs for the same reason.

White nights (**Бе́лые но́чи**) are a feature of midsummer in northern Russia. During this period it never gets completely dark at night and in St Petersburg they celebrate with a music and theatre festival. Locals stay up all night and watch the bridges go up to let the big ships through. Otherwise, if you enjoy going to the theatre or to concerts, all the best plays and concerts are on in winter: most theatres and concert halls close in summer.

Summer or winter the public bath (**ба́ня**) is also a feature of Russian life, similar to a sauna or Turkish bath, and is often featured in films as a place where deals are fixed between businesspeople, sometimes of doubtful honesty. Don't confuse this word with **ва́нная**, which is a perfectly ordinary bathroom.

## ● Language information

### Days of the week

| | | | |
|---|---|---|---|
| понеде́льник | *Monday* | в понеде́льник | *on Monday* |
| вто́рник | *Tuesday* | во вто́рник | *on Tuesday* |
| среда́ | *Wednesday* | в сре́ду | *on Wednesday* |
| четве́рг | *Thursday* | в четве́рг | *on Thursday* |
| пя́тница | *Friday* | в пя́тницу | *on Friday* |
| суббо́та | *Saturday* | в суббо́ту | *on Saturday* |
| воскресе́нье | *Sunday* | в воскресе́нье | *on Sunday* |

To ask what the day is, say **Како́й сего́дня день?** The reply might be: **Сего́дня суббо́та** (*Today is Saturday*). If you ask **Когда́ вы бу́дете игра́ть в футбо́л?** (*When will you play football?*), the reply might be **В суббо́ту** (*On Saturday*). Simply put **в** in front of the word and change **-а** to **-у** when it occurs at the end of the word (the accusative case).

### Months of the year and seasons

| | | | | | |
|---|---|---|---|---|---|
| янва́рь | *January* | в январе́ | *in January* | зима́ | *winter* |
| февра́ль | *February* | в феврале́ | *in February* | | |
| март | *March* | в ма́рте | *in March* | | |
| апре́ль | *April* | в апре́ле | *in April* | весна́ | *spring* |
| май | *May* | в ма́е | *in May* | | |
| ию́нь | *June* | в ию́не | *in June* | | |
| ию́ль | *July* | в ию́ле | *in July* | ле́то | *summer* |
| а́вгуст | *August* | в а́вгусте | *in August* | | |
| сентя́брь | *September* | в сентябре́ | *in September* | | |
| октя́брь | *October* | в октябре́ | *in October* | о́сень | *autumn* |
| ноя́брь | *November* | в ноябре́ | *in November* | | |
| дека́брь | *December* | в декабре́ | *in December* | зима́ | *winter* |

Russian uses capital letters much more sparingly than English. The months and days of the week are all written with a small letter in Russian.

Seasons don't need a separate word to indicate 'in'. They simply change the endings:

зимо́й – *in winter*     весно́й – *in spring*     ле́том – *in summer*     о́сенью – *in autumn*

## Times of the day

| | | | |
|---|---|---|---|
| у́тро | *morning* | у́тром | *in the morning* |
| день | *day* | днём | *during the day, in the afternoon* |
| ве́чер | *evening* | ве́чером | *in the evening* |
| ночь | *night* | но́чью | *at night* |

Like the seasons, the times of the day don't need a word for 'in'. 'In the afternoon' is often translated by the phrase **по́сле обе́да**, which means literally *after dinner*.

## First to tenth

Here are the numbers for first to tenth:

| | | | |
|---|---|---|---|
| пе́рвый | *first* | шесто́й | *sixth* |
| второ́й | *second* | седьмо́й | *seventh* |
| тре́тий | *third* | восьмо́й | *eighth* |
| четвёртый | *fourth* | девя́тый | *ninth* |
| пя́тый | *fifth* | деся́тый | *tenth* |

You should recognise higher numbers of this type without any difficulty.

## Dates

Како́е сего́дня число́?
*What date is it today?*
Сего́дня шесто́е ма́рта (6-ое ма́рта).
*Today is 6th March.*
Сего́дня девя́тое января́ (9-ое января́).
*Today is 9th January.*

....................................

### EXERCISE 1
Look at the dates below. Fill in the boxes with the day, date and month, as in the first example.

| | | | |
|---|---|---|---|
| пя́тница, шестна́дцатое ию́ня | *Fri* | *16* | *June* |
| вто́рник, деся́тое ноября́ | | | |
| понеде́льник, два́дцать пя́тое апре́ля | | | |
| суббо́та, пе́рвое ию́ля | | | |
| среда́, тридца́тое декабря́ | | | |
| воскресе́нье, трина́дцатое октября́ | | | |
| четве́рг, два́дцать девя́тое января́ | | | |

## Future with бу́ду, бу́дешь ...

One way of talking about an event that is going to happen in the future is to use the forms **бу́ду**, **бу́дешь**, etc. combined with the infinitive (the form of the verb that you find in dictionaries). The infinitive usually ends in **-ть**.

**Я бу́ду игра́ть** в футбо́л.
*I will play football. (or I will be playing football)*
Ты **бу́дешь смотре́ть** фильм.
*You will be watching the film.*
Он (Она́) **бу́дет чита́ть** рома́н.
*He (She) will be reading the novel.*
Мы **бу́дем рабо́тать**.
*We shall be working.*
Вы **бу́дете гуля́ть**.
*You will be taking a stroll*
Они́ **бу́дут обе́дать** в час.
*They will have lunch at one.*

You can tell the time that something will take place by simply using the word **бу́дет**. Here are some examples:

Матч бу́дет в пя́тницу.
*The match will be (take place) on Friday.*
Фильм бу́дет за́втра в 8 часо́в.
*The film will be on tomorrow at 8 o'clock.*
Бале́т бу́дет в суббо́ту в 7 часо́в.
*The ballet will be on Saturday at 7 o'clock.*

When you use these expressions, very often you are making plans for the future. To tell someone what you will be doing, you use **бу́ду** with the infinitive. Thus **я бу́ду рабо́тать** (*I shall be working*), **я бу́ду чита́ть** (*I shall be reading*), etc.

## EXERCISE 2

The following exercise consists of sentences you might use when making plans. You have to put in the correct form of the day. The first one is done for you.

**1** Saturday   В ___субботу___ я бу́ду игра́ть в футбо́л.

**2** Monday   В _____ я бу́ду смотре́ть телеви́зор.

**3** Sunday   В _____ я бу́ду гуля́ть в па́рке.

**4** Wednesday   В _____ я бу́ду рабо́тать в университе́те.

**5** Friday   В _____ я буду́ обе́дать в рестора́не.

**6** Thursday   В _____ я бу́ду чита́ть «Войну́ и мир».

**7** Tuesday   Во _____ я бу́ду смотре́ть матч Дина́мо-Спарта́к.

## Of, after, before and the genitive case

The word 'of' is not usually translated into Russian: simply use the genitive case: **1-е ма́рта** (the first *of* March), **центр го́рода** (the centre *of* town). The forms of the genitive case are:

| singular | |
|---|---|
| masculine and neuter nouns end in **-А** | часа́ ме́ста |
| masculine **ь** nouns end in **-Я** | января́ |
| feminine nouns end in **-Ы** or **-И** (KA nouns) | ко́мнаты де́вушки |

| plural | |
|---|---|
| masculine nouns end in **-ОВ** | часо́в |
| feminine nouns remove **-a** | ко́мнат |
| neuter nouns remove **-o** | мест |
| some nouns add **-е** or **-о** to last syllable | де́вушек |
| **ь** nouns end in **ЕЙ** | царе́й |

The genitive case is also used following **по́сле** (*after*) and **до** (*before*): **по́сле обе́да** (*after dinner*), **до у́жина** (*before supper*).

Most Russian numbers are followed by a genitive case. **два** (**две**), **три** and **четы́ре** use the genitive singular: **два часа́** (*two o'clock*), **пять** and above require the genitive plural: **пять часо́в** (*five o'clock*).

## EXERCISE 3

In the following exercise, the endings have been left off some of the nouns. You will either need the genitive case, as explained above, or you may need the prepositional case, when following **в**, **на**, or **о**. Fill in the blanks with the correct form.

Мы за́втракаем в семь [1]час__. По́сле [2]за́втрак __ па́па рабо́тает. Он такси́ст. Он рабо́тает в [3]Москв__, в [4]це́нтр__ [5]го́род__ . До [6]обе́д __мы гуля́ем в [7]па́рк__. Там о́чень краси́во. Мы обе́даем в два [8]час__.

По́сле [9]обе́д __ я смотрю́ телеви́зор. О́чень хорошо́!
Ве́чером в во́семь [10]час__ мы у́жинаем.
По́сле [11]у́жин__ ма́ма рабо́тает на [12]ку́хн__, а папа чита́ет журна́л о [13]футбо́л__.

## EXERCISE 4

Listen to the recording. A guide is describing to a group of tourists their itinerary for a stay in Moscow. They ask him questions about various events that are going to take place.
You have the timetable in front of you, but there are some gaps in it. Fill in the gaps using the information on the recording.

| суббо́та 8-ое ию́ля | |
|---|---|
| 08.00–09.00 | за́втрак |
| [1]_____ | экску́рсия по Москве́ |
| 13.00 | обе́д |
| 14.30 | [2]_____ |
| [3]_____ | Большо́й теа́тр |
| [4]_____ | у́жин |

| воскресе́нье 9-ое ию́ля | |
|---|---|
| 08.00- 09.10 | за́втрак |
| [5]_____ | экску́рсия по Кремлю́ |
| 13.00 | [6]_____ |

## EXERCISE 5

Look at the following notices explaining when places are open. Many Russian shops still close for lunch or for a **санита́рный** (*cleaning*) **час**. Some have a day when they do not open (**выходно́й день**). More and more shops are now opening every day: **без выходны́х**.

1  a  When can you have your photograph taken?

   b  When do they close for lunch?

   c  What day are they closed?

2  When is the department store open

   a  on weekdays?

   b  on Sundays?

3  a  On which days of the week can you buy contact lenses?

   b  At what times is the shop open each day?

4  a  At what times is the cafe open?

   b  What days does it open?

   c  When does it close in the middle of the day?

# ● Looking at words

## Days of the week

Russians start the week with **понеде́льник**, which comes from **неде́ля** (*week*). **вто́рник**, **четве́рг** and **пя́тница** come from the numbers **второ́й** (*second*), **четвёртый** (*fourth*), **пя́тый** (*fifth*). **Среда́** is the 'middle day': the Russian for *middle* is **сре́дний**. **суббо́та** is related to English *sabbath*. **Воскресе́нье** originally meant *Resurrection*. It still does in modern Russian, although it is spelt slightly differently: **воскресе́ние**. It is the title of a novel by Tolstoy.

## Сего́дня

**Сего́дня** is a two-part word: it literally means *of this day*. **Серо́** comes from an old word, **сей**, meaning *this*. You will only see it in a few words and idioms. The modern Russian for *this* is **э́тот**. **-дня** is the genitive case of the word **день**. Be careful, this word is pronounced *sevódnya*: this was mentioned in Unit 5. There are a number of places where **-ого** and **-его** are pronounced with a 'v' instead of a 'g': e.g. **ничег̲о́**.

## Russian version of 'h'

Russian does not have an 'h' sound. When it borrows words which have that sound, it often replaces it with an '**г**'. This may seem strange, until you listen to Russians from the south of the country, or Russian speakers in the Ukraine: they pronounce '**г**' quite close to an 'h'. The horizon in Russian is **горизо́нт**, and if you wish to exclaim 'Aha!', you write '**Ага́!**'.

**EXERCISE 6**

Here are some place names and the names of people (real and fictitious), where 'h' has been replaced by a Russian 'г'. Can you work out the English version?

1 Гонко́нг _____

2 Ги́тлер _____

3 Голла́ндия _____

4 Га́млет _____

5 Копенга́ген _____

# ● Reading

## Summer and winter

**EXERCISE 7**

Read the following passage about how the Kalugin family spend their weekends in summer and winter. Then complete the table below in English. The first entry for **Ива́н Петро́вич** is done for you.

Ива́н Петро́вич Калу́гин о́чень лю́бит спорт. Но он не игра́ет в спорт, то́лько смо́трит спорт по телеви́зору. Зимо́й он хо́дит раз в неде́лю на стадио́н и смо́трит хокке́й. Он всегда́ но́сит *(wears)* тёплое *(warm)* пальто́ и ста́рую уша́нку. Ле́том ка́ждую *(every)* суббо́ту он рабо́тает на да́че, а ка́ждый ве́чер смо́трит футбо́л по телеви́зору.

Его́ жена́ Ири́на не лю́бит спорт. Ка́ждый год она́ покупа́ет *(buys)* абонеме́нт *(season ticket)* и слушает симфо́нии и конце́рты Чайко́вского и Шостако́вича в консервато́рии. Ле́том, когда́ нет конце́ртов, она́ рабо́тает с му́жем *(husband)* на уча́стке, а ка́ждый ве́чер чита́ет рома́ны.

Сын Бо́ря игра́ет в ша́хматы *(chess)* и зимо́й и ле́том: он рабо́тает на да́че то́лько, когда́ на́до. Его́ сестра́ Ма́ша лю́бит му́зыку. Она́ слушает рок-му́зыку с подру́гами. *(female friend)* Ле́том, ка́ждую суббо́ту она́ то́же *(also)* на да́че, но она́ не рабо́тает на уча́стке: она́ лежи́т на со́лнце *(lies in the sun)* и загора́ет.

| | зимо́й | ле́том |
|---|---|---|
| Ива́н | *goes to the stadium to watch ice-hockey* | |
| Ири́на | | |
| Бо́ря | | |
| Ма́ша | | |

# Theatre posters

## EXERCISE 8

Look at the theatre advertisements from a Moscow paper for three theatres, the Bolshoi, the Moscow Arts Theatre (**MXAT**) and the Rossiya concert hall. Then answer the questions below.

| пятница 15 сентября | суббота 16 сентября | воскресенье 17 сентября |
|---|---|---|
| **Государственный академический большой театр** | | |
| Евгений Онегин, опера музыка П. И. Чайковского в 7.30 часов | Коппелия, балет музыка Л. Делиба в 7.30 часов | Борис Годунов, опера М. музыка П. Мусоргского в 7.00 часов |
| **МХАТ (Московский художественный академический театр)** | | |
| Чайка, пьеса А.П. Чехова в 8.00 часов | Гамлет, пьеса Уильяма Шекспира в 7.30 часов | Воскресение, пьеса по роману Л. Н. Толстого в 7.30 часов |
| **Государственный центральный концертный зал «Россия»** | | |
| Иисус Христос — суперзвезда А. Ллойд-Веббер в 7.30 часов | Хит Парад «Арлекино» в 8.00 | Закрыто |

1  a  Where do opera fans go on Friday?
   b  What will they see?
   c  When does it start?

2  a  Which play is on at the Moscow Arts Theatre on Sunday?
   b  Who wrote the novel on which it was based?
   c  When does it start?

3  Name two 'imports' from Britain in this theatre programme.

4  a  Name the ballet on at the Bolshoi Theatre.
   b  What day is it on?
   c  Who wrote the music?

5  a  The Moscow Arts Theatre is famous for its Chekhov productions. Which one can you see?
   b  When is it on?

6  What will you see on Sunday at the Rossiya concert hall?

## A situation to remember

### Making plans

Imagine that you are making plans for tomorrow. Say what time you will have breakfast, lunch and dinner. What will you do before and after dinner?

Here are some things you are going to do:

– play football    – watch a film
– go for a walk in the town    – read a book
– sunbathe    – go for a swim or skate

Alternatively, if you want to go to the cinema, you cay say **Пойдём в кино!** *Let's go to the cinema!*

### A visit by Russians

Make a programme for a group of Russians who are visiting your town and read it out to them. Work with a fellow student if you have the chance.

Activities might be the theatre, a concert, dinner at a restaurant, shops (**магазины**), excursion to London. You should produce a timetable, as in Exercise 4.

## Writing Russian (1)

Over the next five units we will show you how to write Russian letters. As soon as you can you should try writing everything with these forms, rather than printing.

There are some Russian letters which, when written, are easily recognised by an English speaker, but beware of using English variations as you write, as many of these would not be understood by a Russian. When you write, try to get as close as possible to the model. If you enjoy calligraphy you will enjoy the flourishes of written Russian, particularly of the large letters. We shall give you the letters which are difficult or new. Assume that the other letters are as you would expect them to be. Capital letters are given in brackets.

### Examples

т is written *т Т*

and и is written *и И*

п is written *п П*

н is written *н Н*

в is written *в В*

Now you try writing the words.

такси _____
*такси*

парк _____
*парк*

пианист _____
*пианист*

авиа _____
*авиа*

## WHAT YOU KNOW

### What you plan to do
я бу́ду      гуля́ть
вы бу́дете   рабо́тать

### First, second, third ...
пе́рвый, второ́й, тре́тий, четвёртый, пя́тый
шесто́й sixth      девя́тый ninth
седьмо́й seventh   деся́тый tenth
восьмо́й eighth

### Days of the week, months of the year, seasons and times of the day
Како́й сего́дня день?
Сего́дня среда́.

Како́е сего́дня число́?
Сего́дня пя́тое января́.

### When will you do it?
Когда́ вы бу́дете игра́ть  в футбо́л?
Я бу́ду игра́ть в футбо́л  в январе́.
                            весно́й.
                            у́тром.

### *Of, before, after*
1-ое ма́я
по́сле обе́да
до у́жина

## KEY VOCABULARY

| | |
|---|---|
| ба́ня | bath house |
| весна́ | spring |
| выходно́й день | day off |
| гардеро́б | cloakroom |
| да́ча | 'dacha', cottage in the country |
| загора́ть | to sunbathe |
| зима́ | winter |
| ката́ться на конька́х | to skate |
| ката́ться на лы́жах | to ski |
| ката́ться на саня́х | to toboggan |
| купа́ться | to swim |
| ле́то | summer |
| МХАТ | Moscow Arts Theatre |
| о́сень | autumn |
| по́сле обе́да | after dinner, in the afternoon |
| сын | son |
| та́почки | slippers |

# 12

**Talking about the past**

**Famous names in literature**

Genghis Khan

# The origins of Russia

## ● Life in Russia

Traders in old Novgorod

### Early history

Slavic peoples were known in the days of the Roman Empire, but the origin of the Russian kingdom is believed by many historians to be in 862, when Rurik and his two brothers arrived. Rurik settled in Novgorod (**Но́вгород**). The founders of Russia were from Scandinavia, and it was not long before **Ки́ев** became the most important city-state, dominating all the tribes of eastern Slavs by the beginning of the 11th century.

In the 11th and 12th centuries Russia traded with the West and was not isolated until the invasion of the Mongol Tartars under Batu, the great-nephew of Genghis Khan, in 1244. The Tartars lived in encampments outside the towns, demanding homage and regular tribute from the Russian princes. This state of affairs lasted for two centuries, and was known as the 'Tartar Yoke' (**Тата́рское и́го**).

The establishment of Moscow as a city was in 1328 and its importance as the political and religious centre increased until it became acknowledged as the capital of the Russian state. Other important city-states of the period include **Но́вгород**, **Псков**, **Тверь** and **Влади́мир-Су́здаль**. Today they are important historical centres, much visited by tourists.

### Useful words

| | |
|---|---|
| Русь | *Rus', the name given to the country in this period* |
| князь | *prince* |
| тата́рин | *Tartar* |

## Ivan the Terrible, Boris Godunov and the first Romanovs

Ivan III (**Ива́н тре́тий**) was the first **царь** to call himself tsar of all Russia. He reigned from 1462–1505. In 1547 Ivan the Terrible (**Ива́н гро́зный**) was crowned in Moscow. He died in 1584. His name comes from his methods of dealing with the Boyars (**боя́ре**), as the nobility were called, and from his violent, suspicious unpredictability, which led to the murder of his son in a quarrel.

His reign was followed by the 'Time of Troubles' (**Сму́тное вре́мя**), which included the reign of **Бори́с Годуно́в** and finished in 1613 with the accession to the throne of **Михаи́л Фёдорович Рома́нов**, elected by a national assembly. He was the first in the line of Romanovs which came to a violent end after the 1917 Bolshevik revolution.

Ivan the Terrible

Boris Godunov

## Peter the Great and St Petersburg

Peter the Great (**Пётр вели́кий**) came to the throne in 1682. He went on a fact-finding mission to the West, visiting and working in shipyards in Great Britain, Germany and Holland. Some of the time he tried to be incognito – a little difficult when you are well over two metres tall and followed around by a loud retinue. Like **Ива́н гро́зный**, Peter had difficulties with his courtiers, the palace guard (**Стрельцы́**), and dealt with them severely on his return to Moscow.

Russia had fallen behind the West in the years of the Tartar Yoke and Peter set out vigorously to bring the country up-to-date. He reformed the army, and created a ruling class that was rewarded for service rather than birth. Besides his knowledge of ship-building and military matters, he developed an interest in surgery and dentistry, both of which he practised on a less than willing retinue.

Peter the Great

Peter's most spectacular achievement was the foundation in 1703 of St Petersburg (**Санкт-Петербу́рг**), his 'window on the West'. Designed mainly by Italian architects, the city is much more 'Western' than many other Russian cities, its many canals and bridges (**мосты́**) giving it the title of the Venice of the North. The statue of its founder stands proudly on the bank of the river Neva (**Нева́**). **Пу́шкин** wrote one of his most famous poems about it: «**Ме́дный вса́дник**» ('The Bronze Horseman'), in which the statue comes terrifyingly alive. St Petersburg became Peter's capital, and it remained the capital of Russia until the revolution in 1917.

The tsars from Peter onwards were buried in the St Peter and Paul Fortress (**Петропа́вловская кре́пость**) in St Petersburg. Previous tsars were buried in one of the cathedrals of the Moscow Kremlin. St Petersburg has had two other names: in 1914 its name was changed to **Петрогра́д**, and in 1924 it became **Ленингра́д** on the death of Lenin. After a referendum in 1991 the population of the city decided by a narrow majority to return to the old name of **Санкт-Петербу́рг**. During the second world war the siege of Leningrad was one of the most heroic episodes in the history of the Russian people.

## Catherine the Great and the 19th century

Catherine II (**Екатери́на II**) took over the throne from her husband, Peter III. She reigned until 1796, and her attitudes were conditioned by the events in western Europe at the time – liberal philosophy followed by revolution.

The 19th century is the most important century in Russian music and literature. Europe at the start of the century was dominated by Napoleon, who made the mistake of invading Russia. The wars against Napoleon meant that many of the younger nobility, serving in the army, had been able to see parts of western Europe where serfdom had been abolished and autocracy overthrown. They began to want more freedom, and this led to a number of uprisings, one of which involved the Decembrists (**декабри́сты**) in 1825. The atmosphere became strongly anti-censorship and many of the 19th-century writers were in constant conflict with the authorities. The act which freed the serfs (**крепостны́е**) from bondage was passed in 1861, but the process went on until the end of the century, and its protracted nature deprived Russia of the gradual sort of industrial revolution that took place in the West.

## Гла́вные да́ты ру́сской исто́рии

| | |
|---|---|
| 860–1240 | Ки́евская Русь |
| 1113–25 | Влади́мир Монома́х, Князь (Ки́ев) |
| 1147 | Основа́ние Москвы́ |
| 1223 | Чингисха́н и монго́льская а́рмия разби́ли славя́нскую а́рмию |
| 1227 | Смерть Чингисха́на |
| 1240–1480 | Тата́рское и́го |
| 1533–84 | Ива́н IV (Ива́н гро́зный) |
| 1547 | Ива́н IV стал царём |
| 1598–1605 | Бори́с Годуно́в, царь |
| 1682–725 | Пётр I (Пётр вели́кий) царь |
| 1697–8 | Пётр на за́паде, в Голла́ндии и в А́нглии |
| 1703 | Основа́ние Санкт-Петербу́рга |
| 1762-96 | Екатери́на II |
| 1812–4 | Оте́чественная война́ с Наполео́ном |
| 1861 | Крестья́нская рефо́рма (освобожде́ние крестья́н) |
| 1905 | Револю́ция 1905-ого го́да |
| 1914 | Начала́сь Пе́рвая мирова́я война́ |
| 1917 | Октя́брьская револю́ция |
| 1918 | Коне́ц мирово́й войны́<br>Нача́ло гражда́нской войны |
| 1922 | Коне́ц гражда́нской войны́ |
| 1924 | Смерть Ле́нина |
| 1953 | Смерть Ста́лина |
| 1941–45 | Вели́кая оте́чественная война́ |
| 1958–64 | Хрущёв |
| 1985–91 | Горбачёв |
| 1991 | Путч - коне́ц коммуни́зма и Сове́тского сою́за |

## EXERCISE 1

On the left is a list of some of the main dates in Russian history.

The questions below are designed to help you get information from the text.

Do not expect to understand every word. The questions are in order. Use them to work out some of the vocabulary.

1  When was Vladimir Monomakh prince of Kiev?
2  When was the founding of Moscow?
3  When did Genghis Khan defeat the Slav army?
4  When did he die?
5  What were the years of the Tartar Yoke?
6  What happened in 1547?
7  Who became tsar in 1598?
8  Who went where in 1697-8?
9  What happened in 1703?
10 What took place in 1812?
11 When was the peasant reform?
12 When did the October Revolution take place?
13 When was Lenin's death?
14 When was Stalin's death?
15 When did the Soviet Union end?

Russians are very conscious of their historical identity and everywhere you go you will see monuments, plaques and historical museums. Very often a museum devoted to a historical or literary personality will be in the house where they lived and worked. A plaque might have something like this on it:

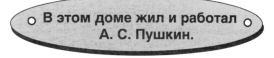

If it were a woman who lived and worked there, it might read:

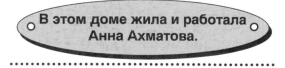

# ● Language information

## Past tense of verbs

| читáть *to read* | |
|---|---|
| я, ты, он | читáл |
| я, ты, онá | читáла |
| мы, вы, они́ | читáли |

The past tense of **читáть** is formed by replacing **-ть** in the infinitive (dictionary form) by **-л** if a man was reading, by **-ла** if a woman was reading and by **-ли** if more than one person was reading. The forms from the verb **быть** (*to be*) are:

| быть *to be* | |
|---|---|
| я, ты, он | был |
| я, ты, онá | былá |
| онó | бы́ло |
| мы, вы, они́ | бы́ли |

The extra form is **бы́ло**, used with **онó** (neuter) nouns.

· · · · · · · · · · · · · · · · · · · · · · · · · ·

### EXERCISE 2

Look at the following passage and note the **past tenses**.

В прóшлом годý *last year* я **был** в Москвé. Пóгода там **былá** óчень хорóшая. Мы **жи́ли** в гости́нице «Росси́я» в цéнтре Москвы́. Я чáсто *often* **ходи́л** *walked* по гóроду. Нéсколько раз *several times* я **смотрéл** футбóльный матч. Однáжды *once* **игрáли** «Дина́мо» Москвá и «Дина́мо» Ки́ев. Пóсле этого мáтча мы **поýжинали** в гости́нице, а потóм **потанцевáли**. Мне нýжно **бы́ло** рабóтать кáждый день. Я **рабóтал** в библиотéке *library*, где **читáл** интерéсные кни́ги.

**1** How can you tell that the author is a man?

**2** How would you have to change the text, if the author were a woman?

· · · · · · · · · · · · · · · · · · · · · · · · · ·

You may notice that some of the past tenses above have **по-** at the beginning. This usually indicates that the action is complete. Other prefixes occur, but **по-** is the most common. More details will appear in Unit 16.

· · · · · · · · · · · · · · · · · · · · · · · · · ·

### EXERCISE 3

Here are some questions asking if you are going to be somewhere tomorrow. You reply that you were there yesterday. The first one is done for you.

**1** Онá зáвтра бýдет в Санкт-Петербýрге?

   Нет, онá __былá__ там вчерá.

**2** Вы зáвтра бýдете в Ки́еве?

   Нет, я _____ там вчерá.

**3** Они́ зáвтра бýдут в Москвé?

   Нет, они́ _____ там вчерá.

**4** Вéра зáвтра бýдет здесь?

   Нет, онá _____ там вчерá.

**5** Вáня бýдет на футбóле?

   Нет, он _____ там вчерá.

**6** Ни́на и Кóля бýдут в рестора́не?

   Нет, они́ _____ там вчерá.

· · · · · · · · · · · · · · · · · · · · · · · · · ·

## The verb *to live*

| жить *to live* | | | |
|---|---|---|---|
| **present tense** | | | |
| я | живý | мы | живём |
| ты | живёшь | вы | живёте |
| он, онá | живёт | они́ | живýт |
| **past tense** | | | |
| я, ты, он | | жил | |
| я, ты, онá | | жилá | |
| мы, вы, они́ | | жи́ли | |

## EXERCISE 4

Look at the diary below. It is also recorded on your cassette. It is written by a young woman student, **Ольга**, at Moscow University (**студéнтка в москóвском университéте**). Notice the endings of the verbs.

---

14ое мáя

Сегóдня я встáла в 7 часóв. Позáвтракала в буфéте. На зáвтрак бы́ли кóфе и яи́чница. Пóсле обéда читáла газéты в библиотéке. Вéчером смотрéла америкáнский фильм «Дóктор Живáго». Фильм стáрый, но óчень хорóший. Мне óчень понрáвился.

15ое мáя

Ýтром сидéла в кóмнате и читáла кни́гу по фи́зике. Потóм написáла письмó пáпе. Пообéдала в столóвой, éла шашлы́к. Пóсле обéда купи́ла грибы́ на ры́нке. Зáвтра бýдет экзáмен по фи́зике. Нýжно рабóтать!

16ое мáя

Сдалá экзáмен. Брат (Ви́тя) пи́шет, что бýдет рабóтать в бáнке. А я дýмала, что он бýдет учи́ться здесь, в Москвé.

---

### New vocabulary

| | |
|---|---|
| фи́зика | *physics* |
| встать | *to get up* |
| письмó | *letter* |
| столóвая | *canteen* |
| купи́ть | *to buy* |
| ры́нок | *market* |
| сдать | *to pass* |
| учи́ться | *to study* |

Answer the questions in English.
1 What did Olga have for breakfast on 14th May?
2 What did she do after lunch?
3 What did she do in the evening? Did she enjoy it?
4 What subject is she studying?
5 What did she buy in the market?
6 Where is her brother going to work?

## EXERCISE 5

Put in the correct form of an appropriate verb. If it happens **зáвтра** (*tomorrow*) you should use the future tense, if it happened **вчерá** (*yesterday*) you should use the past tense.
The first one is done for you.

1 Зáвтра мы ___будем обéдать___ в ресторáне.
2 Вчерá я _____ ромáн «Дóктор Живáго».
3 Зáвтра он _____ телеви́зор.
4 Сейчáс два часá. Сегóдня ýтром мы _____ в пáрке.
5 Вчерá вéчером Ни́на _____ на балалáйке.
6 Зáвтра вы _____ в футбóл.
7 Студéнтка вчерá _____ экзáмены.
8 Моя́ мáма всегдá _____ на кýхне.

# ● Looking at words

## Verbs ending in -ся

A number of Russian verbs have the syllable **-ся** added on at the end. It originally meant *myself, yourself*, etc., although often this meaning has disappeared. Here are a few examples:

| | |
|---|---|
| учи́ть | *to teach* |
| учи́ться | *to study* (literally *to teach yourself*) |
| роди́ть | *to give birth* |
| роди́ться | *to be born* |
| нра́виться | *to like* (literally *to please yourself*) |

The ending **-ся** changes to **-сь** after vowels.

# ● Reading

## Изве́стные ру́сские писа́тели 19-го ве́ка
## Some famous 19th-century Russian writers

**Никола́й Васи́льевич Го́голь** роди́лся в 1809 году́. Он у́мер в 1852 году́. Он писа́л мно́го повесте́й и расска́зов, как наприме́р «Шине́ль» (*The Overcoat*). Он то́же писа́л пье́су «Ревизо́р» (*The Government Inspector*). Он мно́го лет писа́л рома́н «Мёртвые ду́ши» (*Dead Souls*) о крепостны́х, но не ко́нчил его́.

**Алекса́ндр Серге́евич Пу́шкин** роди́лся в 1799 году́. Он у́мер в 1837 году́. В Росси́и он са́мый изве́стный поэ́т, как Шекспи́р в А́нглии. Он писа́л стихи́, как наприме́р «Я вас люби́л», расска́зы «По́вести Бе́лкина» и рома́н в стиха́х «Евге́ний Оне́гин». Чайко́вский писа́л о́перу по э́тому рома́ну.

**Ива́н Серге́евич Турге́нев** роди́лся в 1818 году́. Он у́мер в 1883 году́. Он писа́л рома́ны, как наприме́р «Отцы́ и де́ти». В его́ рома́нах мы чита́ем о «ли́шнем челове́ке». Он то́же писа́л расска́зы и по́вести о любви́ и о приро́де.

**Фёдор Миха́йлович Достое́вский** роди́лся в 1821 году́. Он у́мер в 1881 году́. Он писа́л мно́го рома́нов. Его́ са́мые изве́стные рома́ны «Преступле́ние и наказа́ние» (*Crime and Punishment*), «Идио́т» и «Бра́тья Карама́зовы». Он ча́сто писа́л о го́роде Санкт-Петербу́рге, где он жил.

**Лев Никола́евич Толсто́й** роди́лся в 1828 году́. Он у́мер в 1910 году́. Он роди́лся в «Я́сной поля́не», недалеко́ от го́рода Ту́ла. Там сейча́с откры́т музе́й. Все зна́ют его́ рома́ны «А́нна Каре́нина» и «Война́ и мир».

**Анто́н Па́влович Че́хов** роди́лся в 1860 году́. Он у́мер в 1904 году́. Он рабо́тал врачо́м. Пото́м писа́л юмористи́ческие расска́зы и расска́зы и пье́сы о жи́зни в Росси́и до октя́брьской револю́ции: Ча́йка, Три сестры́, Дя́дя Ва́ня (*Uncle Vanya*), Вишнёвый сад (*The Cherry Orchard*). Он жил в Я́лте в Крыму́ и писа́л о ней в расска́зе «Да́ма с соба́чкой» (*The Lady with the Little Dog*). Он у́мер в Герма́нии.

**New vocabulary**

| | |
|---|---|
| у́мер | (*from* умере́ть) *died* |
| са́мый | *most* |
| изве́стный | *famous* |
| поэ́т | *poet* |
| стихи́ | *poetry* |
| наприме́р | *for example* |
| расска́з | *story* |
| мно́го | *many* |
| по́весть | *(long) story* |
| лет | *years* |
| ко́нчить | *to finish* |
| его́ | *his, him* |
| приро́да | *nature* |
| любо́вь | *love* |
| брат | *brother* |
| все | *everyone* |
| врач | *doctor* |
| юмористи́ческий | *humorous* |
| жизнь | *life* |
| Крым | *Crimea* |
| ли́шний челове́к | *literally 'superfluous man', a recurring theme in 19th-century Russian literature: an idealist, who does not fit in with society* |

## EXERCISE 6

**1** Connect the two parts of the sentence to produce factually correct statements. The first one is done for you.

| | | | |
|---|---|---|---|
| **a** | Лев Толстóй | писáл | ромáн «Преступлéние и наказáние» |
| **b** | Алексáндр Пýшкин | писáл | ромáн «Отцы́ и дéти» |
| **c** | Ивáн Тургéнев | писáл | пьéсу «Три сестры́» |
| **d** | Николáй Гóголь | писáл | ромáн «Войнá и мир» |
| **e** | Фёдор Достоéвский | писáл | стихи́ «Я вас люби́л» |
| **f** | Антóн Чéхов | писáл | пьéсу «Ревизóр» |

**2** What were the first names of the fathers of the above authors and composer? Look them up in the first section.

**3** Using the information in the above texts, answer the following questions in Russian. The first one is done for you.

**a** Кто сáмый извéстный поэ́т в Росси́и?   <u>Пýшкин</u>

**b** Кто писáл «Мёртвые дýши»?   _____

**c** Кто писáл о Санкт-Петербýрге?   _____

**d** Кто писáл о ли́шнем человéке?   _____

**e** Кто роди́лся недалекó от Тýлы?   _____

**f** Какýю (*which*) óперу писáл Чайкóвский?   _____

**g** Какýю пьéсу писáл Гóголь?   _____

**h** Какóй ромáн писáл Тургéнев?   _____

**i** Каки́е ромáны писáл Достоéвский?   _____ _____ _____

**j** Каки́е пьéсы писáл Чéхов?   _____ _____ _____ _____

---

## A situation to remember

### What I did in Russia

Imagine that you are talking to your friend on the telephone discussing what you have been doing. You have been visiting Russia on a two-week excursion. You have been to the theatre several times, the cinema, and you liked the metro system but not the buses. You have been eating in the hotel, and the food has been very good.

## Writing Russian (II)

Be careful of the height of the letters. There are fewer letters which go above and below the line in Russian. This gives printed and written Russian a different profile from English, and it takes a while to adjust to this.

### Example

**д** is written *д Д*

**з** is written *з З*

**х** is written *х Х*

**г** is written *г Г*

Now you try writing the words.

водка _____
*водка*

зоопарк _____
*зоопарк*

Правда _____
*правда*

университет _____
*университет*

хоккей _____
*хоккей*

город _____
*город*

## WHAT YOU KNOW

### What you were doing

| | |
|---|---|
| я/ты/он/Ива́н | чита́л |
| я /ты/она́/Ни́на | чита́ла |
| они́/Ива́н и Ни́на | чита́ли |

### I was, you were ...

быть я был
оня́ была́

там вчера́

э́то бы́ло
мы/вы/они́ бы́ли

### to live

| жить *to live* | | | |
|---|---|---|---|
| **present tense** | | **past tense** | |
| я живу́ | мы живём | я, ты, он | жил |
| ты живёшь | вы живёте | я, ты, она́ | жила́ |
| он, она́ живёт | они́ живу́т | мы, вы, они́ | жи́ли |

## KEY VOCABULARY

| | |
|---|---|
| век | century |
| вели́кий | great |
| война́ | war |
| мирова́я война́ | world war |
| оте́чественная война | 'patriotic' war (on Russian territory) |
| все | everyone |
| вчера́ | yesterday |
| год | year |
| в про́шлом году́ | last year |
| исто́рия | history |
| жить | to live |
| изве́стный | famous |
| коне́ц | the end |
| купи́ть | to buy |
| нача́ло | the beginning |
| не́сколько раз | several times |
| получи́ть | to get, receive |
| расска́з | story |
| роди́ться | to be born |
| рома́н | a novel |
| са́мый | most |
| стихи́ | poetry |
| умере́ть (*past* у́мер, умерла́ ...) | to die |
| ча́сто | often |

Travelling by train

Russian towns

Going on foot or by
vehicle

# Travelling by train

## ● Life in Russia

### Travelling by train

Russia has a highly developed train network, both local and long
distance. Each large town has a number of mainline (terminal)
stations, which are usually named after a major town or region,
served by trains from the station.

**EXERCISE 1**

Can you work out where you would travel to from the following
stations?

**a**  In Moscow
Ки́евский вокза́л
Смоле́нский вокза́л
Ку́рский вокза́л
Яросла́вский вокза́л

**b**  In St Petersburg
Моско́вский вокза́л
Финля́ндский вокза́л
Балти́йский вокза́л
Варша́вский вокза́л

Russian has two words for a station. A mainline station is **вокза́л**.
The word was borrowed from the English 'Vauxhall'. The other
word, **ста́нция**, is used for an underground station or for a
suburban railway station. The Russian for railway is **желе́зная
доро́га**, literally 'iron road'.

When you arrive at a station, look for the following signs:

ПРИ́ГОРОДНЫЕ ПОЕЗДА́  *local trains*

ПОЕЗДА́ ДА́ЛЬНЕГО СЛЕ́ДОВАНИЯ  *long distance trains*

You will also need to recognise the following words and phrases:

ОТПРАВЛЕ́НИЕ                      *departure*
По́езд отправля́ется в 23.00. *The train departs at 11 p.m.*
ПРИБЫ́ТИЕ                         *arrival*
По́езд прибыва́ет в 8.00.      *The train arrives at 8.00 a.m.*

**105**

There are separate local and long distance booking offices (**ка́сса**). If you are going long distance, there are often separate booking offices for different destinations and sometimes separate ones if you want to travel that day. There is usually an enquiry office (**спра́вочное бюро́**), where, amongst other things, you can find out the place to queue for your ticket.

Russian trains are usually identified by numbers, but a few special trains also have names. If you are travelling between Moscow and St Petersburg, you may travel on the Red Arrow (**Кра́сная стрела́**), the famous sleeper, which is painted red after its name, instead of the usual green.

Russian train carriages are divided into soft/hard carriages (**мя́гкий/жёсткий ваго́н**), the equivalent of the British first and second class. Distances in Russia are very great and Russian trains travel very slowly. A fast train (**ско́рый по́езд**) goes faster than a **пассажи́рский по́езд** (passenger train).

Many train journeys are made overnight. If you wish to travel to what Russians call the 'Far East' (**Да́льний восто́к**), for example to **Владивосто́к**, you could be on the train for up to a week.

It is important to choose the appropriate type of sleeper. Sleeping cars can be either the basic open carriage in which you reserve a seat (**плацка́ртный**), or you can travel on one with separate compartments – **купе́йный**, from the word **купе́**, *a compartment*. At the luxury end, there are two-berth compartments (the normal ones have four).

Each carriage on a long distance train has an attendant (**проводни́к**, or **проводни́ца** if the attendant is a woman). It is their job to check your tickets, make any announcements and in a sleeping car to provide you with bed-linen (**бельё**). Be warned, the cost of the bed-linen is not included in your ticket: you will have to pay the **проводни́к** or **проводни́ца** separately. He or she may also provide you with tea or other non-alcoholic drinks for a small fee. If nothing else, you should be able to get hot water.

Most Russians come prepared for a long journey. They bring food supplies with them, as a restaurant car (**ваго́н-ресторáн**) is not always available. Russians also change out of their normal clothes into loose clothing, often into a track-suit, when travelling overnight by train.

## 🔊 EXERCISE 2

Listen to this dialogue, which takes place at a mainline railway station, and answer the questions that follow.

| | |
|---|---|
| Турист: | Скажи́те, пожа́луйста, где здесь ка́сса? |
| Де́вушка: | Куда́ вы е́дете? |
| Турист: | В Санкт-Петербу́рг. |
| Де́вушка: | А когда́? |
| Турист: | Сего́дня. |
| Де́вушка: | Ва́ша ка́сса бу́дет в большо́м за́ле, нале́во. |
| Турист: | Спаси́бо. |

### New vocabulary

Куда́ вы е́дете? *Where are you going to?*
зал             *hall*

1  What is the tourist looking for?
2  Where is she going to?
3  Where can she buy a ticket?

## 🔊 EXERCISE 3

Now listen to her booking her ticket and answer the questions in English. You might find it useful to look at the timetable on page 108.

| | |
|---|---|
| Турист: | Да́йте, пожа́луйста, оди́н биле́т в Санкт-Петербу́рг на сего́дня. |
| Де́вушка: | Вам спа́льный ваго́н? |
| Турист: | Спа́льный. |
| Де́вушка: | Вы хоти́те купе́йный? |
| Турист: | Да, купе́йный. |
| Де́вушка: | У нас есть свобо́дные места́ на по́езде № 6 в 23 часа́ 10 мину́т. Есть ещё оди́н по́езд, № 2, отправле́ние в 23 часа́ 55 мину́т. Это ско́рый по́езд «Кра́сная стрела́». |
| Турист: | Так ... *(ду́мает)* Мне ну́жно быть в Санкт-Петербу́рге у́тром. Когда́ они́ прибыва́ют в Санкт-Петербу́рг? |
| Де́вушка: | По́езд № 6 прибыва́ет в 7 часо́в 35 мину́т, № 2 — в 8 часо́в 25 мину́т. |

| | |
|---|---|
| Турист: | Да́йте биле́т на «Кра́сную стрелу́». С како́й платфо́рмы бу́дет по́езд? |
| Де́вушка: | С пе́рвой. |
| Турист: | Спаси́бо. |
| Де́вушка: | Пожа́луйста. |

### New vocabulary

| | |
|---|---|
| на | *for* |
| ещё оди́н | *another* |
| так | *so* |
| ду́мать | *think* |
| с | *from* |

1  When does she want to travel?
2  What sort of carriage does she book?
3  What choice of trains does she have?
4  Which one does she select?
5  Which platform does it leave from?

The railway line from Moscow to St Petersburg is one of the oldest in Russia: it was built in 1851. It was originally called **Никола́евская желе́зная доро́га**, after **царь Никола́й I**. It is now called **Октя́брьская желе́зная доро́га**.

## EXERCISE 4

Look at the timetable (**расписа́ние**) of trains from Moscow to St Petersburg.
Which train or trains would you choose to meet the conditions below?
Place the number of the train in the box. The first one is done for you.

| Расписание: | | | | | | | | | | | | | |
|---|---|---|---|---|---|---|---|---|---|---|---|---|---|
| | | | Москва — Санкт-Петербург | | | | | | | | | | |
| | | | Октябрьская железная дорога | | | | | | | | | | |
| км | | 20 | 10 | 30 | 158 | 48 | 24 | 160 | 14 | 28 | 26 | 6 | 2 | 4 |
| | | | | | | В-Р | Ю | В-Р | А | | | И | КС | |
| 0 | Москва Ленинградский | 0105 | 0113 | 0156 | 1221 | 1226 | 1328 | 1718 | 2035 | 2200 | 2300 | 2310 | 2355 | 2359 |
| 167 | Тверь | | | | | 1421 | 1537 | 1850 | 2245 | 2355 | 0103 | | | 0202 |
| 331 | Бологое | 0505 | 1515 | 0611 | | 1620 | 1745 | 2013 | 0051 | 0148 | 0302 | 0310 | 0344 | 0352 |
| 650 | Санкт-Петербург Московский | 0916 | 0920 | 1030 | 1720 | 2015 | 2236 | 2319 | 0515 | 0548 | 0710 | 0735 | 0825 | 0829 |

В-Р вагон-ресторан
Ю Юность   А Аврора   И Интурист   КС Красная стрела

**1**  Вы хоти́те прие́хать (*arrive*) в Санкт-Петербу́рг ве́чером.   `48`

**2**  Вы хоти́те обе́дать на по́езде.

**3**  Вы хоти́те у́жинать на по́езде.

**4**  Вы хоти́те прие́хать в Тверь ве́чером.

**5**  Вы хоти́те прие́хать о́чень ра́но (*early*) у́тром в Санкт-Петербу́рг.

**6**  По́езд отправля́ется в 10 часо́в ве́чера.

**7**  По́езд прибыва́ет в Болого́е в три часа́ де́сять мину́т но́чи.

**8**  Вы хоти́те е́хать на «Кра́сной стреле́».

## EXERCISE 5

Look at the following pictures taken in **Моско́вский вокза́л** in St Petersburg and answer the questions that follow.

**Photos 1 and 2:**

**a**  Where are these trains going?
**b**  Are they express trains?
**c**  What are their numbers?

**Photo 3**  Where is this train going?

**Photos 4 and 5:**
Name the places where you would be going if you followed these signs.

Local trains (**электри́чки**) connect the large towns with the surrounding villages. These trains are very basic, often with wooden seats. They go extremely slowly and stop very frequently. Russians use them to go to their **да́ча**. The trains on Friday afternoon out of town and the return ones on Sunday afternoon or evening are often very crowded with **да́чники**.

The price of a ticket on a local train depends on the zone (**зо́на**) you are travelling to. You do not need to book in advance. Give yourself time to queue at the **ка́сса** and name the station you want to go to.

When you are in St Petersburg, you may want to visit some of the summer palaces situated in the small towns surrounding the city. To get there you will usually have to take a local train and then a bus. You may be able to go on foot (**пешко́м**) from the station.

This would be a good time to revise your numbers in Unit 6.

## ⊟ EXERCISE 6

On the tape you will hear four conversations which take place between visitors who are staying with a family, and their host (**хозя́ин**) or hostess (**хозя́йка**). Listen to each conversation and then:

**a** underline where the visitor wants to go;
**b** underline the station in St Petersburg he/she should depart from (**вокза́л**);
**c** underline the local station (**ста́нция**) nearest to the palace;
**d** write in how long it will take him/her;
**e** write in *either* the number of the bus which will take him/her from the station to the palace, *or* write in 'on foot'.

| | Куда́? | вокза́л | ста́нция | ско́лько мину́т | авто́бус № |
|---|---|---|---|---|---|
| 1 | Ломоно́сов Па́вловск Петродворе́ц Ца́рское Село́ | Балти́йский Ви́тебский | Де́тское село́ Но́вый Петерго́ф Ораниенба́ум Па́вловск | | |
| 2 | Ломоно́сов Па́вловск Петродворе́ц Ца́рское Село́ | Балти́йский Ви́тебский | Де́тское село́ Но́вый Петерго́ф Ораниенба́ум Па́вловск | | |
| 3 | Ломоно́сов Па́вловск Петродворе́ц Ца́рское Село́ | Балти́йский Ви́тебский | Де́тское село́ Но́вый Петерго́ф Ораниенба́ум Па́вловск | | |
| 4 | Ломоно́сов Па́вловск Петродворе́ц Ца́рское Село́ | Балти́йский Ви́тебский | Де́тское село́ Но́вый Пстерго́ф Ораниенба́ум Па́вловск | | |

You can also reach **Петродворец** on a hydrofoil (**на Метео́ре**) or by boat (**на теплохо́де**). If you like boat trips, you can go on boat trips along the rivers and canals of St Petersburg. There are also tourist boats that ply up and down the Moskva River (**Москва́-река́**) in Moscow – you get one of the best views of the Kremlin from one of these boats. You could also try a cruise down the Volga.

## ● Language information

### Moving around

Russian distinguishes between going on foot and going in a vehicle.

| **идти́** _to go, come_ (on foot) | | | |
|---|---|---|---|
| **present tense** | | | |
| я | иду́ | мы | идём |
| ты | идёшь | вы | идёте |
| он, она́ | идёт | они́ | иду́т |
| **past tense** _was going (on foot)_ | | | |
| он (я, ты) | шёл | | |
| она́ (я, ты) | шла | | |
| мы, вы, они́ | шли | | |

| **е́хать** _to go, come_ (by vehicle) | | | |
|---|---|---|---|
| **present tense** | | | |
| я | е́ду | мы | е́дем |
| ты | е́дешь | вы | е́дете |
| он, она́ | е́дет | они́ | е́дут |
| **past tense** _was going (in a vehicle)_ | | | |
| он (я, ты) | е́хал | | |
| она́ (я, ты) | е́хала | | |
| мы, вы, они́ | е́хали | | |

## Where are you living, where are you going?

– Где вы живёте?
_Where do you live?_
– Живу́ в це́нтре, на Тверско́й у́лице.
_I live in the centre, on Tverskaya Street._
– Куда́ вы идёте?
_Where are you going?_
– Иду́ в центр, на рабо́ту.
_I am going to the centre, to work._

Russian has two words for _where_. **Где** means _in_ what place; **куда́** means _to_ what place.

### Going to a place

Russian has two words meaning _to_: **в** and **на** followed by the accusative case.

**в** is used with most place words.
**на** is used with words denoting an activity (e.g. **на рабо́ту**).
**на** is used with a few place words:

Я иду́   в це́нтр.
          на вокза́л.
          на по́чту.
          на Тверску́ю у́лицу.
          на Кра́сную пло́щадь.

**на** is sometimes also used to translate _for_:
биле́т на по́езд _a ticket for the train_

### Coming from a place

There are two words to translate _from_. The opposite of **в** is **из** and of **на** is **с**. Both prepositions meaning _from_ are followed by the genitive case:

Я иду́   из це́нтра.
          с вокза́ла.
          с по́чты.

Be careful – **с** can also mean _with_. In this meaning it is followed by the instrumental case (see Unit 9).

Look at how Russian conveys the words *in, on, at, to, from*:

| *in, on, at*<br>в, на + prepositional case | *to*<br>в, на + accusative case | *from*<br>из, с + genitive case |
| --- | --- | --- |
| Я живу́ **в** кварти́р**е** № 5. | Я иду́ **в** кварти́р**у** № 5. | Я иду́ **из** кварти́р**ы** № 5. |
| Я сейча́с **на** Кра́сной пло́щад**и**. | Я иду́ **на** Кра́сн**ую** пло́щад**ь**. | Я иду́ **с** Кра́сной пло́щад**и**. |

If you are measuring distance from one place to another, use the two prepositions **от** and **до**. They are both also followed by the genitive case:

От Москвы́ до Санкт-Петербу́рга 650 киломе́тров.

Notice also the phrase **(не)далеко́ от** *(not) far from*.

## ● Looking at words

### *North, south, east, west*

се́вер

за́пад

восто́к

юг

The four points of the compass – **се́вер** (*north*), **юг** (*south*), **за́пад** (*west*), **восто́к** (*east*) – are always used with **на** to mean *in* and *to*, and **с** to mean *from*.

Мой брат живёт **на** се́вер**е**.
*My brother lives in the north.*
Мы сейча́с е́дем **с** се́вер**а на** юг.
*We are now going from north to south.*

...........................................

**EXERCISE 7**
Complete the following sentences, adding direction phrases. The word **нахо́дится** means *is situated*. The first one is done for you.

1 Санкт-Петербу́рг нахо́дится на  <u>се́вере</u> Росси́и.

2 Владивосто́к нахо́дится на _____ Росси́и.

3 Му́рманск нахо́дится на _____ Росси́и.

4 Ма́нчестер нахо́дится на _____ А́нглии.

5 Сан-Франци́ско нахо́дится на _____ Аме́рики.

6 Аберди́н нахо́дится на _____ Шотла́ндии.
...........................................

## Dividing words up

It is very important to look at the parts of a Russian word. It will help you to work out what words mean that you have never seen before. Here are some examples which start with **при-**:

прийти́      *to arrive (on foot)*
прие́хать     *to arrive (by vehicle)*
прибыва́ть    *to arrive (official)*
прихо́д      *arrival (on foot)*
прие́зд      *arrival (by vehicle)*
прибы́тие     *arrival (official)*

**у-** and **от-** have the opposite meaning: that of departure.

### EXERCISE 8

Can you work out what the following words mean?

| | | | |
|---|---|---|---|
| **1** | уйти́ | **4** | отъе́зд |
| **2** | уе́хать | **5** | ухо́д |
| **3** | отбыва́ть | **6** | отбы́тие |

**в-** means *into*, **вы-** means *out of*.

### EXERCISE 9

Complete the table. The first one is done for you.

| | | Meaning | из | в |
|---|---|---|---|---|
| **1** | вы́йти | *to go out* (on foot) | ✓ | |
| **2** | вы́ехать | | | |
| **3** | вход | | | |
| **4** | вы́ход | | | |
| **5** | въезд | | | |
| **6** | вы́езд | | | |

## идти́

Apart from meaning *to go on foot*, **идти́** has the following meanings:

**1** *to be on* (of film, play, etc.)
Сего́дня идёт интере́сный фильм.
*There is an interesting film on today.*

**2** *to rain, snow*
Идёт дождь.   *It is raining.*
Идёт снег.    *It is snowing.*

## ● Reading

### Find out about Russia

Here are some notes in Russian about three cities of European Russia. Answer the questions which follow each passage in English.

### Москва́

Москва́ – столи́ца Росси́и с 1918-го го́да. Здесь живёт о́коло десяти́ миллио́нов челове́к. В це́нтре го́рода нахо́дятся Кремль, Кра́сная пло́щадь и гла́вная у́лица – Тверска́я у́лица. Недалеко́ от це́нтра нахо́дится Но́вый Арба́т. На э́той у́лице мно́го магази́нов: «Дом кни́ги», гла́вный кни́жный магази́н го́рода и «Мело́дия», где продаю́т пласти́нки, кассе́ты и компа́кт-ди́ски. Москва́ стои́т на Москва́-реке́.

### New vocabulary

| | |
|---|---|
| о́коло | *about* |
| кни́жный магази́н | *bookshop* |
| пласти́нка | *record* |
| стоя́ть | *to stand* |
| река́ | *river* |
| продаю́т | *they sell* |

**1** How many people live in Moscow?
**2** What can you buy on New Arbat Street?

## Санкт-Петербу́рг

В Санкт-Петербу́рге мно́го краси́вых зда́ний, музе́ев, собо́ров. У́лицы в Санкт-Петербу́рге прямы́е и широ́кие. Гла́вная у́лица го́рода – Не́вский проспе́кт. При коммуни́зме Санкт-Петербу́рг называ́лся Ленингра́дом. Здесь нахо́дится Эрмита́ж, о́чень большо́й музе́й и карти́нная галере́я, где вися́т карти́ны за́падных худо́жников. В Санкт-Петербу́рге мно́го рек и кана́лов. Гла́вная река́ – Нева́. Санкт-Петербу́рг – «Се́верная Вене́ция» Росси́и.

### New vocabulary

| | |
|---|---|
| зда́ние | *building* |
| прямо́й | *straight* |
| широ́кий | *wide* |
| при | *in the time of* |
| называ́ться | *to be called* |
| карти́нная галере́я | *art gallery* |
| карти́на | *picture* |
| висе́ть | *to hang* |
| худо́жник | *painter* |

**1** What sort of streets does St Petersburg have?

**2** What is said about the Hermitage?

**3** What is the name of the main street? Can you work out where it gets its name from?

## Яросла́вль

К се́веро-восто́ку от Москвы́ на реке́ Во́лга стои́т ста́рый ру́сский го́род Яросла́вль. По́езд идёт пять часо́в от Москвы́ до Яросла́вля. Он оди́н из городо́в «Золото́го Кольца́» и здесь о́чень мно́го ста́рых зда́ний, наприме́р Спа́сский монасты́рь, постро́енный в шестна́дцатом ве́ке. Говоря́т, что Яросла́в Му́дрый основа́л го́род в 1010 г. Э́тот го́род ста́рше, чем Москва́. Сейча́с он не о́чень большо́й: там живу́т о́коло 600 ты́сяч челове́к.

### New vocabulary

| | |
|---|---|
| к | *to* |
| постро́енный | *built* |
| говоря́т, что | *they say that* |
| му́дрый | *wise* |
| основа́ть | *to found* |
| ста́рше чем | *older than* |

**1** How do you get to Yaroslavl from Moscow? How long does it take?

**2** When was
   a the Spasskiy monastery built?
   b the town of Yaroslavl founded?

## A situation to remember

### Your home town

You are being interviewed for a Russian newspaper. The reporter (**корреспонде́нт**) wants to know about the town where you live. He or she asks you a number of questions. Answer them as fully as you can.

Скажи́те, пожа́луйста, в како́м го́роде вы живёте?

Где нахо́дится го́род?

Расскажи́те мне немно́жко (*a little*) о ва́шем го́роде. Каки́е там зда́ния?

Как мо́жно е́хать отсю́да (*from here*) в ваш го́род?

Ско́лько часо́в на́до е́хать?

Спаси́бо.

Find a partner. You are now a visitor from Britain to Moscow, St Petersburg or Yaroslavl. You meet a friendly person at a party. Ask him or her some questions about the town.

## Writing Russian (III)

Three letters start with a hook:

*л Л м М я Я*

Make sure you do not miss out the hook when you join letters up. Look at the height of the letters in the examples.

**Examples** *дом красная лимонад*

**ы** is written *ы*

**ю** is written *ю Ю*

Now you try writing the words.

литр *литр*

крокоди́л *крокодил*

киломе́тр *километр*

А́нглия *Англия*

вы́ход *выход*

меню́ *меню*

## WHAT YOU KNOW

### Going places
Куда́ вы идёте?
Я иду́ на рабо́ту.

Куда́ вы е́дете?
Я е́ду в Москву́.

### Coming from places
Я иду́ с рабо́ты.
Я е́ду из Москвы́.

### Measuring distance
От Москвы́ до Санкт-Петербу́рга 650 киломе́тров.

### North, south, east, west
се́вер, юг, восто́к, за́пад
Я живу́ на се́вере.
Я е́ду с се́вера на юг.

## KEY VOCABULARY

| | |
|---|---|
| ваго́н | carriage |
| вокза́л | station (mainline) |
| восто́к | east |
| да́ча | dacha |
| е́хать | to go (by vehicle) |
| за́пад | west |
| идти́ | to go (on foot) |
| из + G | from |
| куда́ | where to |
| от ... до + G | from ... to |
| отправле́ние | departure |
| отправля́ться | to depart |
| пешко́м | on foot |
| по́езд | train |
| прибыва́ть | to arrive |
| прибы́тие | arrival |
| проводни́к/проводни́ца | attendant |
| ра́но | early |
| с +G | from |
| се́вер | north |
| ста́нция | station (suburban, underground) |
| электри́чка | train (local) |
| юг | south |

# Going to Russia

## ● Life in Russia

### Getting a visa

To travel to Russia you will need a visa (**ви́за**). If you are going
on a package tour organised by a holiday company, your visa will
be arranged for you. All you will have to do is fill in a visa
application form (**ви́зовая анке́та**). If you are going in any other
way, you will need an invitation (**приглаше́ние**). The company
or educational institution arranging your visit will provide it.

Here is a sample invitation from a Russian university:

---

Московский государственный университет имени
Ломоносова готов принять на курсы русского языка
с 1 сентября 1995 года на три недели следующих
студентов из университета Лондона:

Стивен Джонс          11.01.73 года рождения
паспорт № 007445566
Алан Томас            02.05.74 года рождения
паспорт № 005689023


Проректор по
международным                    Иванов, И.П.
    связям

---

### EXERCISE 1

Read the invitation through and answer the questions which
follow in English. Don't expect to understand every word.

1   Which Russian university has issued the invitation?
2   When does the course start?
3   How long does it last?
4   What are the names of the participants?
5   Where are they studying in Britain?
6   How old were they at the start of the course?

A private citizen can also obtain an invitation for you. Allow plenty of time, as Russian bureaucracy moves slowly. Your host in Russia has to fill in forms and hand them to an organisation called **ОВИР** (**Отде́л виз и регистра́ция иностра́нных гра́ждан,** *Visa Department and Registration of Foreign Citizens*). It will consider the application and eventually issue an official document (**извеще́ние**). You must send this to the consulate with your completed visa form. Here is a sample **извеще́ние**:

ИЗВЕЩЕНИЕ № 2328

ВЕЛИКОБРИТАНИЯ
(гражданство)

БИВОН
(фамилия)

ДЖУЛИЯ
(имя, отчество)

разрешен въезд из Великобритании в СССР
(страна)

г.Москва Хоромный туп. 2/6-20
(наименование города, района)

на 25 в период с „27" 08 1992г.
(суток)

по „ " 19 г.

Начальник ОВИР

(подпись)

Although the Soviet Union no longer exists, some official forms in Russia still have **СССР** on them!

Read through the **извеще́ние** and answer the following questions in English:
1 What is the full name of the person travelling to Russia?
2 In which town is she going to stay?
3 How long can she stay?
4 What is the earliest date that she can arrive?

## Russian airports

You are most likely to travel to Russia by plane (**на самолёте**). You will probably arrive and depart either through Moscow's international airport at **Шереме́тьево** or through St Petersburg's **Пу́лково** airport.

There are two checks at a Russian international airport. First your visa and passport (**па́спорт**) are checked by the border guard (**погра́ни́чник**): he will usually spend a long time looking at you and your visa before letting you through. After that, you must collect your luggage (**бага́ж**). No doubt what you want first is a trolley (**теле́жка**). Here is a sample conversation:

**EXERCISE 3**
Listen to the dialogue on the tape and answer the following questions.

| Тури́ст: | Скажи́те, пожа́луйста, где теле́жки? |
|---|---|
| Пассажи́р: | Вон там они́, нале́во, в углу́. |
| Тури́ст: | Там, где лю́ди стоя́т в о́череди? |
| Пассажи́р: | Да, да. Пойдём вме́сте. *(стоя́т в о́череди)* |
| Тури́ст: | Ой, ой, ой, как не люблю́ стоя́ть в о́череди. |
| Пассажи́р: | Ничего́, ничего́. Бага́ж сейча́с |

будет. Через двáдцать минýт. Вы знáете, что нýжно платúть за телéжку?

Турúст: Нет! Как платúть? Мы не плáтим. У меня тóлько дóллары и фýнты.

Пассажúр: Ничегó. Дáйте им дóллары.

Турúст: А скóлько стóит телéжка?

Пассажúр: Не знáю. Год назáд телéжка стóила два дóллара, а сейчáс кто знáет?

## New vocabulary

| | |
|---|---|
| вон там | *over there* |
| в углý | *in the corner* |
| лю́ди | *people* |
| óчередь | *queue* |
| вмéсте | *together* |
| платúть (за) | *to pay (for)* |
| чéрез | *in (time)* |
| Скóлько стóит ...? | *How much does it cost?* |
| назáд | *ago* |

1 Where does the tourist find the trolleys?
2 Why is the tourist upset?
3 How long do they have to wait to get their luggage?
4 Has the tourist got any roubles?
5 How does the tourist decide to pay?
6 How much did the trolleys cost last year?

When you get your luggage, you need to go through customs (**тамóжня**). You will see a red channel (**крáсный канáл**) and a green channel (**зелёный канáл**). If you wish to register your foreign currency (**валю́та**), you need to go through the red channel. You should have filled in a customs declaration (**тамóженная декларáция**) which you present to the customs officer (**тамóженник**).

## Changing money

One of the first things you will need to do when you arrive is to change some foreign currency into roubles (**рублú**). Look for one of the following signs:

ОБМÉН ВАЛЮ́ТЫ     *change of currency*
ОБМÉННЫЙ ПУНКТ     *exchange point*

You can do it at the airport, or you will find a bewildering number of banks in town. It is worth checking the rate and whether any commission (**комúссия**) is charged. The rates are usually advertised but be careful: there are often two rates – one for the purchase (**покýпка**) and the other for the sale (**продáжа**) of foreign currency. Questions to ask are:

Где мóжно обменя́ть дéньги?
*Where can I change my money?*
Скóлько рублéй за дóллар?
*How many roubles for a dollar?*

Some places will accept a credit card (**кредúтная кáрточка**). Some banks may even give you cash with your card. It is also very useful to take dollars or dollar travellers cheques at the present time rather than sterling.

### EXERCISE 4

Look at the two pictures. If you can change currency here, tick the box.

1

What else can you buy here?

2
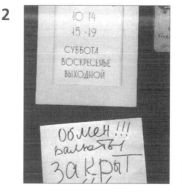

When is the shop open?

## Returning through the airport

When you leave Russia you have to fill in a second **таможенная деклара́ция** and hand both to the customs officer. Sometimes they will want to check what you are taking out of the country.

. . . . . . . . . . . . . . . . . . . . . . . . . . . . . . . . . .

### 🔲 EXERCISE 5

Listen to the tape. You will hear a conversation between a tourist and a customs officer. He is interested in looking at the tourist's suitcase (**чемода́н**) and bag (**су́мка**).

| | |
|---|---|
| Тамо́женник: | *(чита́ет деклара́цию)* Так, у вас оди́н чемода́н и одна́ су́мка. Где они́? Э́то ваш чемода́н? |
| Тури́ст: | Нет, мой чемода́н большо́й и ста́рый. А вот э́тот чемода́н ма́ленький и но́вый. Но где мой чемода́н? А вот он. |
| Тамо́женник: | Откро́йте, пожа́луйста. *(Тури́ст открыва́ет чемода́н).* А что э́то? |
| Тури́ст: | Э́то пода́рки – сувени́ры для ма́мы и па́пы. |
| Тамо́женник: | А что вы купи́ли? |
| Тури́ст: | Купи́л матрёшку, кни́гу о Санкт-Петербу́рге … |
| Тамо́женник: | Покажи́те мне вот э́то. Э́то не пистоле́т? |
| Тури́ст: | Что вы! Э́то игру́шка: у меня́ ма́ленький сын. |
| Тамо́женник: | Хорошо́. А у вас есть икра́? |
| Тури́ст: | Как же! До́рого сто́ит и не люблю́ икру́. |
| Тамо́женник: | А где ва́ша су́мка? |
| Тури́ст: | У меня́ кра́сная су́мка. Вот она́. |
| Тамо́женник: | А там есть пода́рки? |
| Тури́ст: | Нет. Там то́лько оде́жда. На́до откры́ть су́мку? |
| Тамо́женник: | Нет, нет. Проходи́те, пожа́луйста. |

### New vocabulary

| | |
|---|---|
| ма́ленький | *small* |
| откры́ть (откро́йте) | *open* |
| пода́рок | *gift* |
| сувени́р | *souvenir* |
| для | *for* |
| матрёшка | *nested dolls* |
| игру́шка | *toy* |
| сын | *son* |
| оде́жда | *clothes* |
| проходи́те | *to go through* |

Tick the appropriate box to indicate if the sentences are true or false. The first one is done for you.

**1** She has an old suitcase.

true ✓    false ☐

**2** She has bought her mother a present.

true ☐    false ☐

**3** She has bought a toy for her son.

true ☐    false ☐

**4** She is arrested.    true ☐    false ☐

**5** She has a black bag.

true ☐    false ☐

**6** She doesn't have any presents in her bag.

true ☐    false ☐

**7** She opens her bag.

true ☐    false ☐

# ● Language information

## Describing things

Have a look again at the adjective endings explained in Unit 7, and then do Exercise 6.

### EXERCISE 6

Here are three sets of adjectives and nouns. Link the adjectives up to the nouns. You will need to look carefully at the ending. The first one is done for you.

1  ма́ленькая        теле́жки
   моско́вский        су́мка
   но́вые            аэропо́рт

2  де́тская          кана́л
   кра́сный          приглаше́ние
   университе́тское   игру́шка

3  хоро́шие          икра́
   чёрная           тамо́женник
   прия́тный          но́вости

## *My, your, our, his, her, its, their*

The words for *my*, *your* and *our* change their endings, somewhat like adjectives, depending on the gender of the noun:

|            | my   | your (ты) | our   | your (вы) |              |
|------------|------|-----------|-------|-----------|--------------|
| Masculine  | мой  | твой      | наш   | ваш       | дом          |
| Feminine   | моя́  | твоя́      | на́ша  | ва́ша      | кварти́ра     |
| Neuter     | моё  | твоё      | на́ше  | ва́ше      | письмо́ (letter) |
| Plural     | мои́  | твои́      | на́ши  | ва́ши      | кни́ги        |

**Его́** (*his*), **её** (*her*) and **их** (*their*) never change: **его́ дом, его́ кварти́ра, его́ письмо́, его́ кни́ги**.

## Закры́т, откры́т

**Закры́т** (*closed*) and **откры́т** (*open*) have the following forms:

| Masculine | рестора́н | закры́т  | откры́т  |
|-----------|-----------|----------|----------|
| Feminine  | апте́ка    | закры́та  | откры́та  |
| Neuter    | метро́     | закры́то  | откры́то  |
| Plural    | магази́ны  | закры́ты  | откры́ты  |

## *Would like to*

Он хоте́л бы (Она́ хоте́ла бы) обменя́ть де́сять до́лларов.
*He (She) would like to change ten dollars.*
The plural form is **хоте́ли бы**. If you are using any of these forms, you must always use the past tense of the verb.
This is the *conditional* form of the verb, which you will see used in 'if' sentences.

119

## EXERCISE 7

Devise answers to the following questions, as in the example.

### *Example*

Question: Ни́на бу́дет в теа́тре сего́дня ве́чером?
Answer:

| | |
|---|---|
| ~~Он хоте́л бы~~ | закры́т. |
| Она́ хоте́ла бы     пойти́, но теа́тр сего́дня | ~~закры́та~~. |
| ~~Они́ хоте́ли бы~~ | ~~закры́то~~. |

**1** Бори́с бу́дет в рестора́не сего́дня ве́чером?

| | |
|---|---|
| Он хоте́л бы | закры́т. |
| Она́ хоте́ла бы     пойти́, но рестора́н сего́дня | закры́та. |
| Они́ хоте́ли бы | закры́то. |

**2** А́нна и Ка́тя бу́дут в библиоте́ке сего́дня ве́чером?

| | |
|---|---|
| Он хоте́л бы | закры́т. |
| Она́ хоте́ла бы     пойти́, но библиоте́ка сего́дня | закры́та. |
| Они́ хоте́ли бы | закры́то. |

**3** Серге́й бу́дет в кино́ сего́дня ве́чером?

| | |
|---|---|
| Он хоте́л бы | закры́т. |
| Она́ хоте́ла бы     пойти́, но кино́ сего́дня | закры́та. |
| Они́ хоте́ли бы | закры́то. |

**4** Моя́ сестра́ бу́дет на стадио́не сего́дня ве́чером?

| | |
|---|---|
| Он хоте́л бы | закры́т. |
| Она́ хоте́ла бы     пойти́, но стадио́н сего́дня | закры́та. |
| Они́ хоте́ли бы | закры́то. |

**5** Воло́дя бу́дет в кафе́ сего́дня ве́чером?

| | |
|---|---|
| Он хоте́л бы | закры́т. |
| Она́ хоте́ла бы     пойти́, но кафе́ сего́дня | закры́та. |
| Они́ хоте́ли бы | закры́то. |

## ● Reading

### Travelling around

Read the following excerpt from a Russian girl's essay for her school magazine.

В 1992 году́ мы жи́ли в Санкт-Петербу́рге. Па́па там рабо́тал в университе́те. Санкт-Петербу́рг – о́чень краси́вый го́род. Я о́чень люби́ла гуля́ть по Не́вскому проспе́кту, заходи́ть *call in* в ма́ленькое кафе́ и пить сок и́ли Пе́пси.

В 1993 году́ па́па чита́л ле́кции в Ло́ндонском университе́те и мы с ма́мой пое́хали в А́нглию. Там бы́ло о́чень интере́сно. Мы е́хали туда́ на самолёте. Гости́ница в Ло́ндоне была́ о́чень больша́я и комфорта́бельная. Мы бы́ли на Трафальга́рской пло́щади и на Да́унинг-Стрите, где нахо́дится резиде́нция премье́р-мини́стра.

Я хоте́ла бы пое́хать в Вашингто́н и в Нью-Йорк и посети́ть *visit* Бе́лый дом и Эмпа́йр стейт би́лдинг. Я хоте́ла бы подня́ться *go up* на 102-о́й эта́ж!

### EXERCISE 8

Answer the following questions in English.

1 Where did the girl's father work?
2 What did the girl like to do, when she lived in St Petersburg?
3 Why did they go to Britain?
4 Where did they stay?
5 What did they see in London?
6 Where else would she like to go?
7 What would she like to do there?

## ● Looking at words

### Recognising adjectives

Russian commonly makes up new adjectives by adding either **-ный** (**-но́й**) or **-ский** (**-ско́й**) to nouns:

| | |
|---|---|
| интере́с | *interest* |
| интере́сный | *interesting* |
| го́род | *town* |
| городско́й | *municipal* |

In English you can quite commonly put two nouns together to make up a phrase. In Russian you will make the first word into an adjective:

университе́тская ле́кция *university lecture*
мясно́й отде́л *meat section (in shop)*

The last letter of the noun may change when adding **-ный** or **-ский**:

| | |
|---|---|
| поли́тика | *politics* |
| полити́чный | *politic* |

### EXERCISE 9

Translate the following phrases. Try not to look up any words in the dictionary.

1 а́томная эне́ргия
2 кни́жный магази́н
3 въездна́я ви́за
4 Не́вский проспе́кт
5 пивно́й бар
6 Собо́рная пло́щадь
7 телефо́нный разгово́р
8 библиоте́чный день

## Flying

The syllable **-лёт-** or **-лет-** means *flying*. The word for a plane is made up of two roots: **сам** (*oneself*) and **лёт** (*flying*). Don't worry, Russian planes do have pilots! The word for *pilot* is **лётчик** – the ending **-чик** indicates a person, similar to *-er* at the end of English words. You will also see **сам-** at the beginning of some other words: e.g. **самова́р**, which literally means 'self boil'.

## *A situation to remember*

### Going through customs

Russian customs officers are normally not interested in what you are taking out of the country, but occasionally, they see something on their X-ray machines which arouses their suspicions and you may have to open your case. Here is a typical situation for you to recreate with a partner.

**Customs officer     Tourist**

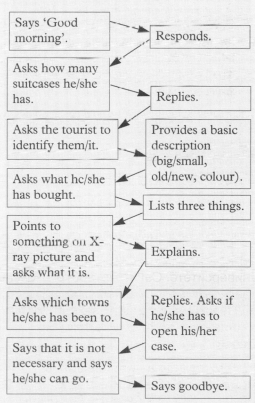

## Writing Russian (IV)

Some of the capital letters are written with a flourish and give written Russian a more ornate appearance. Write all the words below with a capital letter. Note that **ь** is never the first letter in a word and is therefore not normally used as a capital. It is the same height as: *е*  *и*  *л*

### Examples

**Ф** is written  *ф*  *Ф*

**Ч** is written  *ч*  *Ч*

**ь** is written  *ь*

**Б** is written  *б*  *Б*

**Э** is written  *э*  *Э*

Now you try writing the words.

Фо́то _____
  *фото*

Чай _____
  *чай*

Че́хов _____
  *Чехов*

Кремль _____
  *Кремль*

День _____
  *День*

Грибы́ _____
  *Грибы*

Бюро́ _____
  *Бюро*

Бланк _____
  *Бланк*

Экску́рсия _____
  *Экскурсия*

## WHAT YOU KNOW

### My, your, his, her, our, their
мой дом
твоя́ кварти́ра
на́ше письмо́
ва́ши кни́ги
его́ дом
её кварти́ра
их письмо́

### Open, closed
магази́н откры́т/закры́т
библиоте́ка откры́та/закры́та
кафе́ закры́то/откры́то
магази́ны закры́ты/откры́ты

### Would like to
Он хоте́л бы (Она́ хоте́ла бы) обменя́ть де́сять до́лларов.

## KEY VOCABULARY

| | |
|---|---|
| бага́ж | luggage |
| до́ллар | dollar |
| за | for |
| ма́ленький | small |
| обме́н | exchange |
| обменя́ть | to change (money) |
| откры́ть | to open |
| о́чередь | queue |
| па́спорт | passport |
| письмо́ | letter |
| плати́ть | to pay |
| пода́рок | gift |
| приглаше́ние | invitation |
| рубль | rouble |
| Ско́лько сто́ит ...? | How much does ... cost? |
| сувени́р | souvenir |
| су́мка | bag |
| тамо́женник | customs official |
| тамо́жня | customs |
| теле́жка | trolley |
| фунт | pound |
| чемода́н | suitcase |

# Revision

**Russian schools**

**Universities**

**Revision**

## ● Life in Russia

### The school system

Russians go to school (**шкóла**) when they are six years old and most stay in full time education till they are 17. They usually study at the same school for the whole of this period. Such schools are called **срéдняя шкóла**, literally *middle school*. They have numbers, rather than names. The name of a school in St Petersburg might be **Срéдняя шкóла № 21, Москóвского райóна** (*district*).

Under the old Soviet regime, there was a centrally organised curriculum with the same textbooks being used throughout the whole country. Since the fall of communism, there is greater variety and a number of private schools have opened, although costs are high. There was a highly organised network of nursery schools (**ясли**) for children from six months to three years, and kindergartens (**дéтский сад**) for children from three to six years old. These used to be run by the state or state run companies. Nowadays many of them are being run privately and are charging for their services.

Russia has a well established system of higher education institutions (**ву́зы**). At 17, on leaving school, students can go either to a university (**университе́т**) or to an institute (**институ́т**). Most courses last for five years and some lead to a job qualification. If, for example, you study at a **педагоги́ческий университе́т** or **институ́т**, you are trained as a teacher. Under the old system, you were obliged to work as a teacher for a period on graduation from the **вуз**. You had little choice where your first job was. It was often a long way from home in a small town or village. Under the present system you have to look for work and need not take a job teaching if you do not wish to.

Entrance to a **вуз** is by examination and each **вуз** sets its own entrance examination. Examinations in Russia are usually oral. The student arrives and selects a **биле́т** (literally *ticket*) with a topic on it. He or she then has to answer questions on this topic from a panel of lecturers. Most prospective students have to take private lessons if they wish to pass the examination. If they fail the examination, they may be accepted on a **комме́рческий курс** (*commercial course*), for payment, of course.

The Russian education system uses a scale of five marks. The top mark is five (**пятёрка**). This is officially labelled **отли́чно** (*excellent*). Four (**четвёрка**) is **хорошо́** (*good*). Three (**тро́йка**) is **удовлетвори́тельно** (*satisfactory*). The lowest mark normally awarded is **дво́йка** (*two*). This is **неудовлетвори́тельно** (*unsatisfactory*).

Some institutions are now using a ten-point scale, and for entrance to a **вуз** you will need at least eight.

### Useful vocabulary

учи́тель, учи́тельница   *teacher (m/f)*
преподава́тель, преподава́тельница
*teacher (university, senior school)*
учени́к, учени́ца      *pupil (m/f)*
студе́нт, студе́нтка     *student (m/f)*

If you are at school, university or an institute, use the verb **учи́ться**:

Я учу́сь в шко́ле № 23.
*I go to school number 23.*
Он у́чится в МГУ.
*He is a student at Moscow University.*
Вы рабо́таете и́ли у́читесь?
*Are you working or are you a student?*

## ● Language information

### Years

**В 1995 году́ (в ты́сяча девятьсо́т девяно́сто пя́том году́)** – *in 1995*. '**году́**' is often abbreviated to '**г.**'. To recognise years in Russian, listen out for **ты́сяча девятьсо́т**, the equivalent of 'nineteen hundred'. The next number will give you the decade, the final one will be **пе́рвом, второ́м**, etc. These numbers were given in Unit 11.

You will be able to practise them in revision exercises 4–7.

# ● Looking at words

## Number words

Russian has a set of special nouns related to numbers:

**дво́йка** from **два**
**тро́йка** from **три**
**четвёрка** from **четы́ре**
**пятёрка** from **пять**
**шестёрка** from **шесть**
**семёрка** from **семь**
**восьмёрка** from **во́семь**
**девя́тка** from **де́вять**
**деся́тка** from **де́сять**

As you can see from earlier in this unit, **дво́йка** to **пятёрка** are used to refer to marks at school and university. All of the above number words have a variety of other uses:

Cards: **деся́тка пик** is the ten of spades.
Bus, trolleybus and tram numbers: **Я е́ду домо́й на восьмёрке.** (*I am going home on the number eight.*) You will also hear **на восьмо́м авто́бусе (тролле́йбусе ...)**
Horse-driven vehicles: the most famous of them, **тро́йка**, has three.
Groups of people: The film *The Magnificent Seven* is «**Великоле́пная семёрка**» in Russian.

## Abbreviations

Modern Russian makes a lot of use of abbreviations. You have already seen some of these. One word in this lesson is in origin an abbreviation: **вуз** stands for **вы́сшее уче́бное заведе́ние**.

........................................

### EXERCISE 1

Here are some abbreviations we have had in the last few units. Can you remember what they mean in English?

**1** МГУ (Моско́вский госуда́рственный университе́т)
**2** ГУМ (Госуда́рственный универса́льный магази́н)

**3** ОВИР (Отде́л виз и регистра́ция иностра́нных гра́ждан)
**4** МХАТ (Моско́вский худо́жественный академи́ческий теа́тр)

........................................

Sometimes the abbreviations contain not just the first letters of the word but selected syllables.

........................................

### EXERCISE 2

Each of the following is the name of an organisation. One is to do with cars, one with the building industry, one with bread and one with food in general. Which one is which and what else can you work out about each organisation?

**1** Росглавхлеб     **3** Промстройбанк
**2** Минавтопром     **4** Внешторгпродукт

#### New vocabulary

| | |
|---|---|
| мини́сте́рство | *ministry* |
| промы́шленность | *industry* |
| стро́ить | *to build* |
| вне | *outside* |
| торгова́ть | *to trade* |
| проду́кты | *groceries* |

........................................

You will regularly see theatres, concert halls, universities, etc. named after people. Look out for the abbreviation **им.**, short for **и́мени**, literally *of the name of*.

........................................

### EXERCISE 3

Who are the following places named after?

В Москве́
**1** Драмати́ческий теа́тр им. Н. В. Го́голя
**2** Большо́й зал консервато́рии им. П. И. Чайко́вского
**3** Моско́вский госуда́рственный университе́т им. М. В. Ломоно́сова

В Санкт-Петербу́рге
**4** Академи́ческий Большо́й драмати́ческий теа́тр им. А. С. Пу́шкина
**5** Филармо́ния им. Д. Д. Шостако́вича
**6** О́перная сту́дия Консервато́рии им. Н. А. Ри́мского-Ко́рсакова
**7** Музе́й антрополо́гии и этногра́фии им. Петра́ Вели́кого

........................................

# ● Revision exercises

## EXERCISE 4

Here are some dates written out in words. Write the figures in the space provided.

**1** в тысяча двести двадцать третьем году

в _1223_ г.

**2** в тысяча пятьсот сорок седьмом году

в _____ г.

**3** в тысяча шестьсот пятом году

в _____ г.

**4** в тысяча семьсот третьем году

в _____ г.

**5** в тысяча восемьсот шестьдесят первом году   в _____ г.

**6** в тысяча девятьсот сорок первом году

в _____ г.

## EXERCISE 5

All the dates in Exercise 4 refer to events listed in the table of events in Unit 12 (page 98). Answer the question **Что случилось?** (*What happened?*) in Russian or English:

**1** Что случилось в тысяча двести двадцать третьем году?

**2** Что случилось в тысяча пятьсот сорок седьмом году?

**3** Что случилось в тысяча шестьсот пятом году?

**4** Что случилось в тысяча семьсот третьем году?

**5** Что случилось в тысяча восемьсот шестьдесят первом году?

**6** Что случилось в тысяча девятьсот сорок первом году?

## EXERCISE 6

Here are three jumbled lists.
Once again you need to refer to the list of dates in Unit 12 on page 98.
Connect one item from the left-hand column with one from the centre and one from the right-hand column to make a sensible statement.
The first one is done for you.

**1** В 1227 г.   Пётр Великий   первая мировая война.

**2** В 1914 г.   кончилась   Екатерина II.

**3** В 1697 г.   умер   татарское иго.

**4** В 1945 г.   началась   Чингисхан.

**5** В 1480 г.   умерла   поехал в Голландию.

**6** В 1796 г.   кончилось   великая отечественная война.

## ▭ EXERCISE 7

Listen to the recording on your tape, giving information about what events happened in which years this century.
Listen out for **в тысяча девятьсот**, the equivalent of nineteen hundred.
Fill in the table below in English.

|   | Year | Event |
|---|------|-------|
| **1** |  |  |
| **2** |  |  |
| **3** |  |  |
| **4** |  |  |
| **5** |  |  |

## EXERCISE 8

Read through the letter on the next page from **Ваня**, a student in **МГУ**, to his friend **Боря**, who is training to be a teacher at the **педагогический университет** in St Petersburg (**РГПУ им. Герцена**). Then do the exercises.

Москва́

четве́рг 10-ое октября́ 1996 г.

Дорого́й Бо́ря,

Вот я и в Моско́вском Университе́те. Мы $^1$_ꞁ_ ле́кции и семина́ры две неде́ли

наза́д. На́шего профе́ссора по фи́зике $^2$__ Бори́сов, Ива́н Никола́евич. Вчера́

он $^3$__ о́чень интере́сную ле́кцию о ко́смосе. По́сле ле́кции мы $^4$__ в

студе́нческой столо́вой, а пото́м $^5$__ телеви́зор. Америка́нский пиани́ст $^6$__

конце́рт Чайко́вского. За́втра мы бу́дем $^7$__ в лаборато́рии, а ве́чером бу́дем

$^8$__ в библиоте́ке. Мне ну́жно $^9$__ о́чень мно́го рабо́тать, но я то́же $^{10}$__

занима́ться *play* спо́ртом. Здесь мы $^{11}$__ в волейбо́л, хокке́й, те́ннис.

Как ты $^{12}$__ в РГПУ им. Ге́рцена?

Приве́т ма́ме и па́пе

Ва́ня

**1** Here is a list of the words that have been missed out.
Put the letter of the correct word in the space provided in the text.
The first one is done for you.

**a** смотре́ли  **b** зову́т  **c** игра́ем  **d** у́жинали  **e** у́чишься  **f** чита́ть
**g** рабо́тать  **h** чита́л  **i** бу́дет  **j** на́чали  **k** игра́л  **l** бу́ду

**2** Answer the following questions in Russian.

**a** В како́м ме́сяце (*month*) начали́сь ле́кции?   **d** Где Ва́ня бу́дет за́втра?
**b** Как зову́т профе́ссора?   **e** По телеви́зору игра́ет англи́йский
**c** В како́й день профе́ссор чита́л ле́кцию?   пиани́ст?
  **f** В како́м го́роде у́чится Бо́ря?

**EXERCISE 9**

Look at the table, showing how long it takes by plane (**на самолёте**) and by train (**на по́езде**) and giving you information about the zone time (**поясно́е вре́мя**) for the destination (**пункт-назначе́ния**). Then do the task on page 128.

| Пункт назначения (от Москвы) | Время в пути | | Поясное время |
|---|---|---|---|
| | на самолёте | на поезде | |
| ВЛАДИВОСТОК | 9.55 | 170 | + 7 часов |
| ВОЛГОГРАД | 1.35 | 18.15 | + 1 час |
| ВОЛОГДА | 1.15 | 7.32 | Московское время |
| ИРКУТСК | 6.50 | 80.04 | + 5 часов |
| КАЗАНЬ | 1.20 | 14.45 | + 2 часа |
| КРАСНОДАР | 2.25 | 26.06 | + 1 час |
| ЛИПЕЦК | 1.05 | 14.00 | Московское время |
| НИЖНИЙ НОВГОРОД | 1.10 | 6.55 | + 1 час |
| САНКТ-ПЕТЕРБУРГ | 1.20 | 5.59 | Московское время |

A travel agent has a list of people returning from a conference in Moscow. Their means of transport (**вид тра́нспорта**) and departure time (**отправле́ние**) are listed. She uses the table on page 127 to work out when each participant will arrive home. She has done the first one, you do the rest.

| Пассажи́р | вид тра́нспорта | отправле́ние | го́род | прибы́тие |
|---|---|---|---|---|
| Ле́вин | самолёт | семь часо́в | Волгогра́д | 9.35 |
| Алексе́ева | по́езд | во́семь часо́в | Во́логда | |
| Сега́ль | самолёт | де́вять часо́в | Ирку́тск | |
| Моро́зова | по́езд | де́сять часо́в | Ли́пецк | |
| Есе́нин | самолёт | оди́ннадцать часо́в | Владивосто́к | |
| Петро́ва | по́езд | двена́дцать часо́в | Санкт-Петербу́рг | |

## LANGUAGE REVIEW

Look at the words and phrases below. If you don't remember what they mean, look back at the unit given on the right.

| | |
|---|---|
| понеде́льник, вто́рник, среда́; в понеде́льник, во вто́рник, в сре́ду | 11 |
| янва́рь, февра́ль, март; в январе́, в феврале́, в ма́рте | 11 |
| зимо́й, весно́й, ле́том, о́сенью; у́тром, днём, ве́чером, но́чью | 11 |
| пе́рвый, второ́й, тре́тий | 11 |
| 1-е ма́рта, университе́т О́ксфорда | 11 |
| по́сле обе́да, до у́жина | 11 |
| два часа́, пять часо́в | 11 |
| За́втра я бу́ду рабо́тать. | 11 |
| он чита́л, она́ чита́ла, они́ чита́ли | 12 |
| был, была́, бы́ло, бы́ли | 12 |
| живу́, живёшь, живёт, живём, живёте, живу́т | 12 |
| учи́ться, роди́ться | 12 |
| иду́, идёшь, идёт; е́ду, е́дешь, е́дет | 13 |
| где, куда́ | 13 |
| Я иду́ в центр/из це́нтра. Я иду́ на вокза́л/с вокза́ла. | 13 |
| се́вер, юг, восто́к, за́пад; на се́вере, на ю́ге, на восто́ке, на за́паде | 13 |
| прихо́д, ухо́д, вы́ход, вход; прие́зд, отъе́зд | 13 |
| мой, твой, наш, ваш, его́, её, их | 14 |
| закры́т, закры́та, закры́то, закры́ты; откры́т, откры́та, откры́то, откры́ты | 14 |
| хоте́л бы, хоте́ла бы, хоте́ли бы | 14 |

## KEY VOCABULARY

| | |
|---|---|
| вуз | higher educational institution |
| институ́т | institute |
| ме́сяц | month |
| преподава́тель | teacher, lecturer (*m*) |
| преподава́тельница | teacher, lecturer (*f*) |
| учи́тель | teacher (*m*) |
| учи́тельница | teacher (*f*) |
| учени́к | pupil (*m*) |
| учени́ца | pupil (*f*) |
| шко́ла | school |

# 16 More about shopping

Advertising

Opinions

Comparisons

## ● Life in Russia

### Advertising

Russia has changed from a country where there was no advertising (**рекла́мы**) for consumer goods to one which has advertising everywhere. Newspapers and all the television channels are full of adverts. Programmes are often sponsored by big companies. The majority of the advertisers are either Western companies or one of the numerous new Russian banks offering high rates of interest.

It is interesting to browse through Russian newspapers and compare prices (**це́ны**) with those at home, seeing what is cheaper (**деше́вле**) and dearer (**доро́же**). For expensive items such as cars (**автомоби́ли**) the price is usually quoted in dollars because of the unstable nature of the rouble exchange rate. You may, however, have to pay in roubles at the current rate.

Here are some typical advertisements. Don't expect to understand every word in them.

## EXERCISE 1

Look at advertisement **a** below and answer the following questions.

1 What food is the company selling?
2 How many kinds (**виды**) are they offering?
3 Name one type of the food.
4 How much does 1 kilo cost?
5 What would you pay for a 100 gram portion of the processed (**пла́вленный**) variety?

## EXERCISE 2

Below are another two advertisements from the same paper.

1 What is advertisement **b** advertising?
2 How many kinds are available?
3 What is the size of the bottles (**бут.** – short for **буты́лка**)?
4 What is advertisement **c** advertising?
5 How much does it cost?
6 Where does it come from?
7 Where do both companies have their warehouses (**склад**)?

## EXERCISE 3

Look at the advertisement on page 131 from a wholesale importer of food and drink called 'Greenfield' and answer the questions.

1 Link the item to its price. The first one is done for you.

| | | |
|---|---|---|
| **a** | Капу́ста в ви́нном со́усе сто́ит | два́дцать четы́ре до́ллара |
| **b** | Шербе́т с минда́лем сто́ит | де́вять до́лларов |
| **c** | Вино́ десе́ртное «Ви́шня» сто́ит | три́дцать три до́ллара |
| **d** | Сок «Я́ффа» сто́ит | сто шестьдеся́т три до́ллара |
| **e** | Шампиньо́ны стоя́т | сто шестьдеся́т шесть до́лларов |
| **f** | Сок апельси́новый натура́льный сто́ит | два́дцать два до́ллара |
| **g** | Ассорти́ «Се́рдце любви́» сто́ит | сто пятна́дцать до́лларов |
| **h** | Вино́ «Фондатио́н» кра́сное сто́ит | четы́рнадцать до́лларов |
| **i** | Джин «Го́рдонс» сто́ит | де́сять до́лларов |
| **j** | Ви́ски «Джо́нни Уо́лкер рэд лейбл» сто́ит | два́дцать семь до́лларов |

2 How many other items can you work out?

# ТОРГОВЫЙ ДОМ «ГРИНФИЛД»
## Сокольническая площадь, д. 4
### тел. 268-99-07, 268-99-08

### ШОКОЛАД

| | |
|---|---|
| Шоколад Тоблерон черный 100гр. X 20 | 26$ |
| Шоколад горький, 50/100гр. | 39$ |
| Конфеты шоколадные «Лифли», 300гр. X 6 | 22$ |
| Ассорти «Сердце любви», 175гр. X 8 | 24$ |
| Ассорти «Бельгийское», 500гр. X 6 | 36$ |
| Ассорти «Цветы-Нарцис», 175гр. X 10 | 18$ |
| Трюфели, 250гр. X 24 | 33$ |
| Шербет с миндалем, 150гр. X 8 | 22$ |

### КОНСЕРВИРОВАННЫЕ ОВОЩИ

| | |
|---|---|
| Каперсы, 106гр. X 24 | 23$ |
| Оливки, фаршированные красным перчиком 142гр. X 12 | 9$ |
| Маслины 142гр. X 12 | 8$ |
| Фасоль в томатном соусе 400гр. X 12 | 8$ |
| Капуста в винном соусе, 770гр. X 12 | 14$ |
| Огурцы соленые, 720мл. X 12 | 21$ |
| Огурцы маринованные, 370мл. X 12 | 16$ |
| Огурцы по-польски 720мл. X 12 | 21$ |
| Шампиньоны, 170гр. X 12 | 27$ |

### СОКИ

| | |
|---|---|
| Сок «Яффа», 1л. X 12 | 10$ |
| Сок «Дель Монте», ананасовый, 1л. X 12 | 14$ |
| Сок апельсиновый натуральный, 0,7л. X 6 | 9$ |

### ВИНА, ШАМПАНСКОЕ

| | |
|---|---|
| Блу Нан, 0,7л. X 12 | 56$ |
| Шампанское «Асти спуманте», 1.5л. X 6 | 136$ |
| Вино десертное «Вишня», 0,75 л. X 6 | 33$ |
| Шампанское «Кафе Париж» брют, 0,75л. X 6 | 37$ |
| Вино «Фондатион» красное, 0,75л. X 12 | 115$ |

### СПИРТНЫЕ НАПИТКИ

| | |
|---|---|
| Джин «Сигремс», 1л. X 12 | 100$ |
| Джин «Гордонс», 0,75л. X 12 | 163$ |
| Виски «Джонни Уолкер рэд лейбл», 0,75л. X 12 | 166$ |
| Виски «100 пайперс», 0,75л. X 12 | 132$ |
| Водка «Абсолют», 0,75л. X 12 | 101$ |
| Водка «Смирнов» с красной этикеткой, 0,75л. X 12 | 99$ |
| Коньяк «Бисквит», 0,35л. X 24 | 309$ |
| Коньяк «Мартель ВСОП, 0,7л. X 12 | 384$ |

---

## EXERCISE 4

This is an advertisement for business electronic products. You will see that the advertisement has mixed English and Russian. It gives (**даёт**) a guarantee on all goods (**това́ры**). It promises the lowest prices (**са́мые ни́зкие це́ны**) and big discounts (**ски́дки**).

Name as many items as you can which the company sells. You should be able to work out at least ten. If you wanted to fax them, which number would you use?

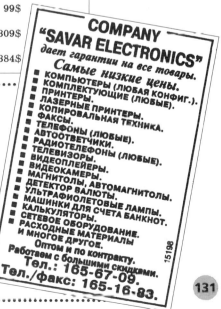

# ● Language information

### Imperfective and perfective verbs

Russian verbs have two forms or *aspects*: *imperfective* and *perfective*.
Here are some examples of the way they are used:

| Imperfective | **Action in progress**<br>Я **сиде́л** до́ма и **чита́л** газе́ту.<br>*I was sitting at home and reading the newspaper.* |
| --- | --- |
| Imperfective | **Action repeated**<br>Ка́ждый день я **чита́л** газе́ту.<br>*Every day I used to read a newspaper.* |
| Perfective | **Action complete on one occasion**<br>Я **прочита́л** газе́ту и **пошёл** в го́род.<br>*I read the newspaper and went to town.* |

Russians make up these forms in a variety of ways. Sometimes they add a prefix at the beginning of the word:

чита́ть/**про**чита́ть   *to read*   писа́ть/**на**писа́ть   *to write*

Sometimes they change the ending:

расска́**зывать**/расска**за́ть** *to tell (a story)*

You will find both forms given in the vocabulary list at the end of the book.

## Comparing things

You have seen a number of words which compare things.
Such comparative forms end in **-e** or **-ee**:

| | | | |
| --- | --- | --- | --- |
| хоро́ший | *good* | лу́чше | *better* |
| плохо́й | *bad* | ху́же | *worse* |
| большо́й | *big* | бо́льше | *bigger, more* |
| ма́ленький | *small* | ме́ньше | *smaller, less* |
| дорого́й | *dear* | доро́же | *dearer* |
| дешёвый | *cheap* | деше́вле | *cheaper* |
| интере́сный | *interesting* | интере́снее | *more interesting* |

*Than* is usually translated by the word **чем**:

Москва́ бо́льше, чем Санкт-Петербу́рг. *Moscow is bigger than St Petersburg.*

## EXERCISE 5

**Это де́ло вку́са**

**It's a matter of taste**

Here are some statements about various nationalities and places.

Match the first part on the left to the ending that best completes the sentence. The first one is done for you.

| 1 | В Шотла́ндии | бо́льше лю́бят вино́, чем пи́во. |
|---|---|---|
| 2 | Во Фра́нции | бо́льше икры́, чем в Ита́лии. |
| 3 | Англича́не | ме́ньше лю́бят хлеб, чем рис. |
| 4 | В Кита́е | ме́ньше лю́бят чай с лимоном, чем с молоком. (*milk*) |
| 5 | Америка́нцы | бо́льше лю́бят ви́ски, чем во́дку. |
| 6 | В Росси́и | бо́льше лю́бят бейсбо́л, чем кри́кет. |

## EXERCISE 6

Each time, the second person in the dialogue below disagrees with the first. Supply the missing word and the nationality of the person making the statement. The first one is done for you.

1 – У вас в А́нглии библиоте́ки лу́чше, чем в Москве́?

– Нет, ху́же. (англича́нин)

2 – Скажи́те, у вас в Нью-Йо́рке бо́льше авто́бусов, чем в Москве́?

– Нет, _____ ( _____ )

3 – Скажи́те, у вас в Росси́и ме́ньше пьют, чем в Япо́нии?

– Нет, _____ ( _____ )

4 – Как вы ду́маете, у вас в Шотла́ндии ме́ньше пьют ви́ски, чем в Аме́рике?

– Нет, _____ ( _____ )

## Prefer

You have come across the expressions **мне нра́вится** (*I like*) and **мне о́чень нра́вится** (*I very much like*). The phrase **мне бо́льше нра́вится** means *I like more*, or *I prefer*. The opposite of this would be **мне ме́ньше нра́вится** (*I like less*). **Мне бо́льше всего́ нра́вится** means *More than anything* (*else*) *I like*.

## EXERCISE 7

In this exercise the second speaker always chooses something different from what is suggested by the first one. You have to fill in the blanks. The first one is done for you.

1 Муж: Вот в меню́ есть бифште́ксы и ры́ба. Мне, пожа́луйста бифште́кс.

Жена́: А мне бо́льше нра́вится ры́ба.

2 Муж: Мо́жно пое́хать и́ли на авто́бусе и́ли на тролле́йбусе. Пое́дем на авто́бусе!

Жена́: Нет, лу́чше _____ ____ _____.

3 Жена́: Фильм идёт в воскресе́нье и четве́рг. Пойдём в воскресе́нье.

Муж: Нет, лу́чше _____ ____ _____.

4 Муж: Сего́дня интере́сная програ́мма по телеви́зору. Я не хочу́ идти́ в теа́тр.

Жена́: А я _____ _____ в теа́тр.

5 Жена́: Что вам бо́льше нра́вится: о́пера или бале́т? Я хоте́л бы послу́шать о́перу.

Муж: А мне _____ _____ бале́т.

## Agreeing

If you want to agree with someone, you say **я согла́сен**, if you are a man, and **я согла́сна**, if you are woman.
To ask them if they agree, you say **Вы согла́сны?**
When you have agreed, you might say **Мы согла́сны**.

## Opinions

When you want to say what you think, you might use the expression **я ду́маю** (*I think*), or **мне ка́жется** (*it seems to me*), or **по-мо́ему** (*in my opinion*).

To ask someone what they think, you say:

Как вы ду́маете?  *What do you think?*
Как по-ва́шему?  *What is your opinion?*

# ● Looking at words

## Giving yourself time to think

Russian, like English, is full of little words and phrases which do not have a great deal of meaning. They are used to fill in time, while you decide on the next thing to say.
**Зна́ете** (*you know*) is used like this in the dialogue between the Muscovite and the two women from Edinburgh in the listening section later in this unit. Other expressions Russians use are:

| | |
|---|---|
| ну | *well* |
| вот | *here* |
| ла́дно | *OK* |
| мне ка́жется | *it seems to me* |
| что́ ли | *well* |
| так | *so* |
| по-мо́ему | *in my opinion* |

These translations are provided as a guide only. If you translate such phrases into English too literally, they will sound artificial. They are extremely useful for the foreign learner, as they may give you time to think of the correct ending!

## Russian proverbs

Russians are very fond of using proverbs and sayings. Many of them make use of the comparative forms we discussed in the 'language information' section. Here are some common ones:

Лу́чше по́здно, чем никогда́
*Better late than never*

Ти́ше е́дешь – да́льше бу́дешь
*More haste, less speed* (literally *the quieter you go, the further you'll be*)

В гостя́х хорошо́, а до́ма лу́чше
*There's no place like home* (literally *it is good visiting, but it is better at home*)

Лу́чше сини́ца в руке́, чем жура́вль в не́бе
*A bird in the hand is worth two in the bush* (literally *it's better to have a tomtit in your hand than a crane in the sky*)

# ● Listening

## Meeting Russians

Russians are very curious about the West, and will be very curious about you and how you live. They may ask very searching questions about the details of your life, some of which can sometimes appear rude, but are usually not intended to be so. Russians, like Ivan in the recording, can hold views which it is difficult to change.

In the following dialogue, recorded on your cassette, two women from Edinburgh are visiting Moscow and staying in a flat with Russian friends. But they are introduced to a very inquisitive Russian friend of the family. He tries to engage them in conversation, but gets put in his place.

Ива́н:   Извини́те, отку́да вы?
А́нна:   Из Великобрита́нии!
Ива́н:   Вы отли́чно говори́те по-ру́сски.
А́нна:   Спаси́бо.
Ива́н:   Вы студе́нтки?
А́нна:   Да.
Ива́н:   Я то́же студе́нт. Прости́те, меня́ зову́т Ива́н Бори́сович. Фами́лия Бело́в.
А́нна:   Я А́нна, а э́то Мэ́ри.
Ива́н:   О́чень прия́тно. Вы из Ло́ндона?
Мэ́ри:   Нет, из Эдинбу́рга.
Ива́н:   Интере́сно. Ну, как дела́ у вас в А́нглии.
Мэ́ри:   Мы не из А́нглии, а из Шотла́ндии.
Ива́н:   Для нас э́то то же са́мое.
Мэ́ри:   А я не согла́сна.
Ива́н:   Скажи́те, у вас в А́нглии – то есть, в Шотла́ндии, же́нщины лю́бят ви́ски?
Мэ́ри:   Нет, я ви́ски не люблю́.
Ива́н:   Я ви́жу, у вас во́дка. Зна́ете, у нас же́нщины лю́бят вино́, шампа́нское, пи́во, коктейли, да́же, мо́жет быть, и конья́к, а во́дку – нет, никогда́.
А́нна:   Э́то де́ло вку́са. Во́дка мне бо́льше нра́вится, чем ви́ски.
Ива́н:   Нет, по-мо́ему, э́то не де́ло вку́са. Де́ло в том, что у нас же́нщины ме́ньше пьют, чем у вас.
А́нна:   Мо́жет быть.
Ива́н:   Коне́чно. А скажи́те, е́сли вы из Шотла́ндии, почему́ вы не в шотла́ндской ю́бке? Говоря́т, что там да́же мужчи́ны но́сят ю́бки. Э́то пра́вда?
Мэ́ри:   Ну, что вы говори́те! Э́то не так! В Шотла́ндии солда́ты но́сят

ю́бки. И пото́м э́то национа́льный костю́м. Иногда́ по пра́здникам мужчи́ны но́сят ю́бки. Вот и всё!
Ива́н:   А милиционе́ры?
Мэ́ри:   Извини́те, но уже́ шесть часо́в. У нас биле́ты в теа́тр.
А́нна:   Пье́са начина́ется в семь часо́в.
Ива́н:   У вас нет ли́шнего биле́та?
А́нна:   К сожале́нию, нет. До свида́ния.
Ива́н:   До свида́ния. Всего́ до́брого. Вы бу́дете здесь за́втра ве́чером?
Мэ́ри:   Я ду́маю, нет.

## New vocabulary

| | |
|---|---|
| Великобрита́ния | *Great Britain* |
| отку́да | *where from* |
| то же са́мое | *same* |
| то есть | *that is* |
| коктейль | *cocktail* |
| да́же | *even* |
| мо́жет быть | *perhaps* |
| никогда́ | *never* |
| де́ло в том, что | *the fact is that* |
| коне́чно | *of course* |
| е́сли | *if* |
| ю́бка | *skirt* |
| солда́т | *soldier* |
| иногда́ | *sometimes* |
| пра́здник | *holiday* |
| милиционе́р | *policeman* |
| уже́ | *already* |
| начина́ться | *to begin* |
| к сожале́нию | *unfortunately* |
| всего́ до́брого | *all the best* |

### EXERCISE 8

Answer the following questions.

1  Where are the British women from?
2  What do Russian women like to drink?
3  Why does the Russian student think it's not just a matter of taste?
4  Why is the Russian student surprised at the way they are dressed?
5  What do they tell him about this?
6  Where are they going?

## A situation to remember

### It's cheaper in Moscow

Your friend wants to buy a television
(**купи́ть телеви́зор**).

Devise a conversation to convince him/her
that it is cheaper to buy it in Moscow than in
St Petersburg.

You tell him/her how much a television costs
in Moscow.

He/she admits it is dearer in St Petersburg.

However, he/she prefers the shops in St
Petersburg.

Don't forget that if you need time to think,
you can add one or more of the words or
phrases from the *Looking at words* section of
this unit.

You can invent similar conversations by
selecting a different item of technical
equipment from the 'Savar Electronics'
advertisement. You could think of other
reasons for shopping in St Petersburg: you
live there, they give a guarantee, you don't
like Moscow, it costs a lot of money to go to
Moscow (**до́рого сто́ит пое́хать в
Москву́**), etc.

## WHAT YOU KNOW

### Comparing things
Москва́ бо́льше, чем Санкт-Петербу́рг

### Expressing preferences
мне бо́льше нра́вится теа́тр

### Agreeing and disagreeing

| я | (не) | согла́сен |
| --- | --- | --- |
| | | согла́сна |
| мы | | согла́сны |

### Expressing your opinion
Я ду́маю, что в Москве́ деше́вле.
Мне ка́жется, что у нас доро́же.
По-мо́ему, в Петербу́рге лу́чше.

## KEY VOCABULARY

| | |
| --- | --- |
| бо́льше | bigger, more |
| деше́вле (дешёвый) | cheaper (cheap) |
| доро́же (дорого́й) | dearer (dear) |
| ду́мать | to think |
| ка́жется | it seems |
| к сожале́нию | unfortunately |
| лу́чше | better |
| ме́ньше | smaller, less |
| никогда́ | never |
| по-мо́ему | in my opinion |
| по-ва́шему | in your opinion |
| согла́сен, согла́сна, согла́сны | agree |
| това́р | goods |
| то есть | that is |
| то же са́мое | the same (the same thing) |
| ху́же | worse |
| цена́ | price |
| чем | than |
| ю́бка | skirt |

## Public and other holidays

## Congratulations and greetings

## More on travel

# Holidays and celebrations

## ● Life in Russia

### Public holidays

Russian holidays follow a fairly similar pattern to ours in the West. Russians tend not to work on Sundays. They have one break in the winter and another at Easter, with a longer spell in the summer, in August. In addition, they have a number of public holidays (**пра́здники**), which may be of more than one day's duration. The current official holidays are as follows:

| | |
|---|---|
| 1-ое и 2-ое января́ | Но́вый год |
| 7-ое января́ | Рождество́ *(Christmas)* |
| 8-ое ма́рта | Междунаро́дный день же́нщин |
| 9-ое ма́я | День побе́ды *(Victory Day)* |
| 12-ое ию́ня | День незави́симости Росси́и *(Russian Independence Day)* |

In addition some people still celebrate:

**1-ое ма́я**  One name for this holiday is День весны́ и труда́ (literally *Day of Spring and Labour*)
**7-ое и 8-ое ноября́**  Годовщи́на Октя́брьской социалисти́ческой револю́ции *(Anniversary of the October Socialist Revolution)*

If you want to check what the official holidays are in any particular year, they are always shown in red on a Russian calendar.

Be careful if you are going to Russia around these public holidays, as it can sometimes be difficult to get things done when places are closed. Two periods to avoid, if you are going on business, are the first weeks of January and May. Many Russians take advantage of two public holidays close together and do not return to work for the intervening period.

Under the old Soviet regime there were a number of holidays celebrating political events. These are officially no longer public holidays, but many people still consider them holidays. There is in fact general confusion as to the status of some public holidays.

By far the most important religious feast is Easter (**Па́сха**), which sometimes coincides with our Easter, but not always. Russian Christians at Easter greet one another with **Христо́с воскре́с** (*Christ is risen*). This is related to the word **воскресе́ние** (*Resurrection*). (See Unit 11.)

The Russian Orthodox church (**Правосла́вие**) still follows the Julian calendar. The Gregorian calendar was adopted in Britain in 1752 but was not introduced into Russia until 1918, after the communist revolution. Since 1900 the Julian calendar has been 13 days behind the Gregorian one. This is why the October revolution had its anniversary in November and why Orthodox Russians celebrate Christmas on January 7th.

## Holidays

Russians usually go away in August. Many go to their dachas and base themselves there for the summer. Others travel to resorts in what used to be part of the Soviet Union. Favourite holiday resorts (**куро́рты**) were the Baltic Republics of Latvia (**Ла́твия**), Lithuania (**Литва́**) and Estonia (**Эсто́ния**) and the Caucasus (**Кавка́з**), which are at present largely out of bounds for political reasons. Russians still go to the Crimea (**Крым**), which is now part of independent Ukraine.

The cost of travel has risen dramatically since the collapse of the Soviet Union and it is only wealthy Russians who can travel. Despite this, many more Russians go abroad (**за грани́цу**) than used to be the case. Many travel agencies (**тураге́нство** or **турфи́рма**) have opened up all over Russia and sell packages (**путёвка**) to cater for all this extra foreign travel. Of course, they claim that prices are reasonable (**досту́пный**).

The Russian for *holiday*, if you are working, is **о́тпуск**; if you are a student, you have **кани́кулы**. On holiday your aim is to have **о́тдых** (*relaxation*) and **развлече́ние** (*entertainment*).

On page 139 is an advertisement from **Интури́ст**, the company which used to organise most travel for foreigners coming to the old Soviet Union. It is now competing for the business of sending Russians abroad. Notice that in this case travel (air fare, **а́виа**, overland travel, **доро́га**) is extra on most of the packages listed.

## EXERCISE 1

Look at the advertisement and answer the following questions.

1 What do you get for $310?
2 What do you get for $515?
3 What do you have to pay to get to Paris?
4 What do you have to pay to get to Holland?
5 How do you get to Bulgaria?
6 What is offered in the Far East?
7 How long has the firm been operating?
8 Which is the cheapest package quoted, excluding flight?

## EXERCISE 2

Look at the poster for the Atlas travel company and answer the following questions.

1 What kind of holiday does Atlas specialise in?
2 How many features of Atlas holidays can you name?
3 Name as many as you can of the ten destinations they have on offer.
4 What are the costs of an Atlas holiday like?
5 Complete the slogan:
'Travel (**Путеше́ствуйте**) with Atlas _____,

| | | |
|---|---|---|
| 13221 | | **30 лет в туризме.** |
| | | **113532, Москва,** |
| | | **Озерковская наб., 50.** |
| | | Факс: (095) 235-60-63. |
| **Кипр** | 8 дней, | 560$ |
| | Тел.: 235-65-76, 235-35-31 | |
| **Греция** | 8 дней, | 210-284$ + авиа + к/с. |
| | Тел.: 235-65-36. | |
| **Австрия** | 7 дней, | 310$ + авиа |
| **Бразилия** | 8 дней, | 550$ + авиа |
| **Нидерланды** | 7 дней, | 400$ + авиа |
| **Сингапур** | 8 дней, | 350$ + авиа |
| | Тел.: 235-22-95. | |
| **Болгария** | 14 дней, | 500$ + дорога |
| Бальнеологический курорт г. Хисаря (под Пловдивом) | Тел.: 235-97-72. | |
| **Франция** (*Париж*) | 7 дней, | 445$ + авиа |
| **Италия** | 8 дней, | 515$ + авиа. |
| | Тел.: 235-13-63. | |
| **Турция** (*Стамбул*) | 5 дней, | 250$. |
| **Турция** (*Анталия*) | 8 дней, | 315-785$. |
| **Тунис** 8 дней (сентябрь, октябрь), | | 200$ + авиа |
| | Тел.: 235-67-72. | |

## Greeting people

Here are some useful phrases for greeting Russians, many of which you have met earlier in the course:

| | |
|---|---|
| Здра́вствуй! (ты )/Здра́вствуйте! (вы) | *Hello.* |
| Приве́т! | *Hi.* |
| Как ты поживáешь?/Как вы поживáете? | *How are you?* |
| Как делá? | *How are things?* |
| До́брое у́тро! | *Good morning.* |
| До́брый день! | *Good afternoon.* |
| До́брый ве́чер! | *Good evening.* |

Apart from these phrases, you will need to know the following construction:

Поздравля́ю
Поздравля́ем  вас  с Но́вым го́дом!
                     с Рождество́м!
                     с Днём побе́ды.

These phrases mean literally *I (We) congratulate you with New Year/Christmas/Victory Day.* If you wish, you can simply say **Поздравля́ю вас с пра́здником!** (*Happy holiday!*) You can often miss out the word **поздравля́ю** or **поздравля́ем** and say simply **С Но́вым го́дом!** etc.

You can also use this same formula for congratulating people on birthdays (**день рожде́ния**), weddings (**сва́дьба**) or name day (**имени́ны**), the religious feast day of the person's patron saint.

Here are some greetings cards. Russians use the word **откры́тки**, which also means *postcards.*

## EXERCISE 3
Work out which holiday or event each card is celebrating.

The last one is a reproduction of a card from the beginning of the century and you may notice extra hard signs (**ъ**) at the end of the words. It has become very fashionable to reproduce cards and books from Tsarist times. You will see several unfamiliar letters and lots of hard signs, which disappeared with the reform of the alphabet in 1918.

## Wishing people well

Russians are often very eloquent when wishing people success, happiness, etc. Here are some sample phrases:

Жела́ю вам сча́стья и успе́хов.
*I wish you happiness and success.*
Жела́ю вам вы́здороветь.
*I hope you recover. (literally I wish you to recover)*
(Sometimes the phrase **жела́ю вам** can be omitted.)

Счастли́вого пути́! *Have a good journey.*
Всего́ хоро́шего! or Всего́ до́брого!
*All the best.*

• • • • • • • • • • • • • • • • • • • • • • • • • •

### EXERCISE 4

Here are some phrases wishing people a variety of things.
When do you think they would be used?

1 Жела́ю вам сдать экза́мен.
2 Прия́тного аппети́та!
3 Поздравля́ем тебя́ с днём рожде́ния!
4 Успе́хов вам!
5 До́лгих (*long*) лет жи́зни!
6 Споко́йной но́чи!
7 Прия́тного сна! (*sleep*)

• • • • • • • • • • • • • • • • • • • • • • • • • •

### EXERCISE 5

Here is a card from a Russian friend. Read it and answer the questions.

1 What was the reason for writing the card?
2 What three things is she wishing her friend?

• • • • • • • • • • • • • • • • • • • • • • • • • •

## Letter writing

Here are some more greetings, this time at the start and finish of a letter in Russian.

**Intimate**
Ми́лая Та́ня!
Целу́ю и обнима́ю!

**Informal**
Дорого́й Бо́ря!
С приве́том!

**Formal**
С уваже́нием!
Уважа́емый Ива́н Петро́вич!

С приве́том!     *Regards*
С уваже́нием!   *With respect*
                        (*Yours sincerely*)
Целу́ю и обнима́ю! *I kiss and embrace you.*

(Russians are much more demonstrative in the way they express affection! This is a standard expression, perhaps translatable by something like 'All my love'.)

Other phrases you will see in letters are:

Переда́йте ему́ (горя́чий) приве́т
*Give him my (warmest) greetings*
Бу́дьте здоро́вы
*Keep well! (literally be well)*
Всего́ до́брого *All the best*

Поздравляем Вас с наступающим Новым 1995 годом! Желаем Вам успехов, здоровья и новых поездок в Петербург.

Ирина

18 / XII / 94

**EXERCISE 6**

Here is a letter with the expressions of greeting omitted. You have to fill them in. Pay attention to the dates when you fill in the first two items.

Notice also that the **ты** form is used, causing the woman to write **передáй** instead of **передáйте**.

**New vocabulary**

| | |
|---|---|
| муж | *husband* |
| сказáть | *to say* |
| получи́ть | *to receive* |
| встречáться | *to meet* |
| рáньше | *earlier, previously* |

Дорогáя Сáша!

Я всегдá дýмаю о тебé в э́то врéмя гóда! Ты, как и я, родилáсь 2-го января́. С ¹_____ _____ и с ²_____ _____! Как твой муж? Передáй емý ³_____ _____. Ми́ла мне сказáла, что твой сын сдал экзáмены в прóшлом годý. ⁴_____! Он дéлает больши́е успéхи! У меня́ есть хорóшие нóвости. Муж получи́л рабóту в Москвé. Мы с тобóй чáсто бýдем встречáться, как и рáньше.
⁵_____ýю и _____ áю
⁶_____ _____

Тáня

# ● Language information

## Case forms used in greetings

The phrase **поздравля́ю вас** is followed by **с** and the instrumental case. We have seen the noun endings for the instrumental case in Unit 9. Adjectives end in **-ым** if the noun is masculine or neuter; they end in **-ой** if the noun is feminine:

Поздравля́ю вас (acc) с Нóв**ым** годом! (instr) *Happy New Year!*
Сын поздрáвил роди́телей (acc) с серéбрян**ой** свáдьбой. (instr)
*The son congratulated his parents on their silver wedding.*

The greeting phrase after **жела́ю вам** is in the genitive case.
The genitive noun endings were given in Unit 11.

Adjectives ending in the genitive are:

| | | | |
|---|---|---|---|
| **Masculine and neuter** | **-ОГО (-ЕГО)** | Всегó дóбр**ого**! | *All the best!* |
| **Feminine** | **-ОЙ (-ЕЙ)** | Спокóйн**ой** нóчи! | *Good night.* |
| **Plural** | **-ЫХ (-ИХ)** | больши́**х** успéхов | *great success* |

## Verbs of going

In Unit 13 we saw the two verbs **идти́** (*to go on foot*) and **éхать** (*to go by vehicle*). There are two further verbs: **ходи́ть** (*to go on foot*) and **éздить** (*to go by vehicle*). They are used either when you are walking or driving *round* (**по**) a place:

Я ходи́л по магази́нам.    Я éздил по гóроду.
*I walked round the shops.*    *I drove round town.*

or when you have made a round trip *there and back*:

Вчерá я ходи́л в кинó.    В прóшлом годý я éздил в Росси́ю.
*I went to the cinema yesterday.*    *Last year I went to Russia.*

# ● Looking at words

## Verbs ending in -овать

There are numerous verbs ending in **-овать**, borrowed from other European languages. The meaning should be obvious from English: for example, **организовáть** (*to organise*), **фотографи́ровать** (*to photograph*).

. . . . . . . . . . . . . . . . . . . . . . . . . . . .

### EXERCISE 7

Look at the following verbs and work out what they mean.

| | | | |
|---|---|---|---|
| 1 | драматизи́ровать | 4 | плани́ровать |
| 2 | эмигри́ровать | 5 | регули́ровать |
| 3 | регистри́ровать | 6 | паковáть |

Note that the present tense of a verb like **целовáть** (*to kiss*) is **я целу́ю, ты целу́ешь, он/онá целу́ет, мы целу́ем, вы целу́ете, они́ целу́ют**. Verbs ending in **-овать** normally form their present tense in this way.

## весь

**Весь** (**вся, всё**) means *all* and is an adjective. The feminine is **вся**, accusative **всю** and neuter **всё**:

| весь день | *all day* |
|---|---|
| всю ночь | *all night* |
| всё утро | *all morning* |

**Всё** also means *everything* and *all the time* (short for **всё врéмя**):

Он знáет всё. *He knows everything.*
Он всё дýмает о Тáне. *He thinks about Tanya all the time.*

The genitive form **всегó** is found in greetings: **всегó дóброго/хорóшего** (*all the best*). **Все** is the plural, so you would say **все рýсские** (*all Russians*). It also means *everybody*, as in **все знáют э́то** (*everyone knows that*). Two useful related words are **всегдá** (*always*) and **совсéм** (*completely*).

# ● Listening

## Travelling round Europe

. . . . . . . . . . . . . . . . . . . . . . . . . . . .

### 🔲 EXERCISE 8

Listen to the passage recorded on your cassette. Two Russians have returned to work after the summer holiday. Answer the questions which follow.

Ири́на: Здрáвствуйте, Ивáн Николáевич! Ну, как делá?

Ивáн: Ири́на Матвéевна, здрáвствуйте! Как вы поживáете?

Ири́на: Спаси́бо, хорошó, а вы?

Ивáн: Тóже хорошó. А скажи́те, кудá вы éздили лéтом?

Ири́на: Ивáн Николáевич, как вам сказáть. По всей Еврóпе éздили!

Ивáн: Интерéсно. А вы бы́ли в Пари́же?

Ири́на: Конéчно. Там óчень краси́во. Домá элегáнтные.

Ивáн: Как мы там вкýсно обéдали! Скажи́те, вы на маши́не бы́ли?

Ири́на: Конéчно, на маши́не. Потóм из Фрáнции мы поéхали в Итáлию.

Ивáн: Ваш муж говори́т по-италья́нски, не прáвда ли?

Ири́на: Нет. Фами́лия нáша италья́нская, но не говори́м.

Ивáн: В Итáлии, мне кáжется, дорóже жить?

Ири́на: Нет, дóрого, но в Пари́же тóже дóрого. В Итáлии бензи́н óчень дóрого стóит.

1 Where did Irina go in the summer?
2 How did she travel?
3 What did she think of Paris?
4 Why does Ivan Nikolayevich think Irina's husband can speak Italian?
5 What did she say about Italy?

# ● Reading

**EXERCISE 9**

Here is an article adapted from a Russian newspaper. Try to answer the questions that follow it. It contains a number of words and constructions that you may not have met.
Do not expect to understand all of the article.
Some key roots are given at the end. Look at these roots and make your best guess at the information in the passage.

---

### Старты и финиши

Москвич Сергей Долматов, набрав 10,5 очка, вышел победителем юношеского первенства мира по шахматам, завершившегося в австрийском городе Граце. На втором месте — теперь уже экс-чемпион мира его земляк Артур Юсупов, отставший от Долматова на 0,5 очка. Третье место занял датчанин Енс Фриз-Нильсен.

Победой русских спортсменов закончилась 16-я велогонка «Тур де Л'авенир» по дорогам Франции. Победителем состязаний (1590 км) стал Сергей Сухорученков из Самары — 42 часа 26 мин. 28 сек. Следующие три места заняли также наши спортсмены — Рамазан Галялетдинов из Самары, москвич Сергей Морозов и победитель велогонки Мира-95 Александр Аверин из Самары.

---

### New vocabulary

| | |
|---|---|
| очко | point |
| юный | young |
| велосипед | bicycle |
| гонки | race |

1 What did Dolmatov win?
2 Where did it take place?
3 What can you learn about Yusupov?
4 What was the surname of the man who came third?
5 Where did the bicycle race take place?
6 Who won the bicycle race and what was his time?
7 Who were the runners-up and which towns did they come from?

---

### A situation to remember

**Passing on greetings and presents**
You have arrived in Russia on 9th May, a public holiday. Your Russian friends **Бо́ря**, **Ната́лья** and **Ви́ктор**, who are living in England, have asked you to pass on their best wishes to their friend **Ва́ня** and his family. They have also given you a large present to pass on (**переда́ть**). You phone **Ва́ня**. His wife **О́ля** answers. Relay the phone conversation.

# ● Playing with words

## Кроссворд

**Across**

1  С____ _____ ! First greeting of the year
10  What Russians sometimes say for *in*
11  She
12  Constrictor or neck-wear
13  **Евге́ний Оне́гин**, for example
15  Along the street _____ у́лице
17  **Апре́ль_____ию́нь**
18  **Не пра́вда ___** ?
19  Nets or networks: after 8, 9, 10 and 19 down you will untangle this one!
20  Sometimes about
21  Sometimes with **зоо-** , but usually not.
22  **Он купи́л пода́рок_____ 10 до́лларов.**
23  Russian Helen
25  С_____ _____!
30  **Покажи́те мне го́род на ка_____ !**
32  **Я о́чень люблю́ на́ши русск_____ блю́да!**
33  **Е́сли у вас нет де́нег, вы́пишите, пожа́луйста_____**
34  Fashion
35  Sometimes used for *and*
36  Moscow sports club
38  I told them = **Я _____ сказа́л**
39  Outside
40  An alternative to **электри́чество**
41  King Arthur had a round one
42  **Он мне пи́шет о _____** (short for 23)
43  A new place in the New World, and historic city
45  German name. Nothing to do with Turkey
48  Aspect or view
50  Three-horse sled
51  He
52  A Russian in Unit 16 thought Scots wore this
53  **В аэропорту́ мо́жно ви́деть _____**

**Down**

1  More emphatic than *a*
2  Clear soup – **буль_____**
3  _____ **нра́вится смотре́ть футбо́л?**
4  **Воло́дя _____** (my) **брат**
5  Gala
6  The place where you register
7  **От семи́ ___ восьми́ бюро́ закры́то**
8  **Пуччи́ни** might have written this
9  Not an obvious way of travelling
10  **В столи́це Ита́лии**
12  Cinderella went to one of these
14  An avenue or path in a park. Looks like an alley but isn't
15  Congratulations!
16  About Mr Chekhov
19  Shops may give this to encourage you to buy
21  **Целу́ю и обнима́ю! _____ приве́т ма́ме и па́пе**
24  **Споко́йной _____ !**
26  They are very kind = **Они́ о́чень _____**
27  **Они́ не брат и сестра́, а муж и _____**
28  Sheet music = __**ты**
29  Novel by Dostoevsky
31  Pupil but not of the eye
37  Somewhere Russians go to rest – **кур _____ р _____ .**
40  Hill or mountain
41  Juice
44  Strong spirit
46  **тот, ___ , то** = *that*
47  They are here!
49  What a Russian bride and groom will say
51  **___ Москвы́ до Ло́ндона бо́льше чем 2000 киломе́тров**

145

# WHAT YOU KNOW

## Greetings

| | | |
|---|---|---|
| доброе утро | добрый день | добрый вечер |
| Поздравляю вас | с Рождеством<br>с Новым годом | с днём рождения |
| Желаю вам | спокойной ночи | всего хорошего/доброго |
| С приветом | С уважением | |

## Verbs of going

Я ходил по магазинам.
Вчера я ходил в кино.
В прошлом году я ездил в Россию.

## KEY VOCABULARY

| | |
|---|---|
| весь, вся, всё, все | all |
| встречаться | to meet |
| день рождения | birthday |
| ездить | to go (by vehicle) |
| желать | to wish |
| милый -ая -ое | dear |
| муж | husband |
| передать | to pass on |
| праздник | holiday |
| прошлый: в прошлом году | last year |
| раньше | earlier, previously |
| Рождество | Christmas |
| сказать | to say |
| уважаемый | respected, dear (letters) |
| уважение | respect |
| ходить | to go (on foot) |
| часто | often |

**The Russian soul –
«Ру́сская душа́»**

**Getting medical
help**

**Parts of the body**

# Expressing feelings

## ● Life in Russia

### The Russian Soul – «Ру́сская душа́»

It often seems to Western observers that the behaviour and
emotions of Russians can be extreme. Extremes of sadness and
depression, extremes of excitement and joy, extremes of
tenderness and violence are all reflected in the works of Russian
authors. Some put this down to the climate, others to the
geography of the country and others to the Russian 'soul' –
**ру́сская душа́**. No doubt all of these play a part. The
atmosphere and air of futility in plays by Chekhov (**Че́хов**), the
introspection and suffering in Dostoyevsky (**Достое́вский**), the
physical involvement of Tolstoy (**Толсто́й**), the 'laughter through
tears' in Gogol (**Го́голь**), all give the work of these writers a
peculiarly 'Russian' flavour. The use of folk songs by composers,
particularly Glinka (**Гли́нка**) and Tchaikovsky (**Чайко́вский**),
also reflect Russian life, and it is this reflection of reality which has
been the constant feature of Russian creative art since the
beginning of the 19th century.

It is perhaps the Russians' love of realism that made Dickens and
Graham Greene two of their most popular English authors, and
Steinbeck and Hemingway are also widely read. On a lighter note,
Russians have long been devotees of Agatha Christie.

**147**

## Russian medical services

The Russian health service is under great pressure. It is underfunded and suffers from a lack of resources. Large state companies, who have now been privatised, can no longer afford to offer their employees in-house health facilities. Doctors are very poorly paid and many medicines are very expensive to buy and beyond the reach of ordinary Russians. You will see Russian chemist's shops (**аптéки**) specialising in foreign medicines with prices in dollars.

There are rapidly developing private medical facilities available for those with the money to pay the high fees. Russians have also learnt the art of providing an appropriate 'gift' to assist in seeing a doctor.

If you are ill in Russia, you may get privileged treatment as a foreigner if you go to the local health centre (**поликлúника**). Alternatively, you can use the private facilities, assuming that you have taken the precaution of buying health insurance (**страхóвка**). From a **поликлúника** you may be referred to a **больнúца** (hospital).

If you are ill, you will need to be able to answer some important questions:

**Как вы себя чýвствуете?**

*How are you?* (literally *How do you feel yourself?*)

**Я чýвствую себя плóхо.**

*I feel ill.* (literally *bad*)

You only use this phrase when inquiring about a person's health. The normal greetings are: **Как делá?** or **Как вы поживáете?**

**Что у вас болúт?**  *What is hurting you?*
**У меня болúт головá.**  *I have a headache.*
**У меня болúт живóт.**  *I have a pain in my stomach.*

If more than one part of the body hurts, use the form **боля́т**:

**У меня боля́т головá и живóт.**
*I have a headache and a pain in my stomach.*

Note that the Russian construction means literally *belonging to me hurts the head/stomach.* English has a variety of ways of indicating the pain.

....................................................

**EXERCISE 1**

Here are some complaints from a patient. Can you work out how an English speaker would express the complaint? Note that Russian has only one way of expressing this idea, English has several.

| | | |
|---|---|---|
| **1** | У меня болúт гóрло. | *throat* |
| **2** | У меня болúт рукá. | *arm* |
| **3** | У меня болúт нос. | *nose* |
| **4** | У меня болúт ногá. | *leg* |
| **5** | У меня болúт зуб. | *tooth* |

If your teeth are causing problems, you should go to a **зубнóй врач** (*dentist*).

You may also be concerned as to whether your temperature (**температýра**) is high (**высóкая**). You may want to tell the doctor how warm you feel:

**Мне хóлодно.**  *I feel cold.*
**Мне теплó.**  *I feel warm.*
**Мне жáрко.**  *I feel hot.*

You may fall ill (**заболéть**) with the flu (**грипп**) or simply a cold (**простýда**). You may get a prescription (**рецéпт**) for some medicine (**лекáрство**) or tablets (**таблéтки**).

The word for doctor is **врач**; **дóктор** is only used when addressing a doctor. In the following dialogue the **медпýнкт** (medical unit) tells the tourist that a **врач** will come. When he comes, the patient calls him **дóктор**.

## 📼 EXERCISE 2

Listen to the dialogue on your tape. It is about someone who falls ill in a hotel in Moscow. The hotel has its own **медпу́нкт**, and the lady at the service desk (**бюро́ обслу́живания**) is very helpful, as are the floor supervisor (**дежу́рная**) and the doctor (**врач**).

Answer the questions which follow.

*Тури́ст набира́ет но́мер*

*Па́уза*

– Бюро́ обслу́живания.
– Скажи́те, пожа́луйста, что мне де́лать? Мне ка́жется, я заболе́л.
– Даю́ вам медпу́нкт.

*Па́уза*

– Медпу́нкт.
– Я говорю́ из но́мера 345. Мне ка́жется, у меня́ высо́кая температу́ра. И о́чень боли́т го́рло.
– Так. Поня́тно. Что ещё?
– Голова́ то́же боли́т, но не о́чень.
– Так. Врач бу́дет у вас че́рез полчаса́. Я ду́маю, что э́то просту́да. Закажи́те че́рез дежу́рную чай с лимо́ном. Э́то иногда́ о́чень помога́ет.
– Спаси́бо.

*Че́рез пять мину́т. Дежу́рная прихо́дит.*

– Здра́вствуйте. Вот вам чай с лимо́ном.
– Спаси́бо.
– Заболе́ли, да? Врач сейча́с бу́дет. Пе́йте чай. Е́сли хоти́те что́-нибудь ещё, позвони́те.
– Спаси́бо большо́е.

*Врач прихо́дит.*

– Мо́жно?
– Пожа́луйста, входи́те.

*Врач вхо́дит в ко́мнату*

– Здра́вствуйте. Я уже́ зна́ю, что у вас боли́т го́рло.
– И голова́.
– А как аппети́т?
– Аппети́та совсе́м нет.
– Покажи́те, пожа́луйста го́рло. Скажи́те «А-а-а»

– А-а-а.
– Гм. Посмо́трим, кака́я у вас температу́ра. Вот термо́метр.

*Па́уза*

– Да, у вас есть температу́ра, но не о́чень высо́кая.
– Э́то грипп, до́ктор?
– Нет, просту́да. Я вам вы́пишу реце́пт. Принима́йте э́ти табле́тки три ра́за в день. Вы должны́ лежа́ть, отдыха́ть. За́втра я бу́ду у вас. Е́сли вам бу́дет ху́же, позвони́те опя́ть в медпу́нкт.

## New vocabulary

| | |
|---|---|
| поня́тно | *understood* |
| че́рез полчаса́ | *in half an hour* |
| че́рез | *through* |
| помога́ет | *helps* |
| что́ нибу́дь | *anything* |
| позвони́ть | *to ring* |
| отдыха́ть | *to relax* |
| опя́ть | *again* |

1  Who does the tourist ring first?
2  To whom is he referred?
3  What are his symptoms?
4  What does he do before the doctor comes?
5  What does the doctor do?
6  Does the tourist have a high temperature?
7  What is the treatment?

## EXERCISE 3

**Иван Петрович** wants to see a doctor and has been recommended to **Наталья Петровна Володина**. He rings up health centre № 23 to make an appointment, only to find she no longer works there. He is given the number of where they think she works. It takes quite a few phone calls to find her. Russian health centres are usually referred to by number and not name.

Listen to the tape and then fill in the table. The first one is done for you.

|   | поликлиника № | телефон |
|---|---|---|
| **1** | 22 | 298 66 38 |
| **2** |  |  |
| **3** |  |  |
| **4** |  |  |
| **5** |  |  |

Which health centre does Dr Volodina work in?

## ● Language information

### Expressing temperature and feelings

As we have seen earlier, when Russians say how hot or cold they are, they use the forms **Мне холодно** (*I'm cold*), **Мне тепло** (*I'm warm*), **Мне жарко** (*I'm hot*). They are saying literally *it is cold to me*. The phrase *to me* is translated by a dative case. These phrases are most commonly used with pronouns:

| я | I | dative | мне | мы | we | dative | нам |
|---|---|---|---|---|---|---|---|
| ты | you | dative | тебе | вы | you | dative | вам |
| он | he | dative | ему | они | they | dative | им |
| она | she | dative | ей |  |  |  |  |

They also use the same form to express a variety of feelings:

| Нам скучно. | *We are bored.* |
|---|---|
| Ему хорошо. | *He feels fine.* |
| Мне плохо. | *I feel ill.* |
| Ей стыдно. | *She is ashamed.* |

## EXERCISE 4

Put the numbers in the appropriate boxes. The first one is done for you.

| | | | |
|---|---|---|---|
| **1** | I'm hot | Мне холодно | 2 |
| **2** | I'm cold | Мне жарко | |
| **3** | I'm ashamed | Мне хорошо | |
| **4** | I feel worse | Мне лучше | |
| **5** | I'm ill | Мне плохо | |
| **6** | I'm bored | Мне тепло | |
| **7** | I feel good | Мне скучно | |
| **8** | I feel warm | Мне стыдно | |
| **9** | I feel better | Мне хуже | |

## EXERCISE 5

On the left you have some English sentences. Show how you would translate them into Russian by linking the words and phrases.

The first one is done for you.

| | | | |
|---|---|---|---|
| 1 | He feels good. | Мне | плóхо |
| 2 | You (fam.) feel hot. | Им | теплó |
| 3 | You feel warm. | Емý | жáрко |
| 4 | We feel ill. | Тебé | хýже |
| 5 | I feel cold. | Вам | скýчно |
| 6 | You are bored. | Нам | сты́дно |
| 7 | She feels better. | Емý | хорошó |
| 8 | He feels worse. | Вам | хóлодно |
| 9 | They are ashamed. | Ей | лýчше |

Notice that you can change these expressions into questions simply by adding a question mark. In speech you make your voice go up on the word you are questioning. Look at the line above the phrase: it indicates where to raise your voice.

Вам плóхо?

Russians often ask negative questions. The meaning is the same, it just sounds less aggressive.

Вам не плóхо?

## EXERCISE 6

Here are three pictures and three captions. Which caption goes with which picture?

1  Вам не жáрко?
2  Мне скýчно.
3  Ей хóлодно.

# Instructing, requesting, advising

Russian has a special form of the verb called the imperative which is used when giving people instructions, making requests and giving advice. The informal (**ты**) form ends in **-и** (or **-й** after a vowel); the formal (**вы**) form, which is also used when addressing more than one person, ends in **-ите** (or **-йте** after a vowel). It is formed from the present tense root. You have already seen some of these forms:

| | | |
|---|---|---|
| покажи́ | покажи́те | *show* |
| извини́ | извини́те | *excuse me* |
| прости́ | прости́те | *excuse me* |
| скажи́ | скажи́те | *tell me* |
| дай | да́йте | *give* |

The words **здра́вствуй** and **здра́вствуйте** (*hello*) originally were advice to 'be healthy'.

You may have noticed some of these forms in the dialogue in Exercise 2: the tourist is told to order (**закажи́те**) and a little later to drink (**пе́йте**) the tea. The tourist tells the doctor to come in (**входи́те**), who in turn tells the tourist to take (**принима́йте**) the tablets twice in the conversation. He is twice encouraged to ring (**позвони́те**) if there is a problem. You will also see examples of **скажи́те** and **покажи́те**.

a          b          c

If you wish to encourage a group of people to do something, you may use a form ending in **-ем**, **-ём** or **-им**. This is the same as the **мы** form of the future tense. In the dialogue the doctor says **посмо́трим** (*let's have a look*). In Unit 4 we saw the form **пойдём** (*let's go*).

You will also hear the forms **Пошли́!** and **Пое́хали!** when you are giving instructions to a group of people or to a bus driver to start moving. This is a colloquial idiom, which means literally *We have gone!* or *We have set off!*

## EXERCISE 7

Pick out a suitable imperative from those listed on the right and put its letter in the correct space. The first one is done for you.

| | | |
|---|---|---|
| **1** Рестора́н о́чень популя́рный. __*d*__ стол. | **a** | позвони́те |
| **2** Е́сли за́втра тебе́ бу́дет ху́же, _____ в медпу́нкт. | **b** | покажи́те |
| | **c** | пойдём |
| **3** _____ чай с лимо́ном. О́чень помога́ет. | **d** | закажи́те |
| **4** Я не люблю́ теа́тры. Лу́чше _____ в кино́. | **e** | пе́йте |
| | **f** | посмо́трим |
| **5** Сего́дня о́чень интере́сный фильм. _____ телеви́зор. | **g** | позвони́ |
| **6** _____ 235 43 67. Там живу́т Ива́н и Та́ня. | **h** | извини́те |
| **7** _____ , пожа́луйста, вы не зна́ете где здесь рестора́н? | **i** | откро́й |
| **8** Мне хо́лодно. _____ , пожа́луйста дверь. (*door*) | **j** | закро́йте |
| **9** Е́сли тебе́ жа́рко, _____ дверь. | | |
| **10** Не хочу́ э́ту кни́гу. _____ , пожа́луйста вот э́ту. | | |

## Should

Another way of giving advice is not to use the imperative form, but simply to tell someone what they ought to do. The doctor in the dialogue says **вы должны́ лежа́ть, отдыха́ть** (*you should lie down, relax*). **До́лжен** is an adjective, i.e. it changes according to the person it describes. Thus **должна́** is what you would use for a woman, and **должны́** for a plural.

## EXERCISE 8

See if you can direct the people via the right boxes. The first one is done for you.

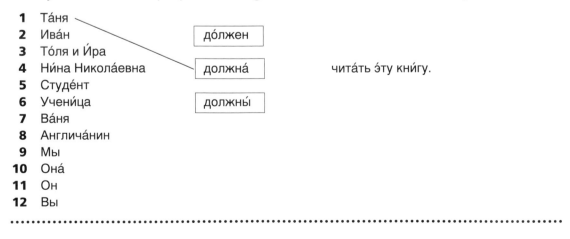

| | |
|---|---|
| **1** Та́ня | |
| **2** Ива́н | до́лжен |
| **3** То́ля и И́ра | |
| **4** Ни́на Никола́евна | должна́ читáть э́ту кни́гу. |
| **5** Студе́нт | |
| **6** Учени́ца | должны́ |
| **7** Ва́ня | |
| **8** Англича́нин | |
| **9** Мы | |
| **10** Она́ | |
| **11** Он | |
| **12** Вы | |

# ● Looking at words

## The root 'бол-'

We have already seen three words with this root:

**боли́т**      *to hurt* (part of the verb **боле́ть**)
**заболе́ть**   *to fall ill*: literally *to begin* (**за-**) *to be ill*
**больни́ца**   *hospital*

**боле́знь** means *an illness* and **он бо́лен, она́ больна́, вы больны́** are ways of saying that *he is ill, she is ill, you are ill*. **больно́й** is a male patient and **больна́я** a female patient.

## Parts of the body

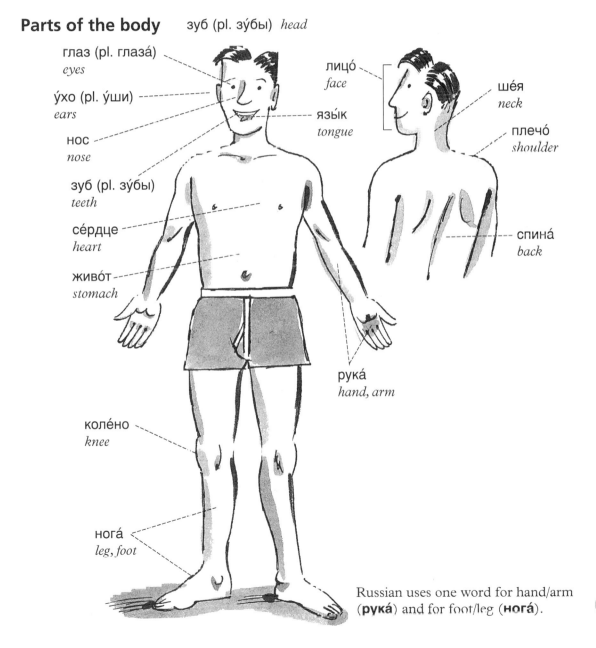

зуб (pl. зу́бы) *head*

глаз (pl. глаза́)
*eyes*

лицо́
*face*

ше́я
*neck*

у́хо (pl. у́ши)
*ears*

язы́к
*tongue*

плечо́
*shoulder*

нос
*nose*

зуб (pl. зу́бы)
*teeth*

се́рдце
*heart*

спина́
*back*

живо́т
*stomach*

рука́
*hand, arm*

коле́но
*knee*

нога́
*leg, foot*

Russian uses one word for hand/arm (**рука́**) and for foot/leg (**нога́**).

153

## A situation to remember

### Ringing a doctor
Devise a telephone conversation as follows:
Your friend is ill and you have to ring the health centre to try and get a doctor.
You are not sure what is wrong with her, but you think it might be something to do with her stomach. She has a pain in her stomach and one in her arm, as well as a headache.
At the moment she is lying down in her room in the hotel.
The person you speak to asks if she has had dinner.
You answer that she hasn't. She has had tea with lemon, but nothing else (**бо́льше ничего́**).

### Complaining
You have an ache or pain.
If you are working with another student, take it in turns to say what is wrong with you. Indicate the part of the body that hurts and say **У меня́ боли́т** _____ .
Your friend may be able to suggest a solution: ringing the doctor, lying down, resting, taking tablets, etc.

## WHAT YOU KNOW

### Expressing how you feel
| | |
|---|---|
| Мне | хо́лодно. |
| Вам, тебе́ | тепло́. |
| Нам | жа́рко. |
| Ему́ | ску́чно. |

| | |
|---|---|
| Как вы себя́ чу́вствуете? | Хорошо́. |
| | Пло́хо. |

### Something hurts
| | | |
|---|---|---|
| Что у вас боли́т? | У меня́ боли́т | зуб. |
| | | го́рло. |
| | | нога́. |

### Instructing, requesting, advising
Позвони́те за́втра.
Откро́йте рот.
Посмо́трим.

### Should
| | | | | | |
|---|---|---|---|---|---|
| он | я | ты | до́лжен | | |
| она́ | я | ты | должна́ | лежа́ть, | отдыха́ть |
| они́ | мы | вы | должны́ | | |

## KEY VOCABULARY
| | |
|---|---|
| боле́ть (боли́т) | to hurt |
| заболе́ть (perfective) | to fall ill |
| больни́ца | hospital |
| врач | doctor |
| высо́кий(-ая,-ое,-ие) | high; tall |
| дава́ть (даю́) | give (I give) |
| дежу́рная | woman on duty (floor supervisor) |
| душа́ | soul |
| набира́ть но́мер | to dial the number |
| пе́йте (from пить) | drink! |
| позвони́ть | to ring |
| поликли́ника | health centre |
| помога́ть | to help |
| посмо́трим | Let's have a look! |
| пошли́, пое́хали | Let's go! |
| принима́ть | to take |
| ску́чно | bored |
| сты́дно | ashamed |
| че́рез полчаса́ | in half an hour |
| чу́вствовать себя́ | to feel |

Russian flats

Finding your way
to a Russian home

Addressing a letter
to Russia

# Visiting a Russian home

## ● Life in Russia

### Russian flats

Most Russians live in small flats (**кварти́ры**) in large apartment blocks. Typical blocks of flats have five or nine storeys (**пятиэта́жный** or **девятиэта́жный дом**) and are often in new districts (**райо́ны**) that have been developed since the second world war. These **райо́ны** are full of tall blocks of flats that stretch as far as the eye can see.

They were built in response to a chronic housing shortage and vast numbers of Russians who were living in overcrowded flats in city centres were rehoused. Many of these city centre flats were communal (**коммуна́льные кварти́ры**), where each family lived in a single room, sharing kitchen and bathroom facilities with a number of other families. The numbers of these have been significantly reduced, if not totally eradicated.

This development was funded by state funds and under the old regime most Russians lived in **госуда́рственные кварти́ры** (*state flats*). Some were built by co-operatives (**кооперати́вы**). Rents were extremely low, as were charges for electricity, gas and telephones (**электри́чество, газ, телефо́н**). Central heating (**центра́льное отопле́ние**) was provided by a boiler, which supplied heating not just for a single apartment block but for a whole district.

Russian flats typically have a **гости́ная** (*living room*), **спа́льня** (*bedroom* – they may have one or two), **ку́хня** (*kitchen*), **ва́нная** (*bathroom*) and **туале́т** (*toilet*). The **гости́ная** will often double as a bedroom: the **дива́н** (*settee*) that you sit on may open out into someone's bed. They usually have double entrance doors and many Russians are installing steel doors for extra security. Flats are categorised by the number of rooms (excluding kitchen and bathroom) that they have. Russians will talk of **одноко́мнатная**, **двухко́мнатная**, **трёхко́мнатная кварти́ра** (*one, two, three room flat*).

Russians now have the opportunity to buy their own flats, which they can then sell on the open market. Flats in big cities, such as Moscow and St Petersburg, can fetch high prices. However, many Russians do not have the money to buy their flats and continue to rent them from the state for low rents.

On the right are some advertisements from a local Moscow paper. People not only want to buy and sell, they also want to let, rent and exchange flats and other property. Essential words to know are:

| | | | |
|---|---|---|---|
| покупа́ть/купи́ть | *to buy* | Куплю́ | *I will buy* |
| продава́ть/прода́ть | *to sell* | Продаю́ | *I am selling* |
| снима́ть/снять | *to rent, hire* | Снима́ем | *We are renting* |
| | | Сни́мем | *We will rent* |
| сдава́ть/сдать | *to rent out* | | |
| меня́ть на | *to exchange for* | Меня́ю | *I exchange* |
| с допла́той | *with extra payment* | | |

**EXERCISE 1**

Read the advertisements and give the phone number or numbers to ring if you want to do the following:

**1** buy a flat near a metro station.
**2** rent out your flat in the centre of Moscow.
**3** rent an office.
**4** exchange a room for a flat, with extra payment.
**5** exchange a one room flat for a larger one, with extra payment.
**6** buy a room.
**7** buy a plot of land in the country to grow your own vegetables.

········································

## Russian addresses

Here are some typical Russian addresses:

Садо́вая у́лица, д. 25, корп. 2, кв.137
Не́вский проспе́кт, д. 236, кв. 343
Можа́йское шоссе́, д. 367, корп. 1, кв 423
Боя́рский переу́лок, д. 53, кв. 98

Abbreviations: **д. (дом)**, **корп. (ко́рпус)**, **кв. (кварти́ра)**.

**Дом** gives you the number of the building, or complex of buildings. Each building can be quite large and you may have to walk further than you think to find your **дом**. If **дом** refers to more than one apartment block, you will be given the block (**ко́рпус**) number. Finally, you will need the flat number. Sometimes addresses are written in an abbreviated form. The first address on our list could be written **Садо́вая у́лица, 25 - 2 - 137**.

**Проспе́кт** is a main street in a town. **У́лица** is an ordinary street. **Переу́лок** is a side street. **Шоссе́** is a main road leading out of town. The name of the **шоссе́** shows you the direction: in our example it leads to the small town of **Можа́йск**, on the Moscow River, near to the site of the Battle of Borodino, where Napoleon defeated the Russian armies in 1812.

You will need to know on which floor (**эта́ж**) someone lives. The question to ask is:

На како́м этаже́ вы живёте?
*What floor do you live on?*

Be careful: Russians start counting floors from the ground, which they call the 'first'. The Russian **второ́й эта́ж** is our first floor, etc. The answers you can expect are:

| | |
|---|---|
| на пе́рвом этаже́ | *on the ground floor* |
| на второ́м этаже́ | *on the first floor* |
| на тре́тьем этаже́ | *on the second floor* |
| на четвёртом этаже́ | *on the third floor* |

The entrance to Russian flats is not normally directly from the street. You usually have to find the entrance into a **двор** and from there find the appropriate **подъе́зд** (*entrance*). To go into many of these **подъе́зды** you have to tap in a code (**код**) to release the door lock.

## Addressing an envelope

Russians write the address (**а́дрес**) in the reverse order, compared with English. You start with the country (**страна́**), if outside Russia, then the town (**го́род**). This is followed by the street. Finally you write the person.

157

Most Russian envelopes are pre-printed with sections labelled **Куда́** (*where to*), **Кому́** (*who to*), and a section on the right to insert the **и́ндекс** (*post code*). There is a space under the address for the **и́ндекс и а́дрес отправи́теля** (*sender*). There will also be a drawing as decoration. In the sample on page 157, it shows Russians' love of mushrooms. There are even dotted lines drawn to help you write the six figures of a Russian **и́ндекс** in the correct way with detailed instructions on the reverse of the envelope.

В н и м а н и е !
Образец написания цифр индекса:

## EXERCISE 2

No doubt, when you return home, you will want to write a letter to your host family. Here is another Russian envelope, this time with a picture of a church. Address it to the family you were staying with. Use one of the addresses given on page 157.

## ● Language information

### Future tense

You have already seen one way of talking about the future:

Я бу́ду жить в Москве́.
*I will live in Moscow.*

This is the *imperfective* future: you are saying that you *will be living* in Moscow. Very often you need to talk about doing something that will be complete in the future. You do this by taking the perfective verb and using forms that look like the present tense. Compare the following two sentences:

**Imperfective, present**
Сейча́с мы **е́дем** в Москву́.
*We are now going to Moscow.*

**Perfective future**
За́втра мы **пое́дем** в Москву́.
*Tomorrow we will go to Moscow.*

You saw some examples of the future tense in the advertisements in Exercise 1:

Куплю́      *I will buy*
Сни́мем    *We will rent*

### Approximate time

Приду́ часо́в в пять.
*I will come at about five o'clock.*
На́до идти́ мину́т де́сять.
*You have to walk for about ten minutes.*

If Russians want to say that you are coming at *about* five o'clock or that something will take *about* ten minutes, they simply put the number after the noun.

## 📼 EXERCISE 3

Sarah is visiting St Petersburg for the first time. She has been invited to go and see a Russian friend, **Воло́дя**, who she has known for a number of years. This is how she makes the arrangements to go and visit him. Listen to the phone conversation and answer the questions that follow.

Са́ра:  (*набира́ет но́мер*) Девятьсо́т два́дцать семь во́семьдесят четы́ре ноль три. До́брое у́тро!

Воло́дя:  Алло́!

Са́ра:  Алло́! Воло́дя? Э́то Са́ра.

Воло́дя:  А Са́ра! Ты прие́дешь к нам сего́дня ве́чером, да? Ната́ша пригото́вит нам вку́сный украи́нский борщ. Мы вы́пьем рю́мку во́дки и поговори́м. Ты здесь надо́лго? Мо́жет быть пое́дем вме́сте в Но́вгород? Я куплю́ биле́ты в теа́тр. Ты лю́бишь бале́т?

Са́ра:  Так, сего́дня ве́чером я к тебе́ пое́ду. Мы всё реши́м тогда́. В кото́ром часу́ мне прие́хать?

Воло́дя:  Часо́в в семь. Ты зна́ешь наш а́дрес?

Са́ра:  Зна́ю. Балка́нская у́лица, дом пятьдеся́т два, кварти́ра но́мер де́вять. А как туда́ дое́хать? Э́то далеко́ от це́нтра?

### New vocabulary

| | |
|---|---|
| к + dative | *to (see)* |
| гото́вить/пригото́вить | *to cook* |
| рю́мка | *glass (small)* |
| говори́ть/поговори́ть | *to have a talk* |
| надо́лго | *for a long time* |
| реша́ть/реши́ть | *to decide* |
| тогда́ | *then, at that time* |
| в кото́ром часу́ | *At what time* |

1  What is Volodya's phone number?
2  What are they going to eat?
3  Who will do the cooking?
4  What are they going to drink?
5  What suggestions has Volodya got to entertain Sarah?
6  At about what time is she expected?

## 📼 EXERCISE 4

Listen to a bit more of the conversation between Sarah and **Воло́дя** and answer the questions which follow.

Воло́дя:  К сожале́нию, мы живём далеко́ от це́нтра, в но́вом райо́не. А где ты живёшь?

Са́ра:  В гости́нице «На Садо́вой». Мой телефо́н три́ста девятна́дцать девяно́сто шесть девяно́сто оди́н.

Воло́дя:  Э́то где? На Садо́вой у́лице?

Са́ра:  Да, да. О́чень удо́бно. Ме́тров пятьсо́т от метро́.

Воло́дя:  Зна́ю. Лу́чше е́хать на метро́. Там две ста́нции: Садо́вая и Сенна́я пло́щадь. Тебе́ нужна́ ста́нция Сенна́я пло́щадь. На́до е́хать до коне́чной ста́нции Ку́пчино.

Са́ра:  Без переса́дки?

Воло́дя:  Без переса́дки. Э́то мину́т два́дцать, два́дцать пять.

Са́ра:  От метро́ мо́жно пешко́м?

Воло́дя:  Мо́жно. Ты идёшь пря́мо, ми́мо остано́вки тролле́йбуса и трамва́я. Пото́м ты свернёшь напра́во: э́то уже́ Балка́нская у́лица. О́коло метро́ там дом двадца́тый и́ли два́дцать второ́й. А наш дом пятьдеся́т второ́й. Та́кже мо́жно сесть на тролле́йбус. От метро́ идёт тролле́йбус но́мер семь.

Са́ра:  Ско́лько остано́вок до твоего́ до́ма?

Воло́дя:  Три. Договори́лись?

Са́ра:  Договори́лись.

Воло́дя:  До ве́чера.

Са́ра:  До ве́чера.

### New vocabulary

| | |
|---|---|
| удо́бный | *convenient* |
| коне́чный | *last* |
| ми́мо | *past* |
| свора́чивать/сверну́ть | *to turn off* |
| договори́лись | *agreed* |

1  Where is Sarah staying?
2  What is her telephone number?
3  What is the simplest way to get to Volodya's flat?
4  Does she have to change trains?
5  How long does it take on the underground?

## 🔊 EXERCISE 5

We now rejoin Sarah. She has found her friend's flat, rings the doorbell (**звони́т в дверь**), the door opens ...

Воло́дя: Входи́, входи́. Снима́й пальто́ и проходи́ в гости́ную.

Са́ра: Я та́кже сниму́ ту́фли.

Воло́дя: Не на́до. Ты наш гость.

Са́ра: На́до. На у́лице идёт дождь.

Воло́дя: Вот тебе́ та́почки. Проходи́ в гости́ную.

Са́ра: Я купи́ла тебе́ пода́рок из А́нглии, нет, не из А́нглии, из Шотла́ндии. Вот, пожа́луйста.

Воло́дя: А что э́то? Зна́ю. Спаси́бо, Са́ра, э́то моё люби́мое ви́ски. Ну проходи́, проходи́.

Са́ра: А где Ната́ша?

Воло́дя: Она́ ещё гото́вит: она́ ско́ро придёт. Сади́сь.

Са́ра: Ско́лько у тебя́ книг! Э́то не гости́ная, а библиоте́ка!

Воло́дя: Я предлага́ю тост за твой прие́зд, за твоего́ му́жа, за твои́х бра́тьев, за твои́х сестёр, за всех мои́х шотла́ндских и америка́нских друзе́й ...

Са́ра: Хва́тит! Дава́й вы́пьем за тебя́, за Воло́дю и за на́шу хозя́йку Ната́шу! Но где она́?

### New vocabulary

| | |
|---|---|
| снима́ть/снять (сниму́) | to take off (clothes) |
| проходи́ть | to go through |
| ту́фли | shoes |
| люби́мый | favourite |
| предлага́ть тост | to propose a toast |
| хва́тит | enough |

1  We looked at imperatives in Unit 18. How many you can find in this dialogue, including repeats?
2  Why does Sarah insist on taking off her shoes?
3  Where is Natasha?
4  What is Sarah's first impression of Volodya's living room?
5  Who does Volodya propose a toast to?
6  Who does Sarah want to drink to?

## Toasts

The Russian construction is:

| | |
|---|---|
| Предлага́ю тост за ... | *I propose a toast to ...* |
| Дава́й(те) вы́пьем за ... | *Let us drink to ...* |

The word **за** (*to, for*) is followed by the accusative case, which for nouns denoting human beings is often identical to the genitive case. Only feminine nouns in the singular have their own form. Here are some examples:

за моего́ бра́та
за мою́ сестру́
за госте́й
за ва́ше (твоё) здоро́вье

Look at Volodya's toasts at the end of the previous conversation for some more examples.

### EXERCISE 6

You are being entertained by some Russian friends, who have already raised their glasses several times to toast you and all their friends in Britain. Now it is your turn to propose a toast. Here are some suggested toasts: you may need them all during the course of the evening! Translate them into Russian.

1  to my Russian friends
2  to Vanya
3  to Sasha
4  to your health
5  to the hostess
6  to happiness
7  to your birthday

# ● Looking at words

## Saying goodbye

Instead of saying **«До свида́ния»** Russians will often use a more specific phrase consisting of **до** and a time word in the genitive case. The conversation for Exercise 5 ends with **до ве́чера** (*till the evening*). A common phrase is **до встре́чи** (*until we meet;* literally *until a meeting*).

### EXERCISE 7

Here are some more examples of phrases which finish conversations. Work out for each one when the speakers hope to meet again.

1 до за́втра
2 до суббо́ты
3 до Рождества́
4 до Па́схи
5 до утра́
6 до Но́вого го́да
7 до сроды́

## Agreeing

If you make an arrangement, Russians usually conclude the discussion with the word **Договори́лись!** (literally *we have agreed*). The other person repeats this to confirm the arrangement. **Воло́дя** and Sarah do this when making the arrangements for her to visit.

## Friends

The standard word for a friend is **друг**. It has a special plural form **друзья́**. If you are referring to a female friend, Russians use **подру́га** instead.

---

### *A situation to remember*

#### Lost in St Petersburg
Actually Sarah got lost! She turned the wrong way out of the underground. Look at the map of the area and you will see where she is. Devise a conversation between Sarah and a passer-by and get some directions to Volodya and Natasha's flat.

#### Giving directions
Volodya has decided to visit Britain once again.
He has arranged to come and see you.
Find out where he is living.
Tell him where you live.
Explain that he has to go by bus.
Tell him how many stops.
Describe your house – is it big, small?
Is it a bungalow? (**одноэта́жный дом**)
How many storeys does it have?
(**двухэта́жный/трёхэта́жный дом ...**)
How long will it take him?

---

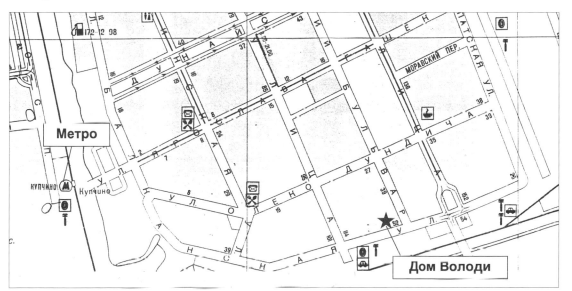

## WHAT YOU KNOW

**Talking about the future**
Я пое́ду в Москву́.
Я куплю́ кварти́ру.
Я бу́ду жить в Москве́.

**Approximate time**
Приду́ часа́ в два.
Вы идёте мину́т пять.

**Drinking people's health**
Предлага́ю тост за на́шего дру́га!
Дава́йте вы́пьем за ва́ше здоро́вье!

**Agreeing and saying goodbye**
Договори́лись!
До за́втра!
До встре́чи!


## KEY VOCABULARY

| | |
|---|---|
| в кото́ром часу́ | at what time |
| ва́нная | bathroom |
| гости́ная | living room |
| гото́вить/пригото́вить | to cook |
| дива́н | settee |
| дом: пятиэта́жный дом | five-storeyed building |
| друг (pl. друзья́) | friend |
| ко́рпус | block |
| кварти́ра: | |
| двухко́мнатная кварти́ра | two-roomed flat |
| меня́ть (на) | to exchange for |
| покупа́ть/купи́ть | to buy |
| продава́ть/прода́ть | to sell |
| сдава́ть/сдать | to rent out |
| ско́ро | soon |
| снима́ть/снять | to let (flat); take off (clothes) |
| спа́льня | bedroom |
| ту́фли | shoes |
| Хва́тит! | Enough! |
| эта́ж: на пе́рвом этаже́ | on the ground floor |

# Revision

Moscow v
St Petersburg

Revision exercises

Peter and Paul Fortress,
St Petersburg

Leningrad station, Moscow

## ● Life in Russia

### Moscow or St Petersburg

Rivalry between St Petersburg and Moscow has existed since the
former was founded as the Russian capital (**столи́ца**), and
intensified when it lost that status at the start of the Soviet state.
Inhabitants of St Petersburg will tell you that it is the Northern
Capital (**се́верная столи́ца**) of Russia. Certainly it rivals, many
would say surpasses, Moscow in the excellence and beauty of its
historic buildings, and the atmosphere is quite different. Moscow
is, of course, much older than St Petersburg, and because it was
formed by the gradual amalgamation of villages (**дере́вни**), it has
evolved in a less organised way. St Petersburg was built more on a
grid system typical of Western architecture of the early 18th century.

Hermitage, St Petersburg

Moscow Kremlin

**163**

Although the patchwork effect of the succeeding styles can still be seen in Moscow, particularly in collections of buildings such as the Kremlin, one has to go to the area around Moscow (**Подмоско́вье**) to see the beautiful wooden houses (**и́збы**) which used to be the typical Russian homes. During the Soviet period there was a conscious attempt, partly for propaganda reasons, to replace all wooden houses with blocks of flats (**жилы́е дома́**). Many other tall buildings (**высо́тные зда́ния**) were built during the Stalin era, including the university and several ministries (**министе́рства**).

## ● Language information

You have met all the cases of nouns in the singular, and most of them in the plural. Here are some of the plurals you have met up to now.

**Nominative case**
грибы́, тури́сты, но́вости, заку́ски, но́чи, поезда́

**Genitive** (*of*) **case**
теа́тров, музе́ев, мину́т, зда́ний

**Dative** (*to* or *for*) **case**
к друзья́м, по у́лицам

**Instrumental** (*by* or *with*) **case**
с гриба́ми, с де́вушками

**Prepositional case**
на лы́жах, на конька́х

The endings of the accusative case are identical to the nominative case (if the nouns refer to inanimate objects) or to the genitive case (if they refer to people or animals).

As you will see, there is a variety of endings in the nominative and genitive. The dative, instrumental and prepositional are always **-ам -ами -ах** or **-ям -ями -ях**.

Adjectives are even simpler! They are the same for all three genders in the plural. In the dative, instrumental and prepositional they have **-ым -ыми -ых** (or **-им -ими -их**): **интере́сным кни́гам** (*interesting books*), **интере́сными кни́гами**, **(в) интере́сных кни́гах**; **ру́сским маши́нам** (*Russian cars*), **ру́сскими маши́нами**, **(о) ру́сских маши́нах**. In the nominative they have **-ые (-ие)**: **интере́сные кни́ги**, **ру́сские маши́ны** and the genitive **-ых (-их)**: **интере́сных кни́г**, **ру́сских маши́н**. Once again, the accusative is like the nominative or genitive case.

## EXERCISE 1

Read the following passage: a letter from two Russian visitors to London written to their children back home in Moscow. Answer the questions which follow.

1 Underline the plural nouns, adjectives and pronouns in the passage.
2 Which city was having the better weather: Moscow or London?
3 Why were they surprised to see a play in English?
4 After the theatre where did they go?
5 Why didn't they eat in a typical British restaurant?
6 What other special features did dad mention?

---

Дороги́е мой!

Вот мы с ма́мой в Ло́ндоне! Здесь о́чень интере́сно, но пого́да не така́я хоро́шая, как у вас в Москве́. Мы бы́ли во мно́гих интере́сных места́х. Здесь о́чень мно́го хоро́ших теа́тров. Вчера́ мы смотре́ли пье́су «Дя́дя Ва́ня» — по-англи́йски! Актёры о́чень хорошо́ игра́ли. Пото́м мы пошли́ в кита́йский рестора́н. Я съел суп из кра́бов, а пото́м креве́тки с гриба́ми и с ри́сом. Все там пи́ли кита́йский чай. Ма́ме там бы́ло хорошо́, а мне не́ бы́ло. Я люблю́ на́ши ру́сские блю́да! Хоте́ли пообе́дать в типи́чном англи́йском рестора́не, но ка́жется, здесь все рестора́ны и́ли кита́йские, и́ли францу́зские, и́ли италья́нские!

Авто́бусы здесь кра́сные, двухэта́жные, и их о́чень мно́го. Здесь о́чень мно́го такси́. Они́ больши́е, чёрные.

Ну, нам пора́! Бу́дьте здоро́вы!
Целу́ем!
Па́па и ма́ма.

---

## ● Revision exercises

### EXERCISE 2

The inhabitants of St Petersburg and those of Moscow usually disagree about which is the better city. Here is a conversation in which this is apparent.
Eleven words have been missed out.
At the end of the passage you will find these eleven words – but not in the correct order.
Fill each space with the correct word from the box below.

A: Мне ка́жется, что в Санкт-Петербу́рге жить о́чень прия́тно. У́лицы у нас широ́кие, зда́ния краси́вые.

B: Пра́вда, но в Москве́ то́же хорошо́.

A: Да, здесь хорошо́, но в Санкт-Петербу́рге [1]лу́чше. Там краси́выс дворцы́ ...

B: В Москве́ дворцы́ то́же [2]_____ . Мне о́чень [3]_____ жить в Москве́. Москва́ [4]_____ Росси́и.

A: Коне́чно, Москва́ хоро́ший го́род, а я о́чень [5]_____ Санкт-Петербу́рг.

B: Я то́же. Но в Москве́ [6]_____ теа́тров, [7]_____ кинотеа́тров, [8]_____ рестора́нов.

A: Пра́вда, у нас [9]_____ рестора́нов, но они́ не [10]_____ чем моско́вские рестора́ны. Как тебе́ ка́жется?

B: Я [11]_____ , что ты бо́льше лю́бишь Санкт-Петербу́рг, а я Москву́. Вот и всё!

| столи́ца | ме́ньше | бо́льше |
|---|---|---|
| ху́же | краси́вые | нра́вится |
| лу́чше | бо́льше | люблю́ |
| ду́маю | бо́льшс | |

## EXERCISE 3

When you have completed Exercise 2 and corrected your responses, answer the following questions in English.

**1** Where does the conversation take place?
**2** Which person speaks first?
**3** Why does the person from St Petersburg think her city is better?
**4** What does she say about the restaurants in St Petersburg?

## EXERCISE 4

If you go to Russia, you are bound to have to fill in forms. At the airport you will have to fill in a customs declaration form; in a hotel you will have to fill in another one when you register, and you will have to fill in yet another at **ОВИР**. Here is a typical form (**анке́та**):

```
            А Н К Е Т А

Фамилия  4 . . . . . . . . . .   Имя . . . . . . . . . . . Отчество . . . . . . . . . . .

Дата рождения . . . . . . . . . . . . . .   Место рождения . . . . . . . . . . . . .

Адрес . . . . . . . . . . . . . . . . . . . . . . . . . . . . . . . . . . . . . . . . . . . . . . . .

. . . . . . . . . . . . . . . . . . . . . . . . . . . . . . . . . . . . . . . . . . . . . . . . . . . . .

Имя отца . . . . . . . . . . . Отчество отца . . . . . . . . . . . . . . . . . . . .

Национальность . . . . . . . . . . . . . . . . . . . . . . . . . . . . . . . . . . .

Профессия . . . . . . . . . . . . . . . . . . . . . . . . . . . . . . . . . . . . . . . . .
```

Here are some answers, all jumbled up. Insert the number against each one in the appropriate place. The first one is done for you.

**1** ул. Чайко́вского 5 кв. 18
**2** Ники́та
**3** Москва́
**4** Су́слова
**5** Ники́тична
**6** А́нна
**7** Петро́вич
**8** студе́нтка
**9** 16-ое апре́ля, 1974 го́да
**10** ру́сская

Now you try to fill in the form, giving your own details.

## EXERCISE 5  Greeting people

Look at the list of greetings and place the number of the appropriate picture in the box.

С Но́вым го́дом! ☐

С днём рожде́ния! ☐

С пра́здником! ☐

Прия́тного аппети́та! ☐

Поздравля́ю! ☐

Fill in the greetings in the sentences below. You should be able to
work them out from the context.

**1** В де́вять часо́в я пошёл в бюро́.

«_____ _____» сказа́л дире́ктор.

«_____ , Ива́н Серге́евич, как вы

_____?»

**2** В рестора́не.

– Вот ваш бифште́кс.

– Спаси́бо.

– _____ _____ !

– _____

**3** –До свида́ния, и _____ до́брого!

– _____ _____

**4** – Уже́ по́здно. Тебе́ пора́ (*time
to*) спать.

– _____ _____

---

## EXERCISE 7  Feeling well and feeling ill
Choose the appropriate alternative.

**1** Ива́н бо́лен. Он чу́вствует себя́  
    хорошо́.  
    сты́дно.  
    пло́хо.

**2** Ни́на больна́. У  
  него́  
  вас  боли́т го́рло.  
  неё

**3** Закро́йте окно́. Мне здесь о́чень  
    хо́лодно.  
    жа́рко.  
    тепло́.

**4** Врач вы́писал мне реце́пт, и я пошёл в  
    медпу́нкт.  
    магази́н.  
    апте́ку.

**5** В апте́ке мне да́ли  
    во́ду.  
    лека́рство.  
    температу́ру.

## EXERCISE 8

Ivan is arranging (**организу́ет**) a birthday party for his sister and wants to order some drink. He rings up a big supermarket he has seen advertising an 'order by phone' service in the paper. He hopes to get a discount (**ски́дка**) or something free (**беспла́тно**) if he orders a lot.

Recorded on your cassette is a conversation between Ivan and a shop assistant. Listen carefully to your cassette and then answer the questions. Try to answer in Russian.

Ива́н: Алло́, э́то магази́н «Арба́т»?

Де́вушка: Да, Арба́т.

Ива́н: В суббо́ту организу́ем вечери́нку для сестры́ – э́то её день рожде́ния. Хочу́ заказа́ть вино́ и во́дку.

Де́вушка: Хорошо́. Како́е вино́ вы хоти́те? У нас сто ви́дов. Вы хоти́те францу́зское и́ли неме́цкое?

Ива́н: Мне пожа́луйста хоро́шее францу́зское кра́сное вино́.

Де́вушка: Рекоменду́ю Кот ду Рон. Отли́чное вино́.

Ива́н: А ско́лько сто́ит буты́лка?

Де́вушка: Де́сять до́лларов. Ско́лько буты́лок вы хоти́те?

Ива́н: Шесть. Вы дади́те мне ски́дку за шесть буты́лок?

Де́вушка: Нет, мы даём ски́дку то́лько за двена́дцать. Вы полу́чите одну́ буты́лку беспла́тно.

Ива́н: Ла́дно, возьму́ двена́дцать буты́лок. А скажи́те, кака́я у вас есть во́дка?

Де́вушка: У нас есть Столи́чная, Сиби́рская и та́кже и́мпортная во́дка.

Ива́н: Мне, пожа́луйста, и́мпортную. «Смирно́в» есть?

Де́вушка: Есть. Де́вять до́лларов за буты́лку. Ско́лько вам?

Ива́н: Возьму́ пять. Я прие́ду в пя́тницу в оди́ннадцать утра́. Ла́дно?

Де́вушка: Ла́дно. До пя́тницы. До свида́ния.

1 Почему́ Ива́н организу́ет ве́чер?
2 Что он хо́чет заказа́ть?
3 Ско́лько ви́дов вин в магази́не?
4 Како́е вино́ де́вушка рекоменду́ет?
5 Ско́лько сто́ит вино́?
6 Ско́лько буты́лок зака́зывает? Почему́?
7 Кака́я во́дка у них есть?
8 Кака́я во́дка бо́льше нра́вится Ива́ну?
9 Ско́лько сто́ит буты́лка э́той во́дки?
10 Когда́ Ива́н прие́дет в магази́н?

## LANGUAGE REVIEW

Here is a list of words and constructions that you have met in the previous five units. If you do not know what they mean, you need to look back at the unit given on the right.

| | |
|---|---|
| Я сиде́л до́ма и чита́л газе́ту. | 16 |
| Я прочита́л газе́ту и пошёл в го́род. | 16 |
| Ка́ждый день я чита́л газе́ту. | 16 |
| Москва́ бо́льше, чем Санкт-Петербу́рг. | 16 |
| Мне бо́льше нра́вится Санкт-Петербу́рг. | 16 |
| Он согла́сен. Она́ согла́сна. | 16 |
| Поздравля́ю вас с Но́вым го́дом! | 17 |
| Жела́ю вам больши́х успе́хов! | 17 |
| Я ходи́л по магази́нам. | 17 |
| В про́шлом году́ я е́здил в Росси́ю. | 17 |
| всё у́тро, весь день, всю ночь | 17 |
| Нам ску́чно. Ему́ хорошо́. Мне жа́рко. | 18 |
| Покажи́те кни́гу! Принима́йте табле́тки! | |
| Позвони́ за́втра! | 18 |
| Та́ня должна́ чита́ть э́ту кни́гу. | 18 |
| Сейча́с мы е́дем в Москву́. За́втра мы пое́дем в Москву́. | 19 |
| Приду́ часо́в в пять. | 19 |
| Предлага́ю тост за моего́ бра́та. | 19 |

# Alphabet: transliteration and pronunciation guide

| Russian | | | |
|---|---|---|---|
| **Capital** | **Small** | **Transliteration** | **Approximate pronunciation (when different or unexpected)** |
| А | а | A | |
| Б | б | B | |
| В | в | V | |
| Г | г | G | 'v' when between two vowels as in -ero, -oro |
| Д | д | D | |
| Е | е | YE★ | 'ye' as in *yet* |
| Ё | ё | YO★★ | |
| Ж | ж | ZH | like 's' in *pleasure* |
| З | з | Z | |
| И | и | I | like 'ee' in *sweet* |
| Й | й | I or Y | like 'y' in *boy* |
| К | к | K | |
| Л | л | L | |
| М | м | M | |
| Н | н | N | |
| О | о | O | |
| П | п | P | |
| Р | р | R | rolled (Scottish) |
| С | с | S | |
| Т | т | T | |
| У | у | U | 'oo' in *boot* |
| Ф | ф | F | |
| Х | х | KH | 'h' but hard, like Scottish *loch* |
| Ц | ц | TS | |
| Ч | ч | CH | but occasionally 'sh' as in что |
| Ш | ш | SH | |
| Щ | щ | SHCH | |
| Ъ | ъ | hard sign★★★ | |
| Ы | ы | Y | like 'y' in *physio* |
| Ь | ь | soft sign★★★ | |
| Э | э | E | 'e' in *Edward* |
| Ю | ю | YU | |
| Я | я | YA | |

★ Initially and after vowels except y, otherwise E
★★ In all positions except after ч and щ, when o is used.
★★★ May be written ' or omitted.

This is not, strictly speaking, a guide to pronouncing Russian, although it may be used as an approximate guide. If you do use it this way, you should take care not to change the sounds in an English way. For example, an English speaker might be tempted to pronounce the Russian word KOSMOS as if it had a 'z' where the first 's' is. A nearer approximation to the Russian might be given by representing the word as 'KOSSMOSS'. There are many other examples of this sort of thing.

You should always try to get your pronunciation as near to the Russian as you can by imitating the sound you hear on the recording. Train yourself to listen without looking at the text, and pay particular attention to the stress, indicated with an accent in the transcriptions. The sound under the stress always carries its full value, but vowels in other positions often sound very different from what you would expect, e.g. the 'o' sounds in **хорошо**. If the transcription system produces a misleading pronunciation, an alternative is given in brackets. Note that KH is the transcription for the Russian **x** and ZH for the Russian **ж**.

## Approximate pronunciation guide for alphabet Units 1–5

### Unit 1

1 KOMÉTA (KOMYÉTA)
2 APPARÁT
3 SAMOVÁR
4 KÁSSA
5 TEÁTR
6 ÁTOM
7 METRÓ
8 ÓPERA
9 SPORT
10 PARK
11 TAKSÍ
12 PIANÍST
13 VINÓ
14 MOSKVÁ
15 RESTORÁN
16 ORKÉSTR
17 ÁVIA
18 MÁRKA
19 NET (NYET)
20 STOP
21 PÁSPORT

## Unit 2

**1** VODÁ
**2** VÓDKA
**3** LIMONÁD
**4** LITR
**5** KILÓ
**6** KILOMÉTR
**7** UNIVERSITÉT
**8** KÓKA-KÓLA
**9** PÉPSI
**10** PRÁVDA
**11** KROKODÍL
**12** KAVKÁZ
**13** ZOOPÁRK
(ZO-OPÁRK)
**14** DOM
**15** DÁTA
**16** KVAS
**17** APTÉKA
**18** MARS
**19** KIÓSK
**20** TOLSTÓY
**21** VOYNÁ I MIR
**22** ROSSÍYSKY
**23** UKRAÍNA
(UKRAÉENA)
**24** ZDRÁVSTVUYTE
(ZDRÁSTVUYTE)

## Unit 3

**1** FUTBÓL
**2** KLUB
**3** VKHOD
**4** KOSTYÚM
**5** MENYÚ
**6** PEREKHÓD
**7** TELEFÓN
**8** BULÓN (BULYÓN)
**9** KAFÉ
**10** BYURÓ
**11** FÓTO
**12** KREML'
**13** FIL'M
**14** YÚMOR
**15** AVTÓBUS
**16** BUFÉT
**17** UZBÉK
**19** DINÁMO
**20** STADIÓN
**21** SPARTÁK
**22** TORPÉDO
**23** LOKOMOTÍV
**24** REMÓNT
**25** ADMINISTRÁTOR
**26** KHOKKÉY
**18** KLÍMAT
**27** KINÓ

## Unit 4

**1** GÓROD
**2** TELEGRÁMMA
**3** GOD
**4** TURÍSTY
**5** AEROFLÓT
**6** SAMOLYÓT
**7** EKSKÚRSIYA
**8** IZVÉSTIYA
**9** GAZÉTA (GAZYÉTA)
**10** ROSSÍYA
**11** GUM
**12** EKSPRÉSS
**13** ENÉRGIYA
**14** PROGRÁMMA
**15** VÝKHOD
**16** VYKHODÍT'
**17** GRIBÝ
**18** ÓL'GA
**19** MAY
(like English 'my')
**20** NEDÉLYA
**21** RYAD
**22** BLANK
**23** EM-GE-Ú (EM GE ÓO)
**24** MÉSTO (MYÉSTO)

## Unit 5

**1** CHÉKHOV
**2** CHÁIKA
**3** MASHÍNA
**4** ELEKTRÍCHESTVO
**5** INFORMÁTSIYA
**6** BIFSHTÉKS
**7** SHASHLÝK
**8** DEMONSTRÁTSIYA
**9** MATCH
**10** BOLSHÓY TEÁTR
**11** MOSKVÍCH
**12** ETÁZH
**13** MÓZHNO
**14** KHOROSHÓ
**15** SHOSSÉ
**16** TSVETÝ
**17** VÉCHER
**18** NOCH'
**19** KRÁSNAYA
PLÓSHCHAD'
**20** SHCHI
**21** SHÁPKA
**22** ZHÉNSHCHINA
**23** TSIRK (TSYRK)
**24** PÓCHTA
**25** TSENTR
**26** KONTSÉRT
**27** POD'YÉZD

# Grammar notes

## 1 Genders

Russian has three genders – masculine, feminine and neuter. Usually the gender can be recognised from the ending (see page 171).

## 2 Cases

Russian nouns, adjectives and pronouns have six cases. This means that words change their endings according to their function in a sentence. The cases are as follows:

● NOMINATIVE. The 'naming' case. This is the one you will find in a dictionary. It is used for the subject of the sentence.

● ACCUSATIVE. This is used for the direct object of a sentence and after some prepositions, mostly indicating movement: notably **в** (*into*), **на** (*onto*) and **чéрез** (*across*). It is also used in many time expressions, either on its own or with a preposition.

● GENITIVE. The 'possession' case, or the 'of' case. It is used with a large number of prepositions (**из**, **от**, **до**, **с**, **у**, etc.) and after numerals.

● DATIVE. The 'to'/'for' case (e.g. **Он дал мне книгу** – *He gave (to) me a book*, **Он купи́л мне книгу** – *He bought (for) me a book*). It is used after some prepositions including **к** (*towards*) and **по** (*along*).

● INSTRUMENTAL. The 'with' or 'by' case. It is used on its own to indicate the instrument used (e.g. **Он писа́л карандашо́м** – *He was writing with a pencil*) and after some prepositions, including **с** – *with* (**чай с лимо́ном**, *tea with lemon*, **сала́т с гриба́ми**, *salad with mushrooms*). It is also used on its own with certain time expressions – **вéчером**, **весно́й**, etc.

● PREPOSITIONAL (sometimes called LOCATIVE). The 'place' case. Only used after the prepositions **в** (*in*), **на** (*on*), **о** (*about*), **при** (*in the time of*).

## 3 Prepositions

All cases except the nominative may have prepositions in front of them, i.e. they may be 'governed' by a preposition. Here is a list of some of the main prepositions with their cases:

| | |
|---|---|
| ACCUSATIVE | **в** (*into*), **на** (*onto*), **за** (*in exchange for*), **чéрез** (*across*) |
| GENITIVE | **у** (*by/at*), **из** (*out of*), **от** (*from*), **до** (*as far as /up to*), **с** (*from*), **для** (*for*), **без** (*without*) |
| DATIVE | **к** (*towards*), **по** (*along, about*), etc. |
| INSTRUMENTAL | **с** (*with*), **под** (*under*), **над** (*above*), **за** (*for*) |
| PREPOSITIONAL (LOCATIVE) | **в** (*in*), **на** (*on*), **о** (*about*) |

# 4 Endings: nouns

You can normally tell which gender a noun is by looking at the ending of the nominative singular case. Here is a table of all the nominative singular endings grouped by gender.

| | Masculine | Feminine | Neuter |
|---|---|---|---|
| **hard endings** | consonant | -а | -о |
| **soft endings** | -й | -я | -е |
| **soft endings** | | -ия | -ие |
| **soft endings** | -ь | -ь | |

The endings in the table appear in nouns which are of Russian origin or in nouns which have become 'Russified' (**футбол**, **чай**, **машина**, etc.). Words which have not (yet) changed in form often do not change their endings at all (**такси**, **кино**, **кенгуру**, etc.).

# 5 Spelling rules

Russian also has a number of spelling rules, which do not allow certain vowels to occur after certain groups of consonants. Two rules that will help in working out the correct endings on nouns and adjectives are:

**Spelling rule 1**: after **г, к, х, ж, ч, ш, щ** write **И** in place of **Ы**

**Spelling rule 2**: after **ж, ч, ш, щ, ц** write **E** in place of unstressed **O**

Note that if the **o** is the stressed syllable, it does not change.

# 6 Tables

Notice that 'hard' and 'soft' types are parallel, in that they involve a difference of one letter only and this is a corresponding vowel. Here is a list of vowels to help you:

| Hard | Soft |
|---|---|
| а | я |
| э | е |
| ы | и |
| о | ё |
| у | ю |

The arrows indicate the corresponding vowels. Thus **Нина** in the accusative is **Нину**, whereas the accusative of **Таня** is **Таню**, etc. Note that **э** occurs mainly in words of foreign origin and never in endings.

# 7 Nouns: masculine

| | Singular | Plural |
|---|---|---|
| **Nom.** | театр | театры |
| **Acc.** | театр* | театры* |
| **Gen.** | театра | театров |
| **Dat.** | театру | театрам |
| **Instr.** | театром | театрами |
| **Prep.** | (в) театре | (в) театрах |

| | Singular | Plural |
|---|---|---|
| **Nom.** | музей | музеи |
| **Acc.** | музея* | музеи* |
| **Gen.** | музея | музеев |
| **Dat.** | музею | музеям |
| **Instr.** | музеем | музеями |
| **Prep.** | (о) музее | (о) музеях |

* In inanimate nouns in both singular and plural the accusative is identical to the nominative; in animate nouns it is identical to the genitive.

Note that masculine nouns in **-ь** behave like **музей** except that they end in **-ей** in the genitive plural.

# 8 Nouns: feminine

| | Singular | Plural |
|---|---|---|
| **Nom.** | комната | комнаты |
| **Acc.** | комнату | комнаты* |
| **Gen.** | комнаты | комнат |
| **Dat.** | комнате | комнатам |
| **Instr.** | комнатой | комнатами |
| **Prep.** | (в) комнате | (в) комнатах |

Feminine nouns ending in **-я** behave very much like those in **-a**, but they have 'soft' endings, e.g. **Таня** → **Таню** (accusative) → **с Таней** (instrumental). The ones in **ия** have **-ий** in the genitive plural and **-ии** in the dative and prepositional singular.

| | Singular | Plural |
|---|---|---|
| **Nom.** | площадь | площади |
| **Acc.** | площадь | площади* |
| **Gen.** | площади | площадей |
| **Dat.** | площади | площадям |
| **Instr.** | площадью | площадями |
| **Prep.** | (на) площади | (на) площадях |

* In inanimate nouns in the plural the accusative is identical to the nominative; in animate nouns it is identical to the genitive.

## 9 Nouns: neuter

Notice that many of the neuter nouns we have used in the course do not change their endings (**кино́, метро́, Дина́мо, кило́, фо́то, кафе́, бюро́, Торпе́до**). Such nouns will be marked *indec* in the vocabulary. One that does change is **ме́сто** (*place*).

|        | Singular    | Plural        |
|--------|-------------|---------------|
| Nom.   | ме́сто       | места́         |
| Acc.   | ме́сто       | места́         |
| Gen.   | ме́ста       | мест          |
| Dat.   | ме́сту       | места́м        |
| Instr. | ме́стом      | места́ми       |
| Prep.  | (в) ме́сте   | (в) места́х    |

The singular of neuter nouns is very much like the masculine singular. Neuter nouns are always inanimate. The genitive plural is very much like feminine in -**a** (it has a 'zero' ending). Notice also the stress shift in the plural. This avoids confusion between the genitive singular and the nominative plural.

|        | Singular     | Plural         |
|--------|--------------|----------------|
| Nom.   | зда́ние       | зда́ния         |
| Acc.   | зда́ние       | зда́ния         |
| Gen.   | зда́ния       | зда́ний         |
| Dat.   | зда́нию       | зда́ниям        |
| Instr. | зда́нием      | зда́ниями       |
| Prep.  | (в) зда́нии   | (в) зда́ниях    |

If you want to learn these by heart it would help if you take note that in all instances the dative, instrumental and prepositional plural are similar in form. The same is true with adjectives. Most, but not all, noun types are listed above. If you want a comprehensive list, you should consult any standard grammar of Russian.

## 10 Pronouns

| Singular |          |         |           |         |
|----------|----------|---------|-----------|---------|
| Nom.     | я        | ты      | он (оно́)  | она́     |
| Acc.     | меня́     | тебя́    | его́       | её      |
| Gen.     | меня́     | тебя́    | его́       | её      |
| Dat.     | мне      | тебе́    | ему́       | ей      |
| Instr.   | мной     | тобо́й   | им        | ей (ею) |
| Prep.    | (обо́)    | (о)     | (о)       | (о)     |
|          | мне      | тебе́    | нём       | нём     |

| Plural |         |         |         |
|--------|---------|---------|---------|
| Nom.   | мы      | вы      | они́     |
| Acc.   | нас     | вас     | их      |
| Gen.   | нас     | вас     | их      |
| Dat.   | нам     | вам     | им      |
| Instr. | на́ми    | ва́ми    | и́ми     |
| Prep.  | (о) нас | (о) вас | (о) них |

Notice that when the pronoun begins with a vowel and is governed by a preposition, **н** is added, e.g. **о нём**, **у них** (genitive), etc.

## 11 Possessive pronouns

|        | Masculine         | | Neuter | Feminine | Plural            |
|--------|-------------------|--|--------|----------|-------------------|
| Nom.   | мой               | | моё    | моя́      | мои́               |
| Acc.   | *as nom. or gen.* | | моё    | мою́      | *as nom. or gen.* |
| Gen.   | моего́             | |        | мое́й     | мои́х              |
| Dat.   | моему́             | |        | мое́й     | мои́м              |
| Instr. | мои́м              | |        | мое́й     | мои́ми             |
| Prep.  | моём              | |        | мое́й     | мои́х              |

|        | Masculine         | | Neuter | Feminine | Plural            |
|--------|-------------------|--|--------|----------|-------------------|
| Nom.   | ваш               | ва́ше | ва́ша | ва́ши    |                   |
| Acc.   | *as nom. or gen.* | | ва́ше  | ва́шу     | *as nom. or gen.* |
| Gen.   | ва́шего            | |       | ва́шей    | ва́ших            |
| Dat.   | ва́шему            | |       | ва́шей    | ва́шим            |
| Instr. | ва́шим             | |       | ва́шей    | ва́шими           |
| Prep.  | ва́шем             | |       | ва́шей    | ва́ших            |

**твой** has the same forms as **мой** and **наш** has the same forms as **ваш**.

## 12 Adjectives

These are much simpler than nouns, in that there are not as many classes, and the plural is the same for all three genders. Masculine and neuter are very much alike, so we have put them together.

|        | Masculine         | Neuter      | Feminine    | Plural            |
|--------|-------------------|-------------|-------------|-------------------|
| Nom.   | интере́сный        | интере́сное  | интере́сная  | интере́сные        |
| Acc.   | *as nom. or gen.* | интере́сное  | интере́сную  | *as nom. or gen.* |
| Gen.   | интере́сного       |             | интере́сной  | интере́сных        |
| Dat.   | интере́сному       |             | интере́сной  | интере́сным        |
| Instr. | интере́сным        |             | интере́сной  | интере́сными       |
| Prep.  | интере́сном        |             | интере́сной  | интере́сных        |

Notice in the feminine the last four endings are the same, and notice the similarity between the adjectival and noun endings, with -**ы** taking the place of -**a** in dative, instrumental and prepositional plural.

Many adjectives end in -**кий** and, following spelling rule 1, will replace all occurrences of the vowel **ы** with **и**. Some adjectives end in -**жий**, -**чий**, -**ший** or -**щий** and will not only replace **ы** with **и**, but also **о** with **е**:

|        | Masculine         | Neuter      | Feminine    | Plural            |
|--------|-------------------|-------------|-------------|-------------------|
| Nom.   | хоро́ший           | хоро́шее     | хоро́шая     | хоро́шие           |
| Acc.   | *as nom. or gen.* | хоро́шее     | хоро́шую     | *as nom. or gen.* |
| Gen.   | хоро́шего          |             | хоро́шей     | хоро́ших           |
| Dat.   | хоро́шему          |             | хоро́шей     | хоро́шим           |
| Instr. | хоро́шим           |             | хоро́шей     | хоро́шими          |
| Prep.  | хоро́шем           |             | хоро́шей     | хоро́ших           |

There are a few 'soft' adjectives, e.g. **вече́рний**, which means that you have a straight substitution of **я** for **а**, **е** for **о**, **и** for **ы** and **ю** for **у**. Thus **вече́рняя газе́та** and **я чита́л вече́рнюю газе́ту**, etc.

Some adjectives have a short form, which is much simpler than the long form, but it is only used in one case, the nominative. For example:

| | |
|---|---|
| Рестора́н откры́т. | *The restaurant is open.* |
| Кафе́ закры́то. | *The cafe is closed.* |
| Апте́ка закры́та. | *The chemist is closed.* |
| Они́ откры́ты. | *They are open.* |

## 13 Adverbs

They are usually derived from adjectives, by taking off the ending and adding **-о**.

| | | |
|---|---|---|
| хоро́ший | хорошо́ | *well* |
| плохо́й | пло́хо | *badly* |
| интере́сный | интере́сно | *interestingly* |

## 14 Comparison

We have used a few short forms of the comparative, as follows:

| | | |
|---|---|---|
| хорошо́ | лу́чше | *better* |
| пло́хо | ху́же | *worse* |
| большо́й | бо́льше | *bigger, more* |
| ма́ленький | ме́ньше | *smaller, less* |

followed by a simple genitive or **чем** (*than*).

## 15 Verbs: present and past tense

The infinitive ends in **-ть** – **рабо́тать, гуля́ть, говори́ть, смотре́ть**, etc. Verbs that end in **-ать** or **-ять** usually have a present tense like **чита́ть** (first conjugation). Those that end in **-ить** have present tense forms like **говори́ть** (second conjugation). Those that end in **-еть** are more difficult to predict, although many common verbs, such as **смотре́ть**, are second conjugation. Look at the examples below.

| Present tense | | | |
|---|---|---|---|
| **чита́ть** | | **говори́ть** | |
| я | чита́ю | я | говорю́ |
| ты | чита́ешь | ты | говори́шь |
| он | чита́ет | он | говори́т |
| мы | чита́ем | мы | говори́м |
| вы | чита́ете | вы | говори́те |
| они́ | чита́ют | они́ | говоря́т |
| stem | чита- | stem | говор- |

In some verbs the stem is slightly different from the infinitive form. If you know the first and second persons singular, you can usually guess the rest. The stress stays fixed from the 'ты' form onwards, and, in such verbs, a stressed ending results in **-ё**. Look at the examples below.

| **е́хать** | | **идти** | |
|---|---|---|---|
| я | е́ду | я | иду́ |
| ты | е́дешь | ты | идёшь |
| он | е́дет | он | идёт |
| мы | е́дем | мы | идём |
| вы | е́дете | вы | идёте |
| они́ | е́дут | они́ | иду́т |

There are one or two exceptions to the above, notably the following:

| **хоте́ть** | |
|---|---|
| я | хочу́ |
| ты | хо́чешь |
| он | хо́чет |
| мы | хоти́м |
| вы | хоти́те |
| они́ | хотя́т |

Past tenses are usually formed from the infinitive, by taking away **-ть** and adding **-л, -ла, -ло, -ли** depending on the gender and number of the persons involved.

| я, ты (m.), он, Ива́н | чита́л, | говори́л |
|---|---|---|
| я, ты (f.), она́, Ве́ра | чита́ла, | говори́ла |
| мы, вы, они́, Ива́н и Ве́ра | чита́ли, | говори́ли |

**оно́** After **оно́**, or neuter nouns, the past tense ends in **-ло**, e.g. **оно́ бы́ло, ра́дио Москва́ говори́ло**. (Exception **идти → шёл шла шло шли**.)

## 16 Verbs: imperatives

Imperatives are formed by taking the stem of the present tense: if it ends in a vowel, add **-й** for the **ты** form or **-йте** for the **вы** form. If it ends in a consonant, add **-и** or **-ите** for the **ты** and **вы** forms respectively. Thus:

| **ты** | **вы** | |
|---|---|---|
| чита́й | чита́йте | *read!* |
| говори́ | говори́те | *speak!* |
| иди́ | иди́те | *go!* |

If you want to say *Let us do it*, use the **мы** form of the perfective future: **Пойдём** (*Let's go!*).

## 17 Verbs: aspects

Most Russian verbs have two aspects, the imperfective and the perfective. The imperfective is used for the present tense, the compound future (**я бу́ду/он бу́дет чита́ть,** etc.) and the past tense. The perfective is used for the simple future and the past.

Aspects are a very complex area of Russian grammar. Only a general indication of when to use each aspect can be given here. You should consult a more detailed Russian grammar if you want further details. The imperfective is used to indicate an action in progress or an action performed on more than one occasion, the perfective is used when stressing that an action is complete on one occasion.

Here are a couple of examples of aspect pairs:

**Imperfective:** покупа́ть смотре́ть е́хать
**Perfective:** купи́ть посмотре́ть пое́хать

We have included both aspects of common verbs in the vocabulary.

## 18 Numerals

| | | | |
|---|---|---|---|
| 1 | оди́н | 30 | три́дцать |
| 2 | два две (f.) | 40 | со́рок |
| 3 | три | 50 | пятьдеся́т |
| 4 | четы́ре | 60 | шестьдеся́т |
| 5 | пять | 70 | се́мьдесят |
| 6 | шесть | 80 | во́семьдесят |
| 7 | семь | 90 | девяно́сто |
| 8 | во́семь | 100 | сто |
| 9 | де́вять | 200 | две́сти |
| 10 | де́сять | 300 | три́ста |
| 11 | оди́ннадцать | 400 | четы́реста |
| 12 | двена́дцать | 500 | пятьсо́т |
| 13 | трина́дцать | 600 | шестьсо́т |
| 14 | четы́рнадцать | 700 | семьсо́т |
| 15 | пятна́дцать | 800 | восемьсо́т |
| 16 | шестна́дцать | 900 | девятьсо́т |
| 17 | семна́дцать | 1,000 | ты́сяча |
| 18 | восемна́дцать | 2,000 | две ты́сячи |
| 19 | девятна́дцать | 3,000 | три ты́сячи |
| 20 | два́дцать | 4,000 | четы́ре ты́сячи |
| 21 | два́дцать оди́н | 5,000 | пять ты́сяч |
| 22 | два́дцать два | 1,000,000 | миллио́н |
| 23 | два́дцать три | | |

After **оди́н/одна́/одно́** the nominative sing. is used; after **два/две**, **три**, **четы́ре** (and numerals ending in these words) the genitive singular is used. After numerals other than these, the genitive plural is used.

## 19 Word building

As you will have seen from our regular *Looking at words* section in the course, it is often possible to make a guess at the meaning of a word by breaking it down into its component parts, i.e. prefix, root (or stem) and ending. Roots can only be learned by constant exposure to Russian. There is only a limited number of prefixes, and a knowledge of these will help you in understanding Russian. Here are some of them with their approximate meanings:

| Prefix | Meaning | Example |
|---|---|---|
| без- бес- | *without* | беспла́тно *free, i.e. without paying* |
| в- | *into (en-)* | вход *entrance* |
| вз- вс- вос- | *upwards* | взлёт *take-off* |
| вы- | *out of (ex-)* | вы́ход *exit* |
| до- | *up to (the end)* | до́читать *to read to the end* |
| за- | *for (purpose)* | заходи́те *come and see us!* |
| из- ис- | *from* | и́здали *from along way away* |
| на- | *onto* | напра́во *to the right* |
| не- ни- | *not, un-* | негра́мотность *illiteracy* |
| о- об- | *about* | описа́ть *to describe* |
| от- | *from* | отходи́ть *to depart* |
| пере- | *across, trans-* | перехо́д *crossing* |
| по- | *a little* | почита́ть *to read a little* |
| при | *towards* | прие́зд *arrival* |
| про- | *through* | проходи́ть *to go through* |
| раз- рас- | *separation* | ра́зный *different* |
| с- со- | *with, together from* | съезд *meeting* сходи́ть *to alight* |
| у- | *away from* | уходи́ть, *to go away* |

Suffixes are the part of a word that appears after the root, and they too can tell you something about the meaning of the word itself. **-ция** can often be the equivalent of the English -tion, as can **-ость**. Words ending in **-ость** are always feminine. They are often the equivalent of the English -ence or -ness: **незави́симый** (*independent*), **незави́симость** (*independence*). Other common suffixes are **-тель** (often -er) as in **чита́тель** (*reader*), and **-ник**, as in **спу́тник** (**с** + **пут** + **ник**): *fellow-traveller, companion,* or, of course, *satellite*. The feminine of words ending in **-ник** ends in **-ница**, which is also added to the -**тель** words: **учи́тельница** (*woman teacher*). Other suffixes are the endings listed in the rest of the grammar section. These give you information about whether the word is a verb, a noun, etc., and about its number, gender, case or person.

# Tapescripts

Included here are all dialogues not printed in the Units.

## Unit 1

### EXERCISE 8
– Здра́вствуйте. Э́то вы хоти́те такси́?
– А такси́! Ма́ма, такси́.
– Хорошо́, я сейча́с.
– Куда́ вы е́дете?
– В Большо́й теа́тр, пожа́луйста.
– Хорошо́.
– Вот Большо́й теа́тр.
– Спаси́бо.
  *(pays)*
– Спаси́бо, и до свида́ния.
– До свида́ния.

## Unit 2

### EXERCISE 7
– Здра́вствуйте!
– Здра́вствуйте!
– А Ва́ня до́ма?
– Да до́ма. Ва́ня! Извини́те, как вас зову́т?
– Ви́ктор Тру́шин.
– Ма́ма, кто э́то?
– Ва́ня, э́то Ви́ктор Тру́шин.
– А, хорошо́. Познако́мьтесь. Это Ви́ктор, э́то ма́ма.
– О́чень ра́да.
– О́чень рад.
– Скажи́те, Ви́ктор, как ва́ша ма́ма?
– Ничего́, спаси́бо. Она́ сейча́с до́ма.

## Unit 3

### EXERCISE 5
**1**
– Скажи́те, пожа́луйста, где метро́?
– Иди́те напра́во, пото́м нале́во и пря́мо.
– Это далеко́?
– Да нет, то́лько оди́н киломе́тр.

**2**
– Извини́те, пожа́луйста, где кино́?
– Кино́? Иди́те пря́мо, напра́во, нале́во и пря́мо.
– Это далеко́?
– Да, далеко́, три киломе́тра.

**3**
– Прости́те, пожа́луйста, где стадио́н?
– Стадио́н? Напра́во, напра́во и пря́мо.
– Это далеко́?
– Да, нет! Здесь ря́дом.

**4**
– Прости́те, пожа́луйста, где здесь рестора́н?
– Рестора́н? Иди́те нале́во, напра́во и опя́ть напра́во.
– Это далеко́?
– Да, но мо́жно взять такси́.
– Спаси́бо вам большо́е.
– Пожа́луйста.

**5**
– Извини́те, пожа́луйста, где здесь стоя́нка такси́?
– Такси́? Иди́те напра́во, напра́во, нале́во и пря́мо. Там стоя́нка.
– Это далеко́?
– Нет, два киломе́тра. Э́то не так далеко́.
– Спаси́бо.
– Пожа́луйста.

### EXERCISE 8
**1**
– Прости́те, где здесь рестора́н?
– Вот там, напра́во.
– Он откры́т?
– Нет, сейча́с закры́т. Кафе́ сейча́с откры́то.

**2**
– Прости́те, вы не зна́ете, где здесь кино́?
– Вот здесь нале́во, но сего́дня кинотеа́тр закры́т.
– Он за́втра бу́дет откры́т?
– Да.

**3**
– Извини́те, где кафе́?
– Кафе́? Пря́мо по коридо́ру.
– Оно́ откры́то?
– Да, кафе́ всегда́ откры́то.

**4**
– Прости́те, пожа́луйста, где здесь буфе́т?
– Вот напра́во, но сего́дня закры́т на ремо́нт.

**5**
– А, вот и кафе́.
– Вот и меню́. Есть пи́во, вино́ и во́дка.

## Unit 4

### EXERCISE 6
– Алло́, э́то О́льга?
– Нет, Ната́ша.
– А, Ната́ша, здра́вствуй! Это И́горь. Как дела́?
– Ничего́, а как ты?
– То́же ничего́. Ната́ша, О́льгу мо́жно?
– Да. О́льга!
– Алло́, И́горь?
– О́ля, слу́шай. У меня́ биле́ты в теа́тр. Пойдём, да?
– Когда́?
– Сего́дня.
– Нет, сего́дня я занята́. А за́втра мо́жно?
– Хорошо́, пойдём за́втра.

## Unit 5

### EXERCISE 4
– Что идёт в па́рке?
– Ну, в па́рке идёт конце́рт.

– Что идёт в кино́?
– Ну, в кино́ идёт фильм «Клеопа́тра».

– Что идёт в Большо́м теа́тре?
– В Большо́м теа́тре идёт о́пера «Князь И́горь».

– Что идёт в университе́те?
– В университе́те ле́кция о ко́смосе.

## Unit 6

### EXERCISE 2
**1**
– Де́вушка, скажи́те, пожа́луйста, у вас есть ма́рки?
– Есть. Ско́лько вам?
– Да́йте, пожа́луйста, шесть.
– Вот, пожа́луйста, шесть ма́рок.
– Спаси́бо.

**2**
– Де́вушка, скажи́те, пожа́луйста, у вас есть биле́ты?
– Есть. Ско́лько вам?
– Да́йте, пожа́луйста, два.
– Вот вам два биле́та.
– Спаси́бо.

**3**
– Де́вушка, скажи́те, пожа́луйста, у вас есть откры́тки?

– Есть. Сколько вам?
– Дайте, пожалуйста, пять.
– Вот вам пять открыток.
– Спасибо.

**4**
– Девушка, скажите, пожалуйста, у вас есть пиво?
– Есть. Сколько вам?
– Дайте, пожалуйста, три бутылки.
– Вот вам три бутылки.
– Спасибо.

**5**
– Девушка, скажите, пожалуйста, у вас есть жетоны?
– Есть. Сколько вам?
– Дайте, пожалуйста, десять.
– Вот вам десять жетонов.
– Спасибо.

### EXERCISE 8
– Здравствуйте.
– Здравствуйте. Скажите, пожалуйста, у вас можно купить билеты в Большой театр?
– Нет, Большой театр сейчас закрыт.
– А в цирк можно?
– Да, пожалуйста, в цирк можно.
– Хорошо. Дайте, пожалуйста, три билета.
– Вот, пожалуйста, три билета.

## Unit 7

### EXERCISE 4
– Здравствуй, как тебя зовут?
– Вера. Меня зовут Вера.
– Как ты поживаешь, Вера?
– Хорошо, спасибо.
– А сколько тебе лет?
– Пять. Мне пять лет.
– А что это у тебя?
– Открытки. Это открытки. Вот, раз, два, три, четыре, пять, шесть, семь, восемь, девять, десять открыток.
– А твой папа инженер, да.
– Да, инженер. И мама тоже инженер.

### TALKING ON THE TELEPHONE
– Алло?
– Слушаю вас.
– Это гостиница Россия?
– Нет, не тот номер. Перезвоните.

– Алло, это гостиница Россия?
– Да.
– А хорошо. Борисова можно к телефону?

## Unit 8

### EXERCISE 5
Здравствуйте. Сегодня передаём следующие передачи:
В 17 часов 30 минут
Концерт музыки Чайковского.
В 19 часов 15 минут
Футбол Спартак Москва и Динамо Санкт-Петербург
В 20 часов 40 минут
«Спокойной ночи, малыши!»
В 21 час 00 минут
Новости
В 21 час 35 минут
Прогноз погоды
В 21 час 45 минут
Художественный фильм «Дядя Ваня» Чехова.
Сейчас передаём последние известия.

### EXERCISE 9
– Саша, почему вы всё смотрите телевизор? Почему вы не гуляете, не играете в теннис, не читаете книгу?
– Потому что не люблю гулять, не люблю играть в теннис.
– Мы все любим смотреть по телевизору фильмы и спорт. Но нельзя же сидеть весь день. Нина, ты доктор. Скажи ему, что это нехорошо.
– Да, это нехорошо, Саша. Анна любит гулять, Виктор играет в футбол, да, Виктор? И ваш брат играет.
– Мой брат сейчас не играет. Он говорит, что не любит футбол.
– Виктор, пойдём в парк, погуляем.
– Нет, спасибо. Простите, я хочу смотреть хоккей по телевизору. Я очень люблю смотреть хоккей.

## Unit 9

### EXERCISE 2
– Свободно?
– Пожалуйста. Садитесь.
– *(to himself)* Ну, здесь очень хороший ресторан.

– Девушка!
– Слушаю вас!
– Сейчас можно ужинать?
– Можно, уже семь часов.

– Дайте, пожалуйста, меню.
– Вот, пожалуйста, меню.
– Посмотрим, какая там рыба.

– Что вы хотите?
– Мне, пожалуйста, икру и шампанское.
– У нас только красная икра.
– Хорошо.

– И потом?
– У вас есть борщ? И судак?
– Есть.
– Хорошо. Дайте, пожалуйста, и борщ и судака. А потом кофе и коньяк.
– Хорошо.

– Вот, пожалуйста, икра и шампанское. Приятного аппетита!
– Спасибо.
– Пожалуйста.
– Ой, как я люблю русское шампанское.

– Девушка, дайте мне, пожалуйста, счёт.
– Вот он.
– Ой-ой-ой!

### EXERCISE 4
– Садитесь, пожалуйста, садитесь!
– Можно здесь?
– Можно, пожалуйста. Вот хлеб и закуски. Типичные русские закуски. Вот чёрная икра, помидоры, колбаса, ветчина, огурцы и сметана. Приятного аппетита! Кушайте на здоровье!
– А извините, какая там рыба?
– Это осетрина, русская осетрина. А потом суп, а второе блюдо курица с картошкой.

## Unit 10

### EXERCISE 5
1 Скажите, пожалуйста, где здесь Большой театр?
2 Мила, здравствуй, как ты поживаешь?
3 Миша, хотите водку?
4 Оля, пойдём со мной в театр.
5 Скажите, ресторан в театре открыт?
6 Игорь, это ваша газета?
7 А вам, Нина, чай или кофе? Тоже кофе?
8 Юрий Иванович, это мой отец.
9 Алло, Вера, это Оля.
10 Что вам, чай или кофе? Чай, да?
11 Здравствуйте, как вы поживаете?

## Unit 11

### EXERCISE 4

– Здра́вствуйте, дороги́е друзья́. Я ваш экскурсово́д. Меня́ зову́т Дми́трий Никола́евич Пу́хов – Ди́ма. Сего́дня у́жин в 8 часо́в. За́втра, зна́чит, в суббо́ту, с 8.00 до 9.10 за́втрак.
– Когда́ бу́дет экску́рсия по Москве́?
– Экску́рсия бу́дет с 9.30 до 12.00 часо́в.
– Что бу́дет в 14.30?
– В 14.30 мы бу́дем в зоопа́рке. Пото́м в 19 часо́в - Большо́й теа́тр и в 23.00 часа́ у́жин.
– В воскресе́нье, 9-ого ию́ля с 8.00 до 9.00 - за́втрак. По́сле за́втрака в 10 часо́в экску́рсия по Кремлю́. В 13 часо́в - обе́д.

## Unit 13

### EXERCISE 6

**1**
– Скажи́те, пожа́луйста, как мне дое́хать до Петродворца́?
– Мо́жно на электри́чке с Балти́йского вокза́ла до ста́нции «Но́вый Петерго́ф».
– Ско́лько мину́т идёт электри́чка?
– Три́дцать пять.
– А пото́м мо́жно пешко́м?
– Лу́чше на авто́бусе но́мер три́ста пятьдеся́т или три́ста пятьдеся́т оди́н.
– Спаси́бо.
– Пожа́луйста.

**2**
– Скажи́те, пожа́луйста, как мне дое́хать до Па́вловска?
– Мо́жно на электри́чке с Ви́тебского вокза́ла до ста́нции «Па́вловск».
– Ско́лько мину́т идёт электри́чка?
– Три́дцать пять.
– А пото́м мо́жно пешко́м?
– Мо́жно че́рез парк, мо́жно та́кже на авто́бусе но́мер три́ста се́мьдесят или три́ста во́семьдесят три.
– Спаси́бо.
– Пожа́луйста.

**3**
– Скажи́те, пожа́луйста, как мне дое́хать до Ца́рского Села́?
– Мо́жно на электри́чке с Ви́тебского вокза́ла до ста́нции «Де́тское Село́».
– Ско́лько мину́т идёт электри́чка?
– Два́дцать пять.
– А пото́м мо́жно пешко́м?
– Лу́чше на авто́бусе но́мер три́ста се́мьдесят оди́н или три́ста во́семьдесят два.
– Спаси́бо.
– Пожа́луйста.

**4**
– Скажи́те, пожа́луйста, как мне дое́хать до Ломоно́сова?
– Мо́жно на электри́чке с Балти́йского вокза́ла до ста́нции «Ораниенба́ум».
– Ско́лько мину́т идёт электри́чка?
– Пятьдеся́т пять.
– А пото́м мо́жно пешко́м?
– Мо́жно.
– Спаси́бо.
– Пожа́луйста.

## Unit 15

### EXERCISE 7

**1** В 1917 г. Октя́брьская револю́ция.
**2** В 1924 г. у́мер Влади́мир Ильи́ч Ле́нин.
**3** В 1945 г. ко́нчилась вели́кая оте́чественная война́.
**4** В 1953 г. у́мер Ио́сиф Виссарио́нович Ста́лин.
**5** В 1991 г. путч в Росси́и.

## Unit 18

### EXERCISE 3

**1**
– Мне, пожа́луйста, Воло́дину, Ната́лью Петро́вну.
– Она́ сейча́с рабо́тает в поликли́нике но́мер два́дцать два.
– А вы не зна́ете телефо́н?
– Две́сти девяно́сто во́семь шестьдеся́т шесть три́дцать во́семь.
– Спаси́бо.
– Пожа́луйста.

**2**
– Мне, пожа́луйста, Воло́дину, Ната́лью Петро́вну.
– Она́ сейча́с рабо́тает в поликли́нике но́мер шестьдеся́т семь.
– А вы не зна́ете телефо́н?
– Четы́реста се́мьдесят два́дцать оди́н се́мьдесят оди́н.
– Спаси́бо.
– Пожа́луйста.

**3**
– Мне, пожа́луйста, Воло́дину, Ната́лью Петро́вну.
– Она́ сейча́с рабо́тает в поликли́нике но́мер девяно́сто три.
– А вы не зна́ете телефо́н?
– Сто три́дцать два со́рок четы́ре шестьдеся́т семь.
– Спаси́бо.
– Пожа́луйста.

**4**
– Мне, пожа́луйста, Воло́дину, Ната́лью Петро́вну.
– Она́ сейча́с рабо́тает в поликли́нике но́мер во́семьдесят оди́н.
– А вы не зна́ете телефо́н?
– Три́ста пятна́дцать два́дцать пять де́сять.
– Спаси́бо.
– Пожа́луйста.

**5**
– Мне, пожа́луйста, Воло́дину, Ната́лью Петро́вну.
– Она́ сейча́с рабо́тает в поликли́нике но́мер пятьдеся́т четы́ре.
– А вы не зна́ете телефо́н?
– Пятьсо́т со́рок два девяно́сто два́дцать пять.
– Спаси́бо.
– Пожа́луйста.

**6**
– Мне, пожа́луйста, Воло́дину, Ната́лью Петро́вну.
– Да, э́то я.

# Key to the exercises

## Unit 1

**EXERCISE 2**
1 pay
2 an airmail letter
3 traffic stops
4 down
5 такси́
6 tea

**EXERCISE 3**
1 Э́то такси́.
2 Э́то рестора́н.
3 Э́то теа́тр.
4 Э́то парк.
5 Э́то метро́.
6 Э́то вино́.
7 Э́то па́па.
8 Э́то ма́ма.
9 Э́то пиани́ст.
10 Э́то орке́стр.

**EXERCISE 5**
1 Нет, э́то не па́па, э́то та́кси.
2 Нет, э́то не пиани́ст, э́то рестора́н.
3 Нет, э́то не парк, э́то теа́тр.
4 Нет, э́то не вино́, э́то парк.
5 Нет, э́то не орке́стр, э́то метро́.
6 Нет, э́то не такси́, э́то вино́.
7 Нет, э́то не ма́ма, э́то па́па.
8 Нет, э́то не теа́тр, э́то ма́ма.
9 Нет, э́то не рестора́н, э́то пиани́ст.
10 Нет, э́то не метро́, э́то орке́стр.

**EXERCISE 6**
1 7     6 1
2 9     7 8
3 4     8 3
4 6     9 2
5 10   10 5

**EXERCISE 7**
1 орке́стр 10   6 парк 4
2 вино́ 6       7 ма́ма 8
3 па́па 7       8 метро́ 5
4 такси́ 1      9 пиани́ст 9
5 рестора́н 2  10 теа́тр 3

**EXERCISE 8**
The Bolshoi Theatre

**EXERCISE 9**
1 Москва́
2 Ко́смос
3 Контине́нт
4 Ка́нторов
5 taxi and underground

**PLAYING WITH WORDS**
1 спорт      4 нет
2 теа́тр      5 такси́
3 рестора́н

## Unit 2

**EXERCISE 2**
1 7     6 1
2 8     7 14
3 4     8 3
4 6     9 2
5 10   10 5

**EXERCISE 3**
1 3     6 12
2 5     7 13
3 9     8 2
4 10   9 1
5 11   10 6

**EXERCISE 4**
1 Вот он. (orchestra)
2 Вот он. (father)
3 Вот она́. (mother)
4 Вот он. (pianist)
5 Вот он. (table)
6 Вот она́. (vodka)
7 Вот она́. (water)
8 Вот оно́. (wine)
9 Вот оно́. (beer)

**EXERCISE 6**
Toronto is in Canada.
The Dynamo stadium is in Moscow.
Ivan is in London.
Madrid is in Spain.
Nina is in the Caucasus.
Kiev is in the Ukraine.

**EXERCISE 7**

**Dialogue:**
Ма́ма, э́то Ví́ktor.
Zdrа́stvuyte, Óchen' rа́da.
Zdrа́stvuyte, Óchen' rad.
Pа́pа, э́то Ví́ktor.
Zdrа́stvuyte óchen' rad.
Zdrа́stvuyte, óchen' rad.

**Expressions from the table:**
Как вас зову́т?
Spasíbo
Nichevó.
Как ма́ма?

**WORD SQUARE 1**
1 КАВКА́З
2 ЗООПА́РК
3 КИНО́
4 О́ПЕРА
5 АППАРА́Т
6 ТЕА́ТР
7 РЕСТОРА́Н
8 НО́МЕР

**WORD SQUARE 2**
КАКА́О
ВИ́СКИ
КВАС
СУП
ЛИМОНА́Д
ПИ́ВО
ВИНО́
ВОДА́
ВО́ДКА

## Unit 3

**EXERCISE 2**
1 11   6 27
2 4     7 20
3 5     8 16
4 9     9 7
5 15   10 2

**EXERCISE 3**
1 15   6 26
2 6     7 17
3 20   8 10
4 8     9 14
5 7     10 22

**EXERCISE 4**
1 ←     5 →
2 →     6 ←
3 ←     7 ←
4 →     8 →

**EXERCISE 5**

|   | 1 | 2 | 3 | 4 | 5 |
|---|---|---|---|---|---|
| 1 | → | ← | ↑ |   |   |
| 2 | ↑ | → | ← | ↑ | ✓ |
| 3 | → | → | ↑ |   |   |
| 4 | ← | → | → |   | ✓ |
| 5 | → | → | ← | ↑ |   |

**EXERCISE 6**
1 4     4 3
2 5     5 1
3 5

**EXERCISE 7**
1 всегда́   4 сейча́с
2 за́втра   5 всегда́
3 сего́дня

**EXERCISE 8**
1 No
2 Tomorrow
3 Always
4 Repairs
5 Beer, wine and vodka

**ALPHABET GAME**
1 ФУТБО́Л   4 БЮРО́
2 КАФЕ́       5 ВХОД
3 ФО́ТО

**JUMBLED WORDS**
1 МЕНЮ́
2 ДИНА́МО
3 ПЕРЕХО́Д
4 ТЕЛЕФО́Н
5 УНИВЕРСИТЕ́Т

## Unit 4

**EXERCISE 2**
1 15   6 17
2 11   7 22
3 18   8 13
4 6     9 4
5 2     10 9

**EXERCISE 3**
1 17   6 10
2 8     7 2
3 15   8 6
4 21   9 13
5 16   10 5

## EXERCISE 4

1 Don't walk on the grass!
2 No entry!
3 Don't take photographs!
4 No exit!
5 No smoking here!
6 No crossing!
7 No smoking!

## EXERCISE 5

1 – Биле́т mózhno?
 – Pozhа́lsta. Вот он.
 –Спаси́бо.
2 – Во́дку mózhno?
 – Pozhа́lsta. Вот она́.
 – Спаси́бо.
3 – Грибы́ mózhno?
 – Pozhа́lsta. Вот они́.
 – Спаси́бо.
4 – Ма́рку mózhno?
 – Pozhа́lsta. Вот она́.
 – Спаси́бо.
5 – Стака́н mózhno?
 – Pozhа́lsta. Вот он.
 – Спаси́бо.
6 – Телефо́н mózhno?
 – Pozhа́lsta. Вот он.
 – Спаси́бо.

## EXERCISE 6

1 Natasha (Ната́ша)
2 Yes (Да)
3 Igor (И́горь)
4 To go to the theatre (Идти́ в теа́тр)
5 She is busy (Она́ занята́)
6 Tomorrow (За́втра)

## JUMBLED WORDS 1

1 ГРИБЫ
2 ПРОГРАММА
3 ЭНЕРГИЯ
4 АЭРОФЛОТ
5 ВЫХОД
Hidden word:ГОРОД

## JUMBLED WORDS 2

1 ГАЗЕТА
2 АВТОБУС
3 ЭКСПРЕСС
4 РОССИЯ
5 ЭКСКУРСИЯ
6 ИЗВЕСТИЯ
Hidden word:ТУРИСТ

## MATCHING SYMBOLS

1 САМОЛЁТ
2 БИЛЕТ
3 РОССИЯ
4 ВЫХОД
5 НЕДЕЛЯ

## Unit 5

### EXERCISE 2

| | | | |
|---|---|---|---|
| 1 | 4 | 6 | 10 |
| 2 | 12 | 7 | 26 |
| 3 | 22 | 8 | 6 |
| 4 | 19 | 9 | 3 |
| 5 | 5 | 10 | 16 |

### EXERCISE 3

| | | | |
|---|---|---|---|
| 1 | 16 | 6 | 20 |
| 2 | 6 | 7 | 22 |
| 3 | 15 | 8 | 17 |
| 4 | 21 | 9 | 25 |
| 5 | 12 | 10 | 7 |

### EXERCISE 4

В па́рке идёт конце́рт.
В кино́ идёт фильм.
В Большо́м теа́тре идёт о́пера.
В университе́те идёт ле́кция.

### EXERCISE 5

1 agency
2 piracy
3 hooliganism
4 administration
5 mobilisation
6 concentration
7 confederation
8 revolution

### EXERCISE 6

Он в рестора́не.
Он в теа́тре.
Она́ в па́рке.
Они́ в па́рке.
Она́ в Москве́.
Он в зоопа́рке.
Она́ в апте́ке.
Он в рестора́не.
Он в кварти́ре.
Он в автома́те.

### EXERCISE 7

1 в Росси́и
2 в це́нтре Москвы́
3 входи́ть
4 входи́ть
5 вхо́да
6 матч

### EXERCISE 8

авто́бусы 4
туале́т(м) 8
ка́сса 1
вы́ход 3
метро́ 6
не кури́ть 10
такси́ 5
Ни́на 2
туале́т(ж) 9
телефо́н-автома́т 7

## JUMBLED WORDS 1

1 МОЖНО
2 ПОЧТА
3 ЧЕХОВ
4 ЦИРК
5 МУЖЧИНА
6 ОПЕРА

## JUMBLED WORDS 2

1 ЧАЙКА
2 ШОССЕ
3 ИНФОРМАЦИЯ
4 ЦЕНТР
5 ЖЕНЩИНА
6 ХОРОШО
7 МАТЧ
8 КОНЦЕРТ

## Unit 6

### EXERCISE 2

| | | | |
|---|---|---|---|
| биле́ты 2 | | ма́рки 6 | |
| пи́во 3 | | жето́ны 10 | |
| откры́тки 5 | | | |

### EXERCISE 3

восемна́дцать 18
двена́дцать 12
девятна́дцать 19
оди́ннадцать 11
пятна́дцать 15
семна́дцать 17
трина́дцать 13
четы́рнадцать 14
шестна́дцать 16

### EXERCISE 4

во́семьдесят 80
два́дцать 20
девяно́сто 90
пятьдеся́т 50
се́мьдесят 70
три́дцать 30
шестьдеся́т 60
со́рок 40

### EXERCISE 5

две́сти 200
пятьсо́т 500
семьсо́т 700
три́ста 300
восемьсо́т 800
четы́реста 400
девятьсо́т 900
шестьсо́т 600
сто 100

### EXERCISE 6

| | | | |
|---|---|---|---|
| 1 | in | 6 | into |
| 2 | in/at | 7 | at |
| 3 | to | 8 | to |
| 4 | to | 9 | into/onto |
| 5 | in | 10 | in |

## EXERCISE 7

Покажи́те, пожа́луйста
Да́йте, пожа́луйста

1 во́дку и вино́
2 ма́рку и откры́тку
3 кни́гу и газе́ту
4 стака́н и ча́шку
5 самова́р и чай

## EXERCISE 8

1 Tickets to the Bolshoi Theatre (Биле́ты в Большо́й теа́тр)
2 It's closed just now (Сейча́с закры́т)
3 The circus (Цирк)
4 Yes, it's possible (Да, мо́жно)
5 Three tickets (Три биле́та)

## Crossword

### Across

1 де́вять
5 нет
6 я
8 три
10 да
11 бале́т
13 во
14 ша́пка
17 эта́ж
19 автома́т
21 щи
22 он
23 но́мер
25 буфе́т
26 дом
27 тасс
29 Оде́сса
30 стоп
31 бу́тсы
32 она

### Down

1 де́вушка
2 вот
3 три
4 кафе́
7 оно́
9 рок
12 а́том
13 вы
15 плане́та
16 авто́бус
17 э́тот
18 Дина́мо
20 анекдо́т
24 ра́да
27 тот
28 суп

**179**

## PUT THINGS IN THEIR PLACE
Дéвушка в Одéссе
Шáпка на дéвушке
Бýтсы в автóбусе
Онá в нóмере (hotel room)

## FIND THE CLUE
нóмер шесть
нóмер одúн
нóмер вóсемь
нóмер два
нóмер дéвять
нóмер пять
нóмер три (вóсемь)
нóмер дéсять
нóмер четы́ре and нóмер семь are missing.

---

## Unit 7

### EXERCISE 1
1 Лéнин (Lenin)
2 Стáлин (Stalin)
3 Хрущёв (Khrushchov)
4 Горбачёв (Gorbachov)
5 Éльцин (Yeltsin)

### EXERCISE 2
1 Алексéй Борúсович
2 Нúна Алексéевна
3 Сергéй Пáвлович
4 Ивáн Николáевич
5 Áнна Ивáновна

### EXERCISE 3
1 здрáвствуй
2 здрáвствуйте
3 здрáвствуйте
4 здрáвствуй
5 здрáвствуйте
6 здрáвствуй
7 здрáвствуйте

### EXERCISE 4
1 Vera
2 Five
3 Postcards
4 Ten
5 He's an engineer
6 She's an engineer as well

They are on 'ты' terms

### EXERCISE 5
1 Россúя большáя странá
2 Олúмпус япóнский фотоаппарáт
3 Дéвушка, у вас есть крáсное винó?
4 Москвá россúйская столúца

5 На столé францýзское шампáнское
6 Динáмовцы хорóшие футболúсты
7 Нью-Йорк Таймс америкáнская газéта
8 Борúс Годунóв рýсский царь
9 Одéсса украúнский порт
10 Мáнчестер англúйский гóрод
(Other combinations may be possible, but make sure they all fit in!)

### EXERCISE 6
1 Russia     5 Ukraine
2 England   6 Poland
3 USA        7 Canada
4 Germany  8 France

### Reading handwriting
СУВЕНИРЫ
ФОТОГРАФИЯ

---

## Unit 8

### EXERCISE 1
1 Мне хóлодно. +1
2 Мне хóлодно. -2
3 Мне теплó. +7
4 Мне теплó. +16
5 Мне хóлодно. -22
6 Мне жáрко. +23
(You may not agree: some people feel colder, or hotter, than others!)

### EXERCISE 2
1 18.20     6 15.25
2 21.05     7 17.03
3 22.10     8 13.35
4 19 15     9 02.49
5 12.22    10 10.55

### EXERCISE 3
1 09 часóв
2 15.00 часóв
3 02 часá
4 22.00 часá
5 15.00 часóв
6 12.00 часóв
7 07.00 часóв
8 20.00 часóв
9 04.00 часá

### EXERCISE 4
1 18.00 News
2 21.00 News
3 18.25 Business Class
4 23.00 Film **Ballad of a Soldier**

5 21.35 Weather forecast
6 19.55 Solzhenitsyn speaks
7 21.40 Concert of Tchaikovsky's music played by Ashkenazy

### EXERCISE 5
1 17.30
2 19.15
3 20.40
4 News
5 News
6 Uncle Vanya

### EXERCISE 6
1 Я игрáю в футбóл.
2 Он/онá лю́бит игрáть на гитáре.
3 Вы гуля́ете в пáрке.
4 Онú говоря́т по-рýсски.
5 Он/онá говорúт по-англúйски.
6 Ты смóтришь телевúзор.
7 Мы не знáем.

### EXERCISE 7
1 Потомý что идёт ремóнт.
2 Потомý что там хорошó.
3 Потомý что хорошó игрáю.
4 Потомý что онá красúвая.
5 Потомý что сегóдня мúнус 20 грáдусов.
6 Потомý что он óчень красúвый гóрод.

### EXERCISE 8
1 video-camera (camcorder)
2 distributor
3 investor
4 yoghurt
5 college
6 computer
7 printer
8 radiator
9 safe
10 supermarket
11 charter
12 shop-tour (shopping trip, usually abroad)

### EXERCISE 9
1 Doctor
2 Walking
3 Watches TV
4 Films and sport
5 Ice-hockey

### Reading handwriting
The advertisement in your office
British tea in Russia
'Fiat' car repairs

ШЕКСПИР
ЧАСЫ

### WORD SQUARE
ФАКС
ДИЛЕР
ДИСК
КСЕРОКС
МАНГО
КОТТЕДЖ
КЛИЕНТ
КОД
ОФИС
ДОК

---

## Unit 9

### EXERCISE 1
Miss Benson 34/4/9/16/ 23/28
Mr Brown 24/7/8/14/22/25
Mr Smith 35/11/15/20/ 32/27
Mr Hart 33/5/12/21/31/26

### EXERCISE 2
1 Yes
2 7 o'clock
3 Fish
4 Black caviar
5 Coffee and brandy
6 He loves Russian champagne
7 Very hefty!

### EXERCISE 3
чёрная икрá  7
шампáнское  8
кýрица  11
фрýкты  9
ры́ба  6
водá  1
салáт  4
шашлы́к  12
кóфе  3
морóженое  5
грибы́  2
вóдка  10

### EXERCISE 4
Black caviar, tomatoes, sausage, ham, cucumbers and smetana (sour cream), sturgeon.
The main course is chicken and potatoes

**EXERCISE 5**

1 mushrooms
2 bill
3 newspaper
4 ticket
5 flowers
6 chicken
7 bread
8 samovar
9 beer
10 metro token

**PLAYING WITH WORDS**

КАРП
ЗАКУСКИ
ПЛОВ
СОК
СУП
ЯИЧНИЦА
САЛАТ
КОТЛЕТ
ЛИМОН
ИКРА

**MISSING LETTERS**

1 Шампа́нское ру́сское (полусухо́е)
2 Сарди́ны в ма́сле
3 Сала́т из помидо́ров
4 Сок тома́тный
5 Бифште́кс натура́льный
6 Икра́ (кра́сная)
7 Вода́ минера́льная
8 Чай с лимо́ном
9 Хлеб с ма́слом

**Reading handwriting**

ЭКСПРЕСС
КАФЕ

## Unit 10

**EXERCISE 1**

1 В    4 А
2 Г    5 Б
3 Б    6 Б

**EXERCISE 2**

1 столе́
2 смо́трит
3 чита́ет
4 идёт
5 по

**EXERCISE 3**

1 c    5 e
2 b    6 g
3 a    7 f
4 d

**EXERCISE 4**

1 A new make of camera
2 A Russian camera, 'Zenith'
3 He doesn't want it, he prefers Japanese
4 A German camera
5 He is in a hurry

**EXERCISE 5**

Хорошо́, а вы? 11
Нет, сейча́с закры́т. 5
Иди́те пря́мо, пото́м нале́во. 1
Нет, то́лько лимона́д. 3
Ничего́, а ты? 2
Здра́вствуйте, о́чень рад. 8
Нет, да́йте, пожа́луйста, ко́фе. 10
Нет, не хочу́. Я сего́дня занята́. 4
Нет, не моя́. 6
Нет, да́йте, пожа́луйста, чай. 7
О́ля, приве́т! Как дела́? 9

**EXERCISE 6**

1 9 ✓ Fisherman's
2 5 Black Stream
3 6 ✓ Ladoga (lake)
4 10 Academic
5 4 ✓ Alexander Nevsky Sq (Russian prince)
6 5 Moscow
7 2 Nevsky Prospect
8 2 Narva (battle of Peter the Great)
9 9 Polytechnic
10 4 ✓ Seaside
11 6 ✓ Lomonosov (Great Russian scholar)
12 2 Dostoyevsky

**Crossword**

Across
1 прости́те
7 и
10 мне
12 ага
14 сто́ит
16 пунш
17 э́тот
19 но
20 арест
22 но
23 АН
24 Ри́ге
25 от
27 ничего́
29 так
33 по
35 нра́вится
37 Дон
38 не
39 Оля
41 ГУМ
42 на
43 гуля́ть
45 лю́бят
51 бар
52 хор
53 за
54 том
55 часо́в

Down
1 пив
2 рестора́не
3 ост
4 смотрю́
5 татари́н
6 МГУ
7 и
8 не
9 де́сять
11 Ни́на
13 АН
15 то́нна
16 при
18 они́
21 сего́дня
22 но́та
26 де́вять
28 час
30 кроль
31 да
32 оян
33 по
34 она́
36 Ту́ла
40 ля
43 газ
44 ура́
46 Юра́
47 бис
48 то
49 Ира
50 по
51 Бр

## Unit 11

**EXERCISE 1**

Fri 16 June
Tues 10 November
Mon 25 April
Sat 1 July
Wed 30 December
Sun 13 October
Thurs 29 January

**EXERCISE 2**

1 суббо́ту
2 понеде́льник
3 воскресе́нье
4 сре́ду
5 пя́тницу
6 четве́рг
7 вто́рник

**EXERCISE 3**

1 часо́в    8 часа́
2 за́втрака  9 обе́да
3 Москве́   10 часо́в
4 це́нтре    11 у́жина
5 го́рода    12 ку́хне
6 обе́да    13 футбо́ле
7 па́рке

**EXERCISE 4**

1 9.30–12    4 23.00
2 зоопа́рк    5 10.00
3 19.00      6 обе́д

**EXERCISE 5**

1 a 10–19.00
  b 15–16.00
  c Sunday
2 a 10–20.00
  b 11–18.00
3 a Tuesday, Thursday, Saturday
  b Tuesday and Thursday 17.00–20.00 Saturday 10–15.00
4 a 9–23.00
  b Every day
  c 13–14.00

**EXERCISE 6**

1 Hong Kong
2 Hitler
3 Holland
4 Hamlet
5 Copenhagen

**EXERCISE 7**

Ива́н (зимо́й) goes to the stadium to watch ice-hockey; (ле́том) works at the dacha on Saturdays and watches football every evening.
Ири́на (зимо́й) goes to concerts in the Conservatoire; (ле́том) works with her husband at the dacha and reads novels in the evenings.
Бо́ря (зимо́й) plays chess; (ле́том) plays chess.
Ма́ша (зимо́й) listens to rock music; (ле́том) sunbathes at the dacha.

**EXERCISE 8**

1 a Bolshoi Theatre
  b *Evgeniy (Eugene) Onegin*
  c 7.30
2 a *Resurrection*
  b Tolstoy
  c 7.30
3 *Jesus Christ Superstar* and *Hamlet*
4 a *Coppelia*
  b Saturday
  c Delibes
5 a *Seagull*
  b Friday
6 Nothing, it's closed!

## Unit 12

**EXERCISE 1**

1 1113–25
2 1147
3 1223
4 1227
5 1240–1480
6 Ivan IV became tsar
7 Boris Godunov
8 Peter went to Holland and Britain
9 Founding of St Petersburg
10 War with Napoleon
11 1861
12 1917
13 1924
14 1953
15 1991

**EXERCISE 2**

1 The past tense after я ends in -л
2 Each time a **я** form (first person singular) occurs, add **-a** to the end of the verb

**EXERCISE 3**

1 была́    4 была́
2 был/-á   5 был
3 бы́ли    6 бы́ли

**EXERCISE 4**

1 Coffee and egg
2 Read a newspaper in the library
3 Watched a film; she enjoyed the film
4 Physics
5 Mushrooms
6 In a bank

**EXERCISE 5**

1 бу́дем обе́дать
2 чита́л/а
3 бу́дет смотре́ть
4 гуля́ли
5 игра́ла
6 бу́дете игра́ть
7 сдала́
8 рабо́тает

**EXERCISE 6**

1
a рома́н «Война́ и мир»
b стихи́ «Я вас люби́л»
c рома́н «Отцы́ и де́ти»
d пье́су «Ревизо́р»
e рома́н «Преступле́ние и наказа́ние»
f пье́су «Три сестры́»
2
a Никола́й
b Серге́й
c Серге́й
d Васи́лий
e Михаи́л
f Па́вел
3
a Пу́шкин
b Го́голь
c Достое́вский
d Турге́нев
e Толсто́й
f Евге́ний Оне́гин
g Ревизо́р
h Отцы́ и де́ти
i Преступле́ние и наказа́ние, Идио́т, Бра́тья Карама́зовы
j Ча́йка, Три сестры́, Дя́дя Ва́ня, Вишнёвый сад

## Unit 13

**EXERCISE 1**

a Kiev      b Moscow
  Smolensk     Finland
  Kursk        Baltic
  Yaroslavl    Warsaw

**EXERCISE 2**

1 The ticket office
2 St Petersburg
3 In the big hall on the left

**EXERCISE 3**

1 Today
2 Sleeper in a compartment
3 No 6 at 23.10 or No 2 at 23.55
4 No 2 'Red Arrow'
5 Platform 1

**EXERCISE 4**

1 48     5 14 or 28
2 48     6 28
3 160    7 6
4 160    8 2

**EXERCISE 5**

1 a Tambov
  b Yes
  c 92
2 a Murmansk
  b No
  c 186
3 Novgorod
4 Underground
5 Exit to the town or Metro

**EXERCISE 6**

1 Петродворе́ц, Балти́йский; Но́вый Петерго́ф; 35; 350/1
2 Па́вловск; Ви́тебский; Па́вловск; 35; 370/383 or on foot
3 Ца́рское Село́; Ви́тебский; Де́тское село́; 25; 371/382
4 Ломоно́сов; Балти́йский; Ораниенба́ум; 55; on foot

**EXERCISE 7**

1 се́вере    4 се́вере
2 восто́ке   5 за́паде
3 се́вере    6 се́вере

**EXERCISE 8**

1 to go away (on foot)
2 to go away (by vehicle)
3 to depart (of a train, etc.)
4 departure (vehicle)
5 departure (on foot)
6 departure (of train, etc.)

**EXERCISE 9**

1 to go out (on foot) из
2 to drive (a vehicle) out из
3 entrance (pedestrian) в
4 exit (pedestrian) из
5 entry (vehicle) в
6 exit (vehicle) из

## Reading

### Moscow

1 About ten million
2 Books, records, cassettes and compact discs

### St Petersburg

1 They are straight and wide

2 It is a very large museum and art gallery, where there are paintings by Western artists
3 Nevsky Prospekt; the River Neva

### Yaroslavl

1 By train; five hours
2 a Sixteenth century
  b 1010

## Unit 14

**EXERCISE 1**

1 Moscow University (MGU)
2 1st September, 1996
3 3 weeks
4 Stephen Jones and Alan Thomas
5 London University
6 23 and 22

**EXERCISE 2**

1 Julia Bivon
2 Moscow
3 25 days
4 27 March 1992

**EXERCISE 3**

1 On the left in the corner
2 He doesn't like queues
3 Twenty minutes
4 No
5 In dollars
6 Two dollars

**EXERCISE 4**

1 ✓books
2 10.00–14.00, 15.00–19.00

**EXERCISE 5**

1 true
2 true     5 false
3 true     6 true
4 false    7 false

**EXERCISE 6**

1 ма́ленькая су́мка моско́вский аэропо́рт но́вые теле́жки
2 де́тская игру́шка кра́сный кана́л университе́тское приглаше́ние
3 хоро́шие но́вости чёрная икра́ прия́тный тамо́женник

## EXERCISE 7

1 Он хотéл бы пойти, но рестора́н сего́дня закры́т.
2 Они́ хотéли бы пойти́, но библиотéка сего́дня закры́та.
3 Он хотéл бы пойти́, но кино́ сего́дня закры́то.
4 Она́ хотéла бы пойти́, но стадио́н сего́дня закры́т.
5 Он хотéл бы пойти́, но кафé сего́дня закры́то.

## EXERCISE 8

1 In the university in St Petersburg
2 Stroll along the Nevsky Prospekt and drink juice in a small cafe
3 Her father was giving lectures at London University
4 In a large comfortable hotel
5 Trafalgar Square and Downing Street
6 Washington and New York
7 Visit the White House and the Empire State Building, and go up to the 102nd floor

## EXERCISE 9

1 atomic energy
2 bookshop
3 entry visa
4 Nevsky Prospekt
5 'beer bar'
6 Cathedral square
7 telephone conversation
8 library day

## Unit 15

### EXERCISE 1

1 Moscow State University
2 State Universal Shop (store)
3 Department of Visas and the Registration of Foreign Citizens
4 Moscow Arts (Academic) Theatre

### EXERCISE 2

1 Bread: main Russian state bakery
2 Cars: ministry of the motor industry
3 Building: building industry bank

4 Food: foreign food import organisation

### EXERCISE 3

1 N.V. Gogol
2 P.I. Tchaikovsky
3 M.V. Lomonosov
4 A.S. Pushkin
5 D.D. Shostakovich
6 N.A. Rimsky-Korsakov
7 Peter the Great

### EXERCISE 4

| | | | |
|---|---|---|---|
| 1 | 1223 | 4 | 1703 |
| 2 | 1547 | 5 | 1861 |
| 3 | 1605 | 6 | 1941 |

### EXERCISE 5

1 Genghis Khan and the Mongol army defeated the Slavs
Чингисха́н и монго́льская а́рмия разби́ли славя́нскую а́рмию
2 Ivan IV became tsar
Ива́н IV стал царём
3 Boris Godunov died
Бори́с Годуно́в у́мер
4 Founding of St Petersburg
Основа́ние Санкт-Петербу́рга
5 Peasant reform
Крестья́нская рефо́рма
6 Second world war
Вели́кая оте́чественная война́ (literally *the Great Patriotic War*)

### EXERCISE 6

1 В 1227 г. у́мер Чингисха́н.
2 В 1914 г. начала́сь пéрвая мирова́я война́.
3 В 1697 г. Пётр Вели́кий поéхал в Голла́ндию.
4 В 1945 г. ко́нчилась вели́кая оте́чественная война́.
5 В 1480 г. ко́нчилось тата́рское и́го.
6 В 1796 г. умерла́ Екатери́на II.

### EXERCISE 7

1 **1917**: October revolution
2 **1924**: Lenin died
3 **1945**: end of second world war
4 **1953**: death of Stalin
5 **1991**: putsch in Russia

## EXERCISE 8

1
| | | | |
|---|---|---|---|
| 1 | j | 7 | g |
| 2 | b | 8 | f |
| 3 | h | 9 | i |
| 4 | d | 10 | l |
| 5 | a | 11 | c |
| 6 | k | 12 | e |

2
a В сентябрé
b Бори́сов, Ива́н Никола́евич
c Во вто́рник
d В лаборато́рии и в библиотéке
e Нет, америка́нский
f В Санкт-Петербу́рге

## EXERCISE 9

Лéвин: **9.35**
Алексéева: **15.32**
Сега́ль: **20.50**
Моро́зова: **24.00**
Есéнин: **03.55**
Петро́ва: **17.59**

## Unit 16

### EXERCISE 1

1 Cheese
2 More than 70
3 Edam
4 $3 10 cents
5 56 cents

### EXERCISE 2

1 Beer
2 7
3 0.5 litre
4 Spaghetti
5 $1.11 for 1 kilo
6 Italy
7 Moscow

### EXERCISE 3

1
a четы́рнадцать до́лларов.
b два́дцать два до́ллара.
c три́дцать три до́ллара.
d дéсять до́лларов.
e два́дцать семь до́лларов.
f дéвять до́лларов.
g два́дцать четы́ре до́ллара.
h сто пятна́дцать до́лларов.
i сто шестьдеся́т три до́ллара.
j сто шестьдеся́т шесть до́лларов.

2
**Chocolate**
Black Toblerone, bitter chocolate, 'Lifley' chocolate sweets, Belgian assortment, 'Narcissus flowers' assortment, truffles
**Preserved vegetables**
Capers, olives stuffed with red pepper, olives (plain), beans in tomato sauce, salted cucumbers, pickled cucumbers, Polish cucumbers
**Juices** Del Monte (pineapple)
**Wine and champagne**
Blue Nun, Asti Spumante, Champagne 'Cafe Paris'
**Spirits** Seagrams gin, 100 Pipers whisky, Absolut and Smirnoff vodka, Bisquit and Martell VSOP cognac

### EXERCISE 4

Some of the items sold by Savar Electronics are: computers, printers, laser printers, fax machines, telephones, mobile phones, televisions, video players, camcorders, false banknote detectors, ultraviolet lamps, calculators, and as the ad says, 'much more'!
Fax number: 165-16-83

### EXERCISE 5

1 бо́льше лю́бят ви́ски, чем во́дку.
2 бо́льше лю́бят вино́, чем пи́во.
3 мéньше лю́бят чай с лимо́ном, чем с молоко́м.
4 мéньше лю́бят хлеб, чем рис.
5 бо́льше лю́бят бейсбо́л, чем кри́кет.
6 бо́льше икры́, чем в Ита́лии.

### EXERCISE 6

1 ху́же. (англича́нин)
2 мéньше. (америка́нец)
3 бо́льше. (ру́сский)
4 бо́льше. (шотла́ндец)

## EXERCISE 7

1 бо́льше нра́вится
2 пое́дем на тролле́йбусе
3 пойти́ в четве́рг
4 хоте́л(а) бы
5 бо́льше нра́вится

## EXERCISE 8

1 Edinburgh
2 Wine, champagne, beer, cocktails, brandy
3 He thinks Russian women drink less
4 Because they are not wearing the kilt
5 That it is a national costume worn by soldiers and men on special days
6 The theatre

## Unit 17

### EXERCISE 1

1 7 days in Austria
2 8 days in Italy
3 $445 + flight
4 $400 + flight
5 By road
6 8 days in Singapore for $350 + flight
7 30 years
8 Tunis

### EXERCISE 2

1 Seaside holidays
2 Comfortable hotels, prestige resorts, excursions, magnificent relaxation and entertainment
3 Spain, Turkey, Italy, Israel, Greece, Cyprus, Bulgaria, Malta, Egypt, Majorca
4 Reasonable, child discounts
5 in comfort, without any problems

### EXERCISE 3

1 New Year
2 Wedding day
3 Congratulations!
4 Christmas
5 New Year

### EXERCISE 4

1 Before exams
2 Before a meal
3 On a birthday
4 Any time (success)

5 On a birthday (long life)
6 At night
7 Before bed

### EXERCISE 5

1 New Year's greeting
2 Success, health and more trips to St Petersburg

### EXERCISE 6

1 Но́вым го́дом
2 днём рожде́ния
3 горя́чий приве́т
4 Поздравля́ю
5 Целу́ю и обнима́ю
6 Всего́ хоро́шего (до́брого/лу́чшего)

### EXERCISE 7

1 dramatise    4 plan
2 emigrate     5 regulate
3 register     6 pack

### EXERCISE 8

1 Around the whole of Europe
2 By car
3 It was very beautiful with elegant houses
4 His surname is Italian
5 It was as expensive as Paris; petrol was very expensive

### EXERCISE 9

1 Junior chess championship of the world
2 Graz, Austria
3 He is also a Russian, a former champion, and he came second, half a point behind.
4 Fries-Nilsen
5 France
6 Sergey Sukhoruchenkov; 42 h 26 min 28 sec.
7 Ramazan Galyaletdinov from Samara, Sergey Morozov from Moscow and Alexander Averin from Samara

### CROSSWORD

Across
 1 новым годом
10 во
11 она
12 боа
13 опера
15 по
17 май
18 ли
19 сети

20 обо
21 парк
22 за
23 Елена
25 днём рождения
30 рту
32 ие
33 чек
34 мода
35 а
36 Динамо
38 им
39 вне
40 газ
41 стол
42 Лене
43 Йорк
45 Отто
48 вид
50 тройка
51 он
52 юбка
53 самолёт

Down
 1 но
 2 он
 3 вам
 4 мой
 5 гала
 6 ОВИР
 7 до
 8 опера
 9 метро
10 в Риме
12 бал
14 аллея
15 поздравляю
16 об Антоне
19 скидка
21 передай
24 ночи
26 милые
27 жена
28 но
29 Идиот
31 ученик
37 о / т
40 гора
41 сок
44 ром
46 та
47 они
49 да
51 от

## Unit 18

### EXERCISE 1

1 I have got a sore throat
2 My arm hurts
3 My nose hurts
4 I have got a pain in my leg
5 I have toothache

### EXERCISE 2

1 The service desk
2 The medical unit in the hotel
3 High temperature, sore throat, slight headache, no appetite
4 Orders tea with lemon
5 Looks at his throat and takes his temperature; writes out a prescription
6 Not very high
7 Tablets three times a day; rest in bed

### EXERCISE 3

1 22   298 66 38
2 67   470 21 71
3 93   132 44 67
4 81   315 25 10
5 54   542 90 25

She works in health centre no. 54.

### EXERCISE 4

1 2    6 8
2 1    7 6
3 7    8 3
4 9    9 4
5 5

### EXERCISE 5

1 Ему́ хорошо́
2 Тебе́ жа́рко
3 Вам тепло́
4 Нам пло́хо
5 Мне хо́лодно
6 Вам ску́чно
7 Ей лу́чше
8 Ему́ ху́же
9 Им сты́дно

### EXERCISE 6

1 b
2 c
3 a

### EXERCISE 7

1 d    6 a
2 g    7 h
3 e    8 j
4 c    9 i
5 f    10 b

## EXERCISE 8

1 Та́ня должна́ чита́ть э́ту кни́гу.
2 Ива́н до́лжен чита́ть э́ту кни́гу.
3 То́ля и Ира должны́ чита́ть э́ту кни́гу.
4 Ни́на Никола́евна должна́ чита́ть э́ту кни́гу.
5 Студе́нт до́лжен чита́ть э́ту кни́гу.
6 Учени́ца должна́ чита́ть э́ту кни́гу.
7 Ва́ня до́лжен чита́ть э́ту кни́гу.
8 Англича́нин до́лжен чита́ть э́ту кни́гу.
9 Мы должны́ чита́ть э́ту кни́гу.
10 Она́ должна́ чита́ть э́ту кни́гу.
11 Он до́лжен чита́ть э́ту кни́гу.
12 Вы должны́ чита́ть э́ту кни́гу.

## Unit 19

### EXERCISE 1

1 186 73 87
2 133 44 22 or 133 44 26
3 124 59 17 or 124 79 17
4 495 40 50
5 491 88 58
6 397 47 61
7 128 29 50 or 128 99 34

### EXERCISE 3

1 927 84 03
2 Borshch
3 Natasha
4 Vodka
5 Go to Novgorod and the theatre
6 About 7

### EXERCISE 4

1 Hotel 'Na Sadovoy'
2 319 96 91
3 Take the underground to Kupchino (last station) and then catch a trolleybus
4 She doesn't
5 Twenty to twenty-five minutes

## EXERCISE 5

1 There are nine occurrences – **входи́** (twice), **снима́й**, **проходи́** (four times), **сади́сь** and **вы́пьем**
2 It's raining outside
3 In the kitchen
4 It's so full of books it looks more like a library
5 To Sarah's visit (arrival), her husband, brothers, sisters and all his Scottish and American friends
6 To Volodya and Natasha

## EXERCISE 6

1 За мои́х ру́сских друзе́й!
2 За Ва́ню!
3 За Са́шу!
4 За ва́ше (твоё) здоро́вье!
5 За хозя́йку!
6 За сча́стье!
7 За ваш (твой) день рожде́ния!

## EXERCISE 7

1 Tomorrow
2 On Saturday
3 At Christmas
4 At Easter
5 In the morning
6 In the New Year
7 On Wednesday

## Unit 20

### EXERCISE 1

1
Дороги́е мои́! Вот мы с ма́мой в Ло́ндоне! Здесь о́чень интере́сно, но пого́да не така́я хоро́шая, как у вас в Москве́. Мы бы́ли во мно́гих интере́сных места́х. Здесь о́чень мно́го хоро́ших теа́тров. Вчера́ мы смотре́ли пье́су «Дя́дя Ва́ня» по-англи́йски! Актёры о́чень хорошо́ игра́ли. Пото́м мы пошли́ в кита́йский рестора́н. Я съел суп из кра́бов, а пото́м креве́тки с гриба́ми и с ри́сом. Все там пи́ли кита́йский чай. Ма́ме там бы́ло хорошо́, а мне не́

было. Я люблю́ на́ши ру́сские блю́да! Хоте́ли пообе́дать в типи́чном англи́йском рестора́не, но ка́жется там все рестора́ны и́ли кита́йские, и́ли францу́зские, и́ли италья́нские!

Авто́бусы здесь кра́сные, двухэта́жные, и их о́чень мно́го. Здесь о́чень мно́го такси́. Они́ больши́е, чёрные.

Ну, нам пора́! Бу́дьте здоро́вы! Целу́ем! Па́па и ма́ма

2 Moscow
3 It was a famous *Russian* play
4 To a Chinese restaurant
5 They didn't see one
6 Taxis and red double-decker buses

### EXERCISE 2

2 краси́вые
3 нра́вится
4 столи́ца
5 люблю́
6 бо́льше
7 бо́льше
8 бо́льше
9 ме́ньше
10 ху́же
11 ду́маю

### EXERCISE 3

1 Moscow
2 The one from St Petersburg
3 The palaces are beautiful
4 They are equal to the Moscow ones

### EXERCISE 4

Фами́лия 4
И́мя 6
О́тчество 5
Да́та рожде́ния 9
Ме́сто рожде́ния 3
А́дрес 1
И́мя отца́ 2
О́тчество отца́ 7
Национа́льность 10
Профе́ссия 0

### EXERCISE 5

С Но́вым го́дом! 5
С днём рожде́ния! 3
С пра́здником! 1
Прия́тного аппети́та! 2
Поздравля́ю! 4

## EXERCISE 6

1 До́брое у́тро
Здра́вствуйте/ поживае́те
2 Прия́тного аппети́та!
Спаси́бо
3 всего́
Всего́ хоро́шего/ до́брого/лу́чшего
4 Споко́йной но́чи

### EXERCISE 7

1 пло́хо
2 неё
3 хо́лодно
4 апте́ку
5 лека́рство

### EXERCISE 8

1 День рожде́ния сестры́ в суббо́ту (It's his sister's birthday on Saturday)
2 Вино́ и во́дку (Wine and vodka)
3 Сто (A hundred)
4 Кот ду Рон (Cotes du Rhone)
5 Де́сять до́лларов ($10)
6 Двена́дцать. Даю́т ски́дку за двена́дцать (Twelve, because he gets a discount)
7 Столи́чная, Сиби́рская и Смирно́в (Stolichnaya, Sibirskaya and Smirnoff)
8 Смирно́в (Smirnov)
9 Де́вять до́лларов ($9)
10 В пя́тницу в оди́ннадцать часо́в утра́ (At 11 in the morning on Friday)

# Russian–English vocabulary

The unit where each word first occurs, or is discussed in detail, is given after each word.

The gender for nouns is given, where not obvious from the ending. Foreign nouns, whose endings never change, are marked *indec* (indeclinable).

Verbs are given in the imperfective form first:
покупа́ть *(imperfective)*/ купи́ть *(perfective)* чита́ть/про- indicates that чита́ть is imperfective and прочита́ть is perfective.

## Abbreviations

+A    + accusative case
+D    + dative case
+G    + genitive case
+I    + instrumental case
+P    + prepositional case
*adj*   adjective
*dim*   diminutive
*f*     feminine
*gen*   genitive
*indec* indeclinable
*m*     masculine
*n*     neuter
*perf*  perfective
*pl*    plural

## А

а 2 *and, but*
абонеме́нт 11 *season ticket*
а́вгуст 11 *August*
а́виа 1 *airmail*
австри́йский 17 *Austrian*
авто́бус 3 *bus*
автома́т 5 *vending machine*
автомоби́ль *m* 8 *car*
ага́ 11 *aha*
аге́нтство 5 *agency*
администра́тор 3 *manager*
администра́ция 5 *administration*
а́дрес 10 *address*
академи́ческий 11 *academic*
актёр 20 *actor*
актри́са 10 *actress*
Алекса́ндр 7 *Alexander*
Алекса́ндра 7 *Alexandra*
Алексе́й 7 *Alexei*
Алёша 7 *Alyosha* (*dim of* Алексе́й)

алло́ 7 *hello* (*on phone*)
Аме́рика 5 *America*
америка́нец 7 *American m*
америка́нка 7 *American f*
америка́нский 7 *American adj*
англи́йский 7 *English adj*
англича́нин *pl* англича́не 7 *Englishman*
англича́нка 7 *Englishwoman*
А́нглия 5 *England*
анке́та 14 *form*
А́нна 2 *Anna*
Анто́н 2 *Anton*
антрополо́гия 15 *anthropology*
А́ня 7 *Anya* (*dim of* А́нна)
апельси́новый сок 16 *orange juice*
аппара́т 1 *camera*
аппети́т 18 *appetite*
апре́ль *m* 11 *April*
апте́ка 2 *chemist*
Арба́т 6 *Arbat* (*street in Moscow*)
а́рмия 12 *army*
ассорти́ *indec* 16 *assortment*
а́том 1 *atom*
а́томный 14 *atomic*
аэропо́рт 14 *airport*
Аэрофло́т 4 *Acroflot*

## Б

ба́бушка 5 *old woman, grandmother*
бага́ж 14 *luggage*
балала́йка 8 *balalaika*
бале́т 5 *ballet*
балко́н 4 *balcony*
балла́да 8 *ballad*
банк 12 *bank*
ба́ня 11 *bath house*
бар 14 *bar*
бежа́ть/по- 10 *to run*
без + *G* 11 *without*
бейсбо́л 16 *baseball*
бе́лый 9 *white*
бельё 13 *bed-linen*
бензи́н 17 *petrol*
беспла́тно 20 *free* (*of charge*)
бефстро́ганов 9 *beef Stroganoff*
библиоте́ка 12 *library*
библиоте́чный 14 *library adj*
би́знес 8 *business*
бизнесме́н 8 *businessman*
биле́т 4 *ticket*
бифште́кс 5 *rissole, steak*
бланк 4 *form*
блины́ 9 *pancakes*
блю́до 9 *dish*

Бог 10 *God*
Бо́же 10 *God* (*form of address*)
боле́знь *f* 18 *illness*
бо́лен, больна́, больны́ 18 *ill*
боле́ть (боли́т) 18 *to hurt*
больни́ца 18 *hospital*
больно́й, больна́я 18 *patient*
бо́льше 16 *bigger, more*
бо́льше ничего́ 18 *nothing else*
большо́е спаси́бо 9 *thanks very much*
большо́й 3 *big*
Большо́й теа́тр 3 *Bolshoi Theatre*
Бори́с 7 *Boris*
Бори́с Годуно́в 12 *Boris Godunov* (*Russian tsar*)
борщ 9 *borshch*
Бо́ря 7 *Borya* (*dim of* Бори́с)
боя́рин *pl* боя́ре 12 *boyar*
брат *pl* бра́тья 12 *brother*
бу́ду, бу́дешь ... 11 *I will, you will* ...
бу́дь(те) 17 *be*
бульо́н 3 *clear soup*
бу́тсы 4 *football boots*
буты́лка 6 *bottle*
буфе́т 3 *snack bar*
бы: хоте́л бы 14 *would: I would like*
быть 12 *to be*
бюро́ *indec* 3 *office*
бюро́ обслу́живания 6 *service bureau*

## В

в (во) + *P* 2 *in*
в (во) + *A* 6 *into, to*
в кото́ром часу́ 19 *at what time*
ваго́н 13 *carriage*
ваго́н-рестора́н 13 *restaurant car*
валли́ец 7 *Welshman*
валли́йка 7 *Welsh woman*
валли́йский 7 *Welsh adj*
валю́та 14 *hard currency*
вам 8 *you* (*dative of* вы)
ва́нная 11 *bathroom*
Ва́ня 7 *Vanya* (*dim of* Ива́н)
варе́нье 11 *jam*
ваш, -а, -е, -и 14 *your*
век 12 *century*
вели́кий 12 *great*
великоле́пный 15 *magnificent*
Великобрита́ния 16 *Great Britain*
велосипе́д 17 *bicycle*
Верхоя́нск 8 *Verkhoyansk* (*town in Siberia*)

весна́ 11 *spring*
ве́сти 8 *news*
весь 9 *all*
ветчина́ 9 *ham*
ве́чер 5 *evening*
вечери́нка 20 *party*
вид 16 *type, kind*
видеока́мера 8 *camcorder*
ви́деть (я ви́жу)/у- 16 *to see*
ви́за 14 *visa*
ви́зовая анке́та 14 *visa form*
Ви́ктор 2 *Viktor*
ви́нный 16 *wine adj*
вино́ 1 *wine*
висе́ть 13 *to hang*
ви́ски *indec* 9 *whisky*
Ви́тя 7 *Vitya* (*dim of* Ви́ктор)
Вишнёвый сад 12 *The Cherry Orchard*
ви́шня 16 *cherry*
вкус 16 *taste*
вку́сный 7 *tasty*
Владивосто́к 8 *Vladivostok*
Влади́мир 10 *Vladimir* (*town near Moscow*)
Влади́мир 2 *Vladimir* (*man's name*)
вме́сте 14 *together*
вне + *G* 15 *outside*
вода́ 2 *water*
води́тель *m* 6 *driver*
во́дка 2 *vodka*
возьму́ 10 (*I*) *will take*
война́ 12 *war*
Война́ и мир 2 *War and Peace*
вокза́л (на вокза́ле) 13 *station (main) (in the station)*
Во́лга 5 *Volga (river and car)*
Волгогра́д 8 *Volgograd*
волейбо́л 15 *volleyball*
Воло́дя 7 *Volodya* (*dim of* Влади́мир)
вон там 14 *over there*
восемна́дцать 6 *eighteen*
во́семь 6 *eight*
во́семьдесят 6 *eighty*
восемьсо́т 6 *eight hundred*
воскресе́ние 11 *resurrection*
воскресе́нье 11 *Sunday*
восто́к (на восто́ке) 13 *east (in the east)*
восьмёрка 15 *eight*
восьмо́й 11 *eighth*
вот 2 *here (is)*
врач 12 *doctor*
вре́мя *n* 8 *time*
все 12 *everyone*
всегда́ 3 *always*
Всего́ до́брого/ хоро́шего/ лу́чшего! 17 *All the best*

всё 6 *everything*
вставать/встать 12 *to get up*
встреча 19 *meeting*
встречаться/встретиться
  17 *to meet (each other)*
вторник 11 *Tuesday*
второй 9 *second*
вуз 15 *higher educational
  institution*
вход 3 *entrance*
входить/войти 5 *to go in*
вчера 12 *yesterday*
въезд 13 *entrance (vehicle)*
въездная виза 14 *entry visa*
вы 7 *you (formal)*
Вы не туда попали 7 *wrong
  number*
Вы сейчас выходите?
  6 *Are you getting off?*
выезд 13 *exit (vehicle)*
выезжать/выехать 13
  *to go out (by vehicle)*
выздоравливать/
  выздороветь 17 *to recover
  (health)*
выписывать/выписать
  18 *to write out*
высокий 18 *high; tall*
высотное здание 20
  *skyscraper*
выход 4 *exit*
выходить/выйти 4 *to exit,
  go out (on foot)*
выходной день 11 *day off*

## Г

газ 19 *gas*
газета 4 *newspaper*
газон 4 *lawn*
галерея 13 *gallery*
Галина 7 *Galina*
галоши 11 *overshoes,
  galoshes*
Галя 7 *Galya (dim of Галина)*
Гамлет 11 *Hamlet*
гардероб 11 *cloakroom*
где 2 *where*
Германия 7 *Germany*
гитара 8 *guitar*
Гитлер 11 *Hitler*
главный 10 *main*
глаз pl глаза 18 *eye (eyes)*
Глинка 18 *Glinka
  (Russian composer)*
говорить/сказать 7 *to speak*
говорить/поговорить 19 *to
  have a talk*
Гоголь m 10 *Gogol*
год (в прошлом году) 4
  *year (last year)*
годовщина 17 *anniversary*
Голландия 11 *Holland*
голова 18 *head*
гонки 17 *race*
Гонконг 11 *Hong Kong*
Горбачёв 12 *Gorbachev*
горизонт 11 *horizon*
горло 18 *throat*
город 4 *town, city*

городской 14 *municipal,
  town adj*
горячий 17 *hot, warmest
  (greetings)*
гостиная 19 *living room*
гостиница 10 *hotel*
гость m (в гостях) 16 *visitor
  (visiting)*
государственный 11 *state*
готов, -а, -ы 9 *ready*
готовить/приготовить 19
  *to cook*
гражданин 14 *citizen*
гражданская война 12
  *civil war*
граница (за границу) 17
  *border (abroad)*
гриб 4 *mushroom*
грибной 9 *mushroom (adj)*
грипп 18 *flu*
грозный 12 *threatening,
  'terrible'*
грузинский 9 *Georgian*
гулять 8 *to walk*
ГУМ 3 *GUM*

## Д

да 1 *yes*
Давай выпьем 19 *Let us drink*
Давайте на ты! 7 *Let's say
  ты*
давать (даю, даёшь)/дать
  16 *to give*
даже 16 *even*
Дайте, пожалуйста ...?
  6 *Give (me) please*
далеко 3 *far*
Дальний восток 13 *Far East
  (also of Russia)*
дальше 17 *further*
дама 5 *lady*
Дама с собачкой 12
  *The Lady with the Little Dog*
дата 2 *date*
датчанин 17 *Dane*
дача 11 *dacha, country
  cottage*
дачник 13 *dacha owner*
два 6 *two*
двадцать 6 *twenty*
двенадцать 6 *twelve*
двери закрываются 6
  *doors are closing*
дверь f 6 *door*
двести 6 *two hundred*
двойка 15 *two*
двор 5 *courtyard*
дворец 20 *palace*
двухкомнатная квартира
  19 *two-roomed flat*
двухэтажный дом 19
  *two-storeyed building*
девочка 6 *girl (little)*
девушка 6 *girl (form of
  address in shop)*
девяносто 6 *ninety*
девятиэтажный дом 19
  *nine-storeyed building*
девятка 15 *nine*

девятнадцать 6 *nineteen*
девятый 11 *ninth*
девять 6 *nine*
девятьсот 6 *nine hundred*
дежурная 18 *woman on duty
  (floor supervisor)*
декабрист 12 *Decembrist*
декабрь m 11 *December*
декларация 14 *declaration*
делать/с- (делать пересадку)
  6 *to do, make (to change
  trains)*
дело в том, что 18 *the fact
  is that*
дело вкуса 16 *matter of taste*
демонстрация 5
  *demonstration*
день m 11 *day*
день рождения 17 *birthday*
деньги pl 14 *money*
деревня 20 *village*
десертное вино 16 *dessert
  wine*
десятка 15 *ten*
десятый 11 *tenth*
десять 6 *ten*
дети 12 *children*
детский 14 *children's*
дешевле 16 *cheaper*
дешёвый 16 *cheap*
джин 16 *gin*
диван 19 *settee*
дилер 8 *dealer*
Динамо 2 *Dynamo*
динамовец 7 *Dynamo player*
директор 20 *director*
диск 8 *disc*
дистрибьютер 8 *distributor*
для + G 14 *for*
до + G 9 *until, before, up to*
до свидания 1 *goodbye*
доброе утро 17
  *good morning*
добрый вечер 5
  *good evening*
добрый день 17
  *good afternoon*
договорились 19 *agreed*
доезжать/доехать до + G
  13 *to get to*
дождь m (идёт дождь)
  13 *rain (it is raining)*
док 8 *dock (maritime)*
доктор 18 *doctor*
долгий 17 *long (time)*
должен, -жна, -жны 18 *should*
доллар 14 *dollar*
дом 2 *house*
дома 2 *at home*
доплата 19 *extra payment*
дорога 17 *road*
дорогой 10 *expensive*
дороже 16 *more expensive*
доступный 17 *reasonably
  priced; affordable*
драматический 15 *dramatic*
друг (plural друзья) 19 *friend*
думать 13 *to think*
душа 18 *soul*
Дядя Ваня 12 *Uncle Vanya*

## Е

Евгений 7 *Eugene*
Евгения 7 *Eugenia*
Европа 17 *Europe*
его 14 *his*
единый билет 6 *season ticket*
её 14 *her*
ездить 17 *to go (by vehicle)*
Екатерина 12 *Catherine*
Елена 7 *Yelena, Helen*
Ельцин 7 *Yeltsin*
если 16 *if*
есть/съ- 9 *to eat*
есть 6 *there is, are, (I) have*
ехать/по- 13 *to go (by vehicle)*
ещё 13 *still, another*

## Ж

жареный 9 *roast, fried*
жарко 8 *hot*
желать 17 *to wish*
железная дорога 13 *railway*
жена 9 *wife*
женщина 5 *woman*
Женя 7 *Zhenya
  (dim of Евгений and Евгения)*
жетон 6 *token
  (on underground)*
жёсткий 13 *hard, second-
  class (train)*
живот 18 *stomach*
Жигули 5 *Zhiguli (car)*
жизнь f 12 *life*
жилой дом 20 *apartment block*
жираф 3 *giraffe*
жить 12 *to live*
журавль m 16 *crane*

## З

за + A (За ваше здоровье!)
  9 *for (Your health!)*
заболевать/заболеть 18
  *to fall ill*
завтра 3 *tomorrow*
завтрак 9 *breakfast*
завтракать/по- 9 *to have
  breakfast*
загорать 11 *to sunbathe*
Загорск 10 *Zagorsk
  (now Сергиев посад)*
заказывать/заказать 9
  *to order, book*
закрыт, -а, -ы 3 *closed*
закрывать(ся)/закрыть
  (ся)(закройте) 6 *to close
  (Close imperative)*
закуски 9 *hors d'oeuvre*
зал 13 *hall*
заниматься + I 15 *to do,
  study*
занят, -а, -ы 9 *occupied*
занимать/занять 17 *to occupy*
запад (на западе) 13 *west
  (in the west)*
заходить/зайти (к+ D) 14
  *to call in (to see)*
звезда 11 *star*
звонить/по- 18 *to ring*
здание 13 *building*

**187**

май 4 *May*
ма́ленький 14 *small*
малы́ш 8 *child*
ма́ма 1 *mother, mum*
ма́нго *indec* 8 *mango*
Марии́нский теа́тр 6 *Mariinsky Theatre*
ма́рка 1 *stamp, model (of camera, etc.)*
Марс 2 *Mars*
март 11 *March*
ма́сло 9 *butter, oil*
матрёшка 14 *nested dolls*
матч 5 *match (sports)*
маши́на 5 *car*
МГУ 4 *Moscow University*
Ме́дный вса́дник 12 *Bronze Horseman*
медпу́нкт 18 *medical unit*
ме́ньше 16 *smaller, less*
меню́ *indec* 3 *menu*
Меня́ зову́т ... 2 *My name is ...*
меня́ть (на + A) 19 *to exchange for*
ме́сто 4 *place, seat*
ме́сяц 15 *month*
Метео́р 13 *hydrofoil (make of)*
метр 19 *metre*
метро́ *indec* 1 *underground*
Мёртвые ду́ши 12 *Dead Souls*
Ми́ла 17 *Mila (dim of Людми́ла)*
милиционе́р 16 *policeman*
миллио́н 13 *million*
ми́лый 17 *dear*
ми́мо + G 19 *past*
минда́ль *m* 16 *almond*
минера́льная вода́ 9 *mineral water*
министе́рство 15 *ministry*
ми́нус 6 *minus*
мину́та 8 *minute*
мир 17 *world*
мисс 9 *Miss*
мирово́й 12 *world*
ми́ссис *indec* 9 *Mrs*
ми́стер 9 *Mr*
Михаи́л 7 *Mikhail, Michael*
Ми́ша 7 *Misha (dim of Михаи́л)*
мне 8 *me (dative of я)*
Мне ... лет. 7 *I am ... years old*
мне, пожа́луйста, ... 9 *Can I please have ...*
мно́го + gen 12 *many*
мобилиза́ция 5 *mobilisation*
мо́жет быть 16 *perhaps*
мо́жно 4 *possible*
Мо́жно на ты? 7 *Can I call you ты?*
мой, моя́, моё, мои́ 14 *my*
моли́ться 10 *to pray*
молоко́ 16 *milk*
монасты́рь *m* 10 *monastery, convent*
монго́льский 12 *Mongol*
мо́ре 17 *sea*
морж 11 *walrus*

моро́женое 9 *ice-cream*
Москва́ 1 *Moscow*
москви́ч 5 *Muscovite (and make of car)*
моско́вский 8 *Moscow adj*
моско́вское вре́мя 8 *Moscow time*
мост 12 *bridge*
му́дрый 13 *wise*
муж 11 *husband*
мужчи́на 5 *man*
музе́й 5 *museum, art gallery*
му́зыка 8 *music*
мультфи́льм 8 *cartoon*
Му́рманск 8 *Murmansk*
Му́соргский 11 *Mussorgsky*
МХАТ 11 *Moscow Arts Theatre*
мы 8 *we*
мя́гкий 13 *soft*
мясно́й 9 *meat adj*
мя́со 9 *meat*

## Н

на + P 2 *on*
на + A 6 *onto, for*
набира́ть/набра́ть 18 *dial*
на́до 10 *necessary*
надо́лго 19 *for a long time*
наза́д 14 *ago*
называ́ться/назва́ться 13 *to be called*
нале́во 3 *to the left, on the left*
напи́ток 9 *drink*
напиши́те 6 *write*
напра́во 3 *to the right, on the right*
наприме́р 12 *for example*
напро́тив 6 *opposite*
наступа́ющий 17 *coming*
Ната́лья 7 *Natalya*
Ната́ша 7 *Natasha (dim of Ната́лья)*
натура́льный 9 *natural*
находи́ться 13 *to be situated*
национа́льность f 20 *nationality*
национа́льный 16 *national*
нача́ло 12 *beginning*
начина́ть(ся)/нача́ть(ся) 12 *to begin*
наш, -а, -е, -и 14 *our*
не 1 *not*
Не зна́ю. 7 *I don't know*
Не тот но́мер 7 *wrong number*
не́бо 16 *sky*
Нева́ 12 *Neva (river in St Petersburg)*
Не́вский проспе́кт 3 *Nevsky Prospekt*
недалеко́ 3 *not far from*
неде́ля 4 *week*
незави́симость f 17 *independence*
незави́симый 8 *independent*
нельзя́ 4 *impossible*
не́мец 7 *German m*
неме́цкий 7 *German adj*

не́мка 7 *German f*
немно́жко 13 *little*
не́сколько 12 *several, a few*
нет 1 *no*
неудовлетвори́тельно 15 *unsatisfactory*
ни́зкий 16 *low*
никогда́ 16 *never*
Ники́та 7 *Nikita*
Ни́на 2 *Nina*
ничего́ 2 *OK*
но 1 *but*
Но́вгород 19 *Novgorod*
Новосиби́рск 8 *Novosibirsk*
но́вости 8 *news*
но́вый 5 *new*
нога́ 18 *leg, foot*
но́мер 1 *number, hotel room*
нос 18 *nose*
носи́ть 11 *to wear*
ночь f 5 *night*
ноя́брь *m* 11 *November*
нра́вится (мне нра́вится) 8 *like (I like)*
ну 16 *well*
ну́жно 10 *must, necessary*

## О

о (об) 10 *about*
обе́д 9 *dinner*
обе́дать/по- 9 *to have dinner*
обме́н 14 *change (money)*
обме́нный пункт 14 *exchange point*
обме́нивать/обменя́ть 14 *to change (money)*
обнима́ть/обня́ть 17 *to embrace*
ОВИ́Р 14 *OVIR (visa registration office)*
огуре́ц 9 *cucumber*
оде́жда 14 *clothes*
оди́н 1 *one*
оди́ннадцать 6 *eleven*
одна́жды 12 *once*
однокомнатная кварти́ра 19 *one-room flat*
одноэта́жный дом 19 *bungalow, single-storeyed house*
о́коло + G 13 *about, near*
октя́брь *m* 11 *October*
октя́брьский 12 *October*
О́льга 4 *Olga*
О́ля 7 *Olya (dim of О́льга)*
Омск 8 *Omsk*
он, она́, оно́, они́ 2 *he, she, it, they*
о́пера 1 *opera*
о́перная сту́дия 15 *opera studio*
опя́ть 18 *again*
организова́ть 17 *to organise*
орке́стр 1 *orchestra*
Оруже́йная пала́та 10 *Armoury museum*
освобожде́ние 12 *liberation*
о́сень f 11 *autumn*
осетри́на 9 *sturgeon*

основа́ние 12 *foundation*
осно́вывать/основа́ть 13 *to found*
Оста́нкино 8 *Ostankino (TV channel and Moscow district)*
остано́вка 6 *stop*
осторо́жно 6 *be careful*
от + G 13 *from*
отбыва́ть/отбы́ть 13 *to depart*
отбы́тие 13 *departure*
отде́л 14 *department*
о́тдых 17 *relaxation*
отдыха́ть/отдохну́ть 18 *to relax*
оте́ц 7 *father*
оте́чественная война́ 12 *'patriotic' war (on Russian territory)*
Вели́кая оте́чественная война́ 12 *second world war*
откры́т, -а, -ы 3 *open*
откры́тка 5 *(post)card*
открыва́ть/откры́ть (откро́йте) 14 *to open (Open imperative)*
отку́да 16 *where from*
отли́чный 15 *excellent*
отопле́ние 19 *heating*
отправи́тель *m* 19 *sender*
отправле́ние 13 *sending, departure*
отправля́ться/отпра́виться 13 *to depart*
о́тпуск 17 *holiday*
отсю́да 13 *from here*
о́тчество 7 *patronymic*
отъе́зд 13 *departure (by vehicle)*
о́фис 8 *office*
о́чень 2 *very*
О́чень прия́тно! 7 *Pleased to meet you!*
о́чередь f 14 *queue*
очко́ 17 *point*

## П

Па́вел 7 *Pavel, Paul*
Па́влова 7 *Pavlova*
пальто́ *indec* 11 *overcoat*
па́па *m* 1 *father, dad*
Пари́ж 8 *Paris*
парк 1 *park*
парте́р 4 *stalls*
па́спорт 1 *passport*
пассажи́рский 13 *passenger*
Па́сха 17 *Easter*
па́уза 18 *pause*
педагоги́ческий 15 *pedagogical*
пе́йте (from пить) 18 *drink!*
Пе́пси *indec* 2 *Pepsi*
пе́рвенство 17 *championship*
пе́рвый 7 *first*
Передаём после́дние изве́стия 8 *Here is the latest news*
передава́ть/переда́ть 17 *to pass on, broadcast*

свини́на 9 pork
свобо́дно 9 free
свобо́дный 13 free
свора́чивать/сверну́ть
  19 to turn off
сдава́ть/сдать 12
  to take/pass (exams)
сдава́ть/сдать 19 to rent out
се́вер (на се́вере) 13 north
  (in the north)
се́верный 20 northern
сего́дня 3 today
седьмо́й 11 seventh
сейф 8 safe
сейча́с 3 now
сельдь f 9 herring (salted)
семёрка 15 seven
семина́р 15 seminar
семна́дцать 6 seventeen
семь 6 seven
се́мьдесят 6 seventy
семьсо́т 6 seven hundred
сентя́брь m 11 September
Серге́й 7 Sergei
Се́ргиев Поса́д 10
  Sergiyev Posad
  (formerly Заго́рск)
се́рдце 16 heart
сере́бряный 17 silver
Серёжа 7 Seryozha
  (dim of Серге́й)
сестра́ 2 sister
сиде́ть 16 to sit
симфо́ния 11 symphony
сини́ца 16 tit, tomtit
скажи́ (те) 7 tell (me)
сказа́ть 17 to say
  (perf of говори́ть)
ски́дка 16 discount
склад 16 warehouse
ско́лько 6 how many
Ско́лько сейча́с вре́мени?
  8 What's the time?
Ско́лько сто́ит ...? 6
  How much does ... cost?
Ско́лько тебе́/вам лет?
  7 How old are you?
ско́ро 19 soon
ско́рый 13 fast
ску́чно 18 bored
славя́нский 9 Slavonic
Славя́нский база́р 9
  (restaurant in Moscow)
сла́дкий 9 sweet
сла́дкое 9 dessert
сле́дующий 6 next
слу́шать/по- 11 to listen
слу́шаю вас 7 hello
  (on phone), yes
  (waiter in restaurant)
смерть f 12 death
смета́на 9 smetana,
  sour cream
смотре́ть/по- (телеви́зор)
  8 to watch (television)
смотре́ть/по- на + A 10
  to look at
Сму́тное вре́мя 12
  The Time of Troubles

снег 13 snow
снима́ть/снять (сниму́,
  сни́мешь) 19 to let (flat);
  to take off (clothes)
собо́р 10 cathedral
собо́рный 14 cathedral adj
Сове́тский Сою́з 12
  Soviet Union
совсе́м 17 completely, quite
согла́сен, -сна, -сны 16
  agree
сок 9 juice
солда́т 8 soldier
солёный 9 salted
со́лнце (на со́лнце) 11
  sun (in the sun)
сом 9 catfish
сон 17 sleep
со́рок 6 forty
со́ус 16 sauce
социалисти́ческий 17
  socialist
спа́льный ваго́н 13
  sleeping carriage
спа́льня 19 bedroom
Спарта́к 3 Spartak
спаси́бо 1 thank you
спина́ 18 back
споко́йной но́чи 5 good night
спорт 1 sport
спортсме́н 2 sportsman
спортсме́нка 2 sportswoman
спра́вочное бюро́ 13
  enquiry office
среда́ 11 Wednesday
сре́дний 11 middle
стадио́н 2 stadium
стака́н 9 glass
Ста́лин 12 Stalin
Станисла́вский 10
  Stanislavsky
ста́нция 6 station
ста́рше чем 13 older than
ста́рый 5 old
стать (perf of станови́ться)
  12 to become
стихи́ 12 poetry
сто 6 hundred
сто́ить 6 to cost
сто́йте 6 stop
стол 2 table
столи́ца 7 capital
Столи́чная 9 (type of vodka
  – from the capital)
столо́вая 12 canteen
стоп 1 stop
стоя́ть 13 to stand
страна́ 7 country
страхо́вка 18 insurance
Стрельцы́ 12 streltsy (Peter
  the Great's bodyguard)
стро́ить/по- 15 to build
студе́нт 2 student m
студе́нтка 2 student f
студе́нческий 15 student adj
сту́дия 15 studio
сты́дно 18 ashamed
суббо́та 11 Saturday
сувени́р 14 souvenir

суда́к 9 zander
Су́здаль m 10 Suzdal'
су́мка 14 bag
суп 9 soup
суперма́ркет 8 supermarket
сухо́й 9 dry
счастли́вый 17 happy
сча́стье 17 happiness, luck
счёт 9 bill
США 7 USA
съесть 20 to eat perf of есть
сын 14 son
сыр 9 cheese

# Т

табле́тка 18 tablet
так 13 so
та́кже 13 also
тако́й 20 so, such
такси́ indec 1 taxi
такси́ст 1 taxi driver
тало́н 8 ticket (on bus), coupon
там 6 there
Тама́ра 7 Tamara
тамо́женная деклара́ция
  14 customs declaration
тамо́женник 14
  customs official
тамо́жня 14 customs
танцева́ть/по- 12 to dance
та́почки 11 slippers
тата́рин 12 Tartar
Тата́рское и́го 12
  Tartar Yoke
Тверь f 12 Tver'
твой, твоя́, твоё, твои́ 14
  your (familiar)
творо́г 9 curd cheese
теа́тр 1 theatre
тебе́ 8 you (dative of ты)
телеви́дение 8 television
телеви́зор 8 television (set)
телегра́мма 4 telegram
теле́жка 14 trolley
телефо́н 3 telephone
телефо́н-автома́т 5
  telephone box
телефо́нный 14 telephone
температу́ра 18 temperature
те́ннис 8 tennis
тепло́ 8 warm
теплохо́д 13 motor vessel,
  boat
термо́метр 18 thermometer
технологи́ческий 10
  technological
тёплый 11 warm
ти́ше 16 quieter
то есть 16 that is
то же са́мое 16 same
това́ры pl 16 goods
тогда́ 19 then (at that time)
то́же 11 also
Толсто́й 2 Tolstoy
то́лько 9 only
тома́тный 9 tomato adj
торгова́ть 15 to trade
Торпе́до 3 Torpedo
торт 9 gateau

тост 19 toast
трамва́й 6 tram
тре́тий 10 third
Третьяко́вская галере́я
  6 Tretyakov Gallery
трёхко́мнатная кварти́ра
  19 three room flat
три 6 three
три́дцать 6 thirty
трина́дцать 6 thirteen
три́ста 6 three hundred
Тро́ица 10 Trinity
Тро́ице-Се́ргиева ла́вра 10
  Trinity-St Sergius Monastery
тро́йка 15 three
тролле́йбус 6 trolley bus
труд 17 labour
туале́т 3 toilet
туда́ 14 there (motion)
тураге́нство 17 travel agency
тури́ст 4 tourist
турфи́рма 17 travel company
ту́фли pl 19 shoes
ты 7 you (informal)
ты́сяча 6 thousand

# У

У вас есть ...? 6 Do you
  have ...?
У меня́/нас есть 6 I/We have
У тебя́/вас есть 6 You have
уважа́емый 17 respected,
  dear
уваже́ние 17 respect
у́гол (в углу́) 14 corner
  (in the corner)
удо́бный 19 convenient
удовлетвори́тельно 15
  satisfactory
уезжа́ть/уе́хать 13 to leave
  (by vehicle)
уже́ 16 already
у́жин 9 supper
у́жинать/по- 9 to have supper
узбе́к 3 Uzbek man
Узбекиста́н 3 Uzbekistan
Украи́на (на Украи́не)
  2 Ukraine (in the Ukraine)
украи́нец 7 Ukrainian man
украи́нка 7 Ukrainian woman
украи́нский 7 Ukrainian adj
у́лица 8 street
умира́ть/умере́ть (past у́мер,
  умерла́...) 12 to die
университе́т 2 university
университе́тский 14
  university adj
Успе́нский собо́р 10
  Assumption Cathedral
успе́х 17 success
у́тро 11 morning
у́хо (pl у́ши) 18 ear (ears)
ухо́д 13 departure (on foot)
уходи́ть/уйти́ 13 to leave
  (on foot)
уча́сток 11 plot of land
учени́к 15 pupil m
учени́ца 15 pupil f
учи́тель m 15 teacher m

уци́тельница 15 *teacher f*
учи́ть/на- 12 *to teach*
учи́ться 12 *to study*
уша́нка 11 *hat with ear flaps*
Уэльс 7 *Wales*

**Ф**

факс 8 *fax*
фами́лия 7 *surname*
февра́ль *m* 11 *February*
федера́ция 7 *federation*
фи́зика 12 *physics*
филармо́ния 15
 *philharmonic*
филе́ *indec* 9 *fillet*
фильм 3 *film*
фи́рма 8 *firm*
флот 4 *fleet*
фо́то *indec* 3 *photograph*
фотоаппара́т 7 *camera*
фотографи́ровать 4
 *to photograph*
фотогра́фия 10 *photograph*
Фра́нция 7 *France*
францу́женка 7
 *French woman*
францу́з 7 *French man*
францу́зский 7 *French adj*
фру́кты 9 *fruit*
фунт 14 *pound*
 (*money and weight*)
футбо́л 3 *football*
футболи́ст 7 *footballer*
футбо́льный 10 *football adj*

**Х**

Хва́тит! 19 *Enough!*
хлеб 9 *bread*
ходи́ть 4 *to go* (*on foot*)
хозя́йка 13 *hostess, landlady*
хозя́ин 13 *host, landlord*
хокке́й 3 *ice-hockey*
хо́лодно 8 *cold*
хоро́ший 7 *good*
хорошо́ 1 *fine; good*
хоте́ть 9 *to want*
храм 10 *church, cathedral*
Храм Васи́лия Блаже́нного
 10 *St Basil's Cathedral*
Христо́с (Христо́с воскре́с!)
 17 *Christ (Christ has risen!)*

Хрущёв 10 *Khrushchev*
худо́жественный 8 *artistic*
худо́жник 13 *artist*
ху́же 16 *worse*
хулига́нство 5 *hooliganism*

**Ц**

царь *m* 7 *tsar*
цветы́ 5 *flowers*
целова́ть/по- 17 *to kiss*
цена́ 16 *price*
центр 5 *centre*
центра́льный 11 *central*
це́рковь *f* 10 *church*
цирк 5 *circus*

**Ч**

чай 6 *tea*
ча́йка 5 *seagull*
Чайко́вский 5 *Tchaikovsky*
ча́ртер 8 *charter*
час 8 *hour, o'clock*
час пик 8 *rush hour,*
 *peak hour*
ча́сто 12 *often*
часы́ 10 *watch, clock*
ча́шка 6 *cup*
чек 6 *receipt* (*from* ка́сса)
челове́к 12 *person*
чем 16 *than*
чемода́н 14 *suitcase*
чемпио́н 17 *champion*
че́рез + *A* 14 *in* (*time*),
 *through, across*
четве́рг 11 *Thursday*
четвёрка 15 *four*
четвёртый 11 *fourth*
четы́ре 6 *four*
четы́реста 6 *four hundred*
четы́рнадцать 6 *fourteen*
Че́хов 5 *Chekhov*
Чёрное мо́ре 17 *Black Sea*
чёрный 9 *black*
Чингисха́н 12 *Genghis Khan*
чита́ть/про- 8 *to read*
что 1 *what*
что ли 16 *well*
что случи́лось 15
 *What happened*
что-нибу́дь 18 *something*
чу́вствовать себя́ 18 *to feel*

**Ш**

шампа́нское 6 *champagne*
шампиньо́н 16 *mushrooms*
 (*cultivated*)
ша́пка 5 *hat*
ша́хматы 11 *chess*
шашлы́к 5 *kebab*
шашлы́чная 5 *kebab*
 *restaurant*
Шекспи́р 11 *Shakespeare*
шербе́т 16 *sherbet*
Шереме́тьево 14
 *Sheremetevo* (*Moscow's*
 *international airport*)
шестёрка 15 *six*
шестна́дцатый 13 *sixteenth*
шестна́дцать 6 *sixteen*
шесто́й 15 *sixth*
шесть 6 *six*
шестьдеся́т 6 *sixty*
шестьсо́т 6 *six hundred*
ше́я 18 *neck*
Шине́ль *f* 12 *The Overcoat*
широ́кий 13 *wide*
шко́ла 15 *school*
шоп-тур 8 *shopping tour*
шоссе́ *indec* 5 *highway*
Шостако́вич 11 *Shostakovich*
шотла́ндец 7 *Scotsman*
Шотла́ндия 7 *Scotland*
шотла́ндка 7 *Scotswoman*
шотла́ндский 7 *Scottish adj*
шпро́ты 9 *sprats*

**Щ**

щи 5 *cabbage soup*
щипцы́ 5 *pincers*
щу́ка 9 *pike*

**Э**

Эдинбу́рг 16 *Edinburgh*
экза́мен 17 *examination*
экску́рсия 4 *excursion*
экспре́сс 4 *express*
элега́нтный 17 *elegant*
электри́чество 5 *electricity*
электри́чка 13 *local train*
эне́ргия 4 *energy*
Эрмита́ж 3 *Hermitage*
эскала́тор 6 *escalator*
Эсто́ния 17 *Estonia*

эта́ж 5 *floor, storey*
этногра́фия 15 *ethnography*
э́то 1 *this, it*
э́тот, э́та. э́то, э́ти 8 *this*

**Ю**

ю́бка 16 *skirt*
юг (на ю́ге) 13 *south*
 (*in the south*)
ю́мор 3 *humour*
юмористи́ческий 12
 *humorous*
ю́ный 17 *young*
Ю́ра 7 *Yura* (*dim of* Ю́рий)
Ю́рий 7 *Yuriy*
Ю́рий Долгору́кий 12 *Yuriy*
 '*Longhand*'

**Я**

я 1 *I*
язы́к 18 *tongue*
яи́чница 9 *fried egg*
яйцо́ 9 *egg*
Я́лта 12 *Yalta*
янва́рь *m* 11 *January*
Япо́ния 16 *Japan*
япо́нский 7 *Japanese adj*
Яросла́вль *m* 13 *Yaroslavl*
я́рус 4 '*Gods*' (*theatre*)
я́сли *pl* 15 *nursery school*
Я́сная Поля́на 12
 (*Tolstoy's estate*)

---

### Acknowledgements

We thank Natalya Levina of Moscow State Pedagogical University and Larissa Wymer of the University of Essex. Sue Purcell, of Surrey Adult Education Service, made many detailed and constructive suggestions, most of which we gratefully included.

Thanks to Martin Moore for starting us on the right track, to Damien Tunnacliffe and Louise Elkins for keeping us more or less on the straight and narrow, to Giles Davies for designing the book, and to Alan Wilding for so ably producing the recordings.

Thanks also to Terry Doyle for his continued interest and support over the years, and to Julia Bivon and Jo Mullis for their patience and help.